Particularities

Studies in the
Postmodern Theory of Education

Joe L. Kincheloe and Shirley R. Steinberg
General Editors

Vol. 44

PETER LANG
New York • Washington, D.C./Baltimore • Boston
Bern • Frankfurt am Main • Berlin • Vienna • Paris

George W. Noblit

Particularities

Collected Essays on Ethnography and Education

PETER LANG
New York • Washington, D.C./Baltimore • Boston
Bern • Frankfurt am Main • Berlin • Vienna • Paris

Library of Congress Cataloging-in-Publication Data

Noblit, George W.
Particularities: collected essays on ethnography
and education/ George W. Noblit.
p. cm. — (Counterpoints; v. 44)
Includes bibliographical references.
1. Educational anthropology—United States. 2. Educational
sociology—United States. I. Title. II. Series:
Counterpoints (New York, N.Y.); vol. 44.
LB45.N57   306.43—dc21   97-17054
ISBN 0-8204-3674-7
ISSN 1058-1634

Die Deutsche Bibliothek-CIP-Einheitsaufnahme

Noblit, George W.:
Particularities: collected essays on ethnography and education /
George W. Noblit.–New York; Washington, D.C./Baltimore; Boston;
Bern; Frankfurt am Main; Berlin; Vienna; Paris: Lang.
(Counterpoints; Vol. 44)
ISBN 0-8204-3674-7

Cover design by Andy Ruggirello

The paper in this book meets the guidelines for permanence and durability
of the Committee on Production Guidelines for Book Longevity
of the Council of Library Resources.

Printed in the United States of America

Contents

Acknowledgments

A book such as this owes the debts of a lifetime. My students and colleagues have taught me more than I could ever repay. For what is good in the following chapters, my coauthors deserve credit. The failings are clearly my own.

Jo Cook and Jodie Sirls prepared the manuscript, put up with my frenetic behavior, and reassured me when I had doubts that we could get this done.

My family wonder why I do this type of thing, but put up with me and encourage me with their love. Clayton, Ben, and Mary deserve more than an acknowledgment. I can only offer my love in return.

Introduction

"And you're not even dead yet!" One of my graduate students sees the opportunity to collect a set of my essays as an honor that is usually accorded to those who have left the living. I was stopped cold (but not dead) by this comment. It is true that the honor this volume represents is exceptional, but I also hope that it does not mean that my work is over. I do not feel that I am done, that I can seek early retirement to my farm and spend the time with my family and friends that is so unavailable during my academic life. Such musings may or may not lead to life-changing revelations, and for me they do not. Indeed, they cause me to do what I usually do. I thought about the particularities of the people I have worked with over the years, the writing I do, and what I am currently doing and pursuing. I am not dead; I am particular.

What first attracted me to ethnography was its dedication to understanding people and situations in emic terms. It seemed to promise a respect toward people that the dominant positivism in sociology did not allow. As we well know now, this promise is at best partial. Respect is on our terms, not on theirs. We invade everyday life and use people's lives to render interpretations and critiques important to the ethnographer's world. In the twenty years of research and writing that this volume spans, I have experimented with various ways of addressing this partiality. My early ethnographic writings on school desegregation and race (see Part 2) were written against the views of whites and policy makers. My more recent writings on race and education continue to do this. Yet, I also write against prevalent views in the academy and, finally, against myself.

The particular for me includes not just the others I create when I write an ethnographic account but the disciplinary, policy, and self understandings that are particular to my everyday life as an ethnographer in education. The writings in Part 1 reflect my conscious attempt to think carefully about how ethnographers construct their work. These essays address the various genres of qualitative research in education (ethnography, action or teacher research, evaluation, and policy research) and my attempts to rehumanize ethnographic methods. While technique is important to me, I am writing against the view that our methods somehow raise our enterprise to a special form of human endeavor. To my way of thinking, ethnography is simply particular forms of the everyday realms of politics, morality, and understanding. That I do not write much about technique reflects my concern that we need to expose what ethnographers do in private as well as in public.

Let me use the artwork on the cover of this book to demonstrate what particularity can offer. The painting from which the cover is copied was done by Julie Longhill, an artist in Cleveland, Ohio. Looking closely, we see two elderly people at a wall. The man is looking over the wall while the woman holds a line that is dropped over the side of the wall. In the original painting, the leaves would tell us it is the peak of fall, when leaf colors are their brightest. We can try to infer from the scene what is going on. We could correctly conclude the woman is fishing and the man gazing over the water. We might even conclude from our own point of view that it is a nice day for fishing. Indeed, she is lightly dressed for fall, and the weather seems clear. We may also note an incongruity with our usual views of fishing. She is fishing without a pole. Why is she fishing and he watching? I would also ask questions about gender and power in this scene. I could go on, but my point here is to demonstrate one meaning of particularity. It refers to the close examination of a scene and grounded inferences about the scene.

There are other meanings of particularity that this painting allows. Interviewing the artist, I learn that the couple is married and both are originally from Italy. The artist asked if she could paint them and was given permission. Julie set up her easel and canvas and began to sketch on the canvas. In turn, the woman altered her stance and her movements. She "posed" for her portrait. The man changed his actions less but also restricted himself into a "pose."

Julie took some time to rough in the painting and thanked the couple, who broke their pose to come see what Julie had drawn. They were subdued but closely examined the art work. Julie recalls her feelings: "It was intimate . . . and beautiful . . . and reflective." The last term had multiple connotations for Julie. The couple seemed reflective; the scene caused Julie to be reflective about the couple, the day, and her art; and finally the fall colors were reflected in the water. Again, more detail can be given, but the point is that another meaning of particularity is the close examination of how the scene got recorded. Julie loved painting the scene, and loves this painting. This is not a neutral recording but a passionate, if quiescent, rendering of the artist's experience.

Julie did not tell me what she changed from the scene to make the painting, but I know from her other paintings that she regularly changes details to give a more accurate sense of the scene. Like an ethnographer, she translates the scene so that it will be better understood by an imagined audience. She points to the power of those who inscribe others.

This painting also can give another sense of particularity. There is a context to Julie's being there to inscribe the scene. First, the scene is Cleveland's Metroparks. Cleveland is a city proud of its ethnic heritages, a city where people such as this couple identify themselves by the country of their origin or the origin of their families. Second, Julie moved to Cleveland because it seemed to offer a conducive climate for an artist, stemming from a history of philanthropy fueled by the exploitive profits of now defunct heavy industry. Third, Julie lives next to the Metroparks and often uses them as both scene and inspiration for her art. Thus, this scene was incidental, but not accidental. It is the product of Julie's work patterns, the physical environment surrounding her, and the nature and history of the city itself. The economic reality of being an artist also means the Metroparks are a cheap source of inspiration.

It is also important to understand the context to the art appearing on the cover of this volume. The particularities involved may not be the same that put an ethnography into a publication, but they remind us to attend to an even wider context. Julie is my sister-in-law, and I have admired this painting for some time. I was negotiating this volume at the American Educational Studies Association meetings in Cleveland, and part of that discussion briefly touched on the cover design. That evening, Julie agreed I could use this painting for the cover. I saw it as a way to do what I have just done—explore how a focus on particularities pushes an ethnographer to consider the details of the entire ethnographic process, not just the details of the scene being studied. I used what little power I had to pull this off, and

Joe Kincheloe understood the importance of this to me. Clearly, particularities enable a different sense of ethnography.

Abu-Lughod (1991, p. 149) taught me the fuller meaning of "ethnographies of the particular." In her view, ethnographies of the particular constitute "writing against culture" in which "Culture is the essential tool for making other" (p. 143).

Abu-Lughod's apt critiques of the well-intended attempts to move toward a view of cultural critique by Marcus and Fischer (1986) and Clifford and Marcus (1986) reveal that a focus on the particular is one strategy to use to work against ethnography's historical relationships of power. For me, this means increasingly particularistic accounts of the production of ethnographic accounts as well as the "refusing to generalize" Abu-Lughod (p.153) advocates. In this way, I can write not only against culture but against myself.

In my life, ethnography has become a quest to construct an identity for myself. I started this quest as a blue-collar kid growing up with a large group of peers who eventually became a small-town gang. The gang gave me both a sense of self and clear evidence of protection and support. These were arrayed against others who would challenge us or who were simply not us. In college I learned more than academics. I found a new gang who let me locate my identity in issues and peoples to whom I was not directly and personally attached. Radicalism in graduate school deepened my commitments and gave them intellectual depth.

However, I was only to have those ideals brought into question as I worked with African Americans in Memphis during school desegregation. As a young sociology professor, I had not considered that being in favor of an abstract leftist view would put me into conflict with people struggling for equality. They brought me back to the lessons of the gang of my youth—trust comes from committing to particular people and situations, not from one's abstract political leanings. The twist, of course, was that while the gang of my youth was defined by the given similarities of neighborhood, working-class lifestyles, troublesome and broken families, race, and gender, African Americans taught me that similarities can be constructed out of shared struggles.

I had learned to use my ethnographic research on school desegregation not only to advance a struggle for equality and to work against racism, but to write against myself. My political beliefs did not dramatically change, but I learned that the abstract did not have much meaning to those whose lives were jeopardized by their struggles against injustice. In a commitment to particular people, struggles, and situations, my life had meaning to, and with, others. Ethnography became more than a methodology. It is my pedagogy to allow writing against myself.

I also came to understand research and publication as more than efforts to advance a discipline, career, or theory. In those days, ethnography was in ill-repute in sociology and in education. It was not scientific or even objective. For many of my generation of ethnographers, the quest was to gain legitimacy for the method and for the work of valuing particular peoples and their beliefs. In this way, research was a moral endeavor, a way to write against dominant cultural beliefs and political practices. The lessons of the particular led me to what we now would term a postmodern struggle—how to end dominance without inscribing new grand narratives, new hegemonies. Politically, it is clear that ethnography is yet to be successful in this. We see quantitative researchers now complaining of the "hegemony of narrative" (Cizek, 1995). My explanation for this is that in the "paradigm wars" we have inscribed ethnography as primarily a research methodology and, in doing so, replicated the professionalization of research that Mills (1959) so aptly critiqued. As I recently put it:

> Once critiqued as overly subjective, qualitative research is now professionalizing subjectivity. We know that professions use exclusion to increase status, distancing themselves from the people they are to serve. Let us . . . undercut the tendencies to objectify, reify, legitimate, and professionalize qualitative research (Noblit, 1995, p. 404).

One way we can avoid reinscribing dominance in society and in research is by embracing gerunds over nouns. Gerunds put you in action, in the particular, and in abeyance. Nouns make something, give it existence and definiteness. In life and in social thought, the particular teaches us that words and deeds take on new meaning when they are reified. Indeed, it is on reifications that people build fortifications. I also understand the contradictions this creates for all of us, including myself in this book. As Berger and Luckmann (1967) have taught us, humans make social constructions and reifications essential to such constructions. For me, the quest is to try to remember that *we* made the reifications and *we* can change them. In my life, ethnography's pushing me into the particular allows me to remind myself and others of the dangers of knowing: to remind myself that when I reify, I fortify.

The works in this volume show that I had to learn this lesson repeatedly, and learn to actively dereify, to question, to be uncertain. Since you will see in the subsequent chapters where I have come from, I want to show you where I am going. As I think this volume may be best used in a second course on qualitative research methods, I will focus on reading and writing ethnographies in this introduction. These are the gerunds—*reading* and *writing*—that I am now considering in earnest. I would also recommend Atkinson's book (1992) on reading and writing ethnography. He and I share a set of concerns. I think my understanding of reading and writing, however, has a larger context, in a set of other gerunds that are my personal approach to ethnography and education: committing, working, and theorizing.

Committing

Ethnographic research, beyond anything else, involves committing. There are four commitments I wish to highlight: first to people, second to understanding, third to learning, and fourth to advocating. Committing to people is ultimately what this work is about. It is people who construct culture. It is people that we interview and observe, and it is people who create the documents that we peruse so assiduously. This means committing to people that we do not always like. I recall during my desegregation ethnography one of the people I liked the least in the school was the Reserve Officers Training Corps (ROTC) instructor. But the ROTC instructor was someone who was doing something very interesting. I had to commit enough to get beyond my original distaste for what ROTC instructors represented to me. The ROTC instructors, in my mind, were people that represented the worst of the culture. They had been part of the Vietnam War, which I had actively opposed, and part of demeaning many of the values that I thought were central to American life: democracy, freedom of expression, and peace. But in Crossover High School (pseudonym) the ROTC class was one of the few places where races were, actually, being treated equally.

I learned much by watching through my distaste and by trying to understand. There was a formal equality in ROTC classes. It was the formal equality of the armed forces. People of equal rank were treated equally no matter what. Respect would be shown. In this class, students would rotate through leadership roles regardless of race. This was something particularly important to the working-class African-American and white young men in the high school. ROTC was one of the places where the formal nature of school could get beyond the dreadful politics of race taking place in the community and elsewhere in the school. There were other places, primarily band, chorus—places that were less "academic." Yet the point is that I had to learn to commit to someone I disliked, to commit to understanding what he was about in order to learn an important lesson about something I valued: desegregation.

I have also committed to people that I liked, people who I thought were doing the right thing, only to learn that in the end what I had thought initially was right was really misguided or what I had thought was particularly moral was much more seedy than I would have imagined. Nonetheless, these incidences have taught me that ultimately ethnographers have to commit to people if we are going to do this work. We have to commit to people if we are going to understand what is going on in the worlds in which we live. We have to commit to people if we are going to try to change our culture.

The second commitment is to understanding. Understanding is not easily wrought through research. In positivistic research, it almost seems as though procedure gets in the way of understanding. The formalized research methodology creates obstacles to our having insight. In ethnographic research, we pride ourselves on pursuing understanding. Yet, as we proceed to do our research, there are many things that can get in the way of our actual understanding of what people are doing. There is the insecurity about method, "Did I ask the interview question correctly?" "Have I been appropriate in how I observed?" Even the necessary prior planning can sometimes make us focus more on our procedure than on what people are saying—to focus on *us* rather than on the particulars of the other people's lives. Another impediment to understanding in ethnographic research is the values that we ourselves hold. If we do not work against ourselves, work against our values and identities, then they always get in the way of our understanding someone else's point of view. Understanding is also thwarted by our commitments to our careers, to our theories, to our past research, and to our past writings (Van Galen & Eaker, 1995). We try to make our careers build by moving from one study to another, citing ourselves again and again to establish a line of research for which we are known. As a result, we track *our own* cultural construction of the lives of others more than we emically understand those lives. It is also true that theory may be an impediment to understanding others. Theory is itself a social construction through which we filter our understanding of someone else's life. Yet the social theories that we employ were created by people who live rather different lives from those we are trying to understand. It is our commitment to others' values, the theorists' in this case, that makes it difficult to understand the people with whom we are working.

Another commitment that we must make is to learning. The ethnographer is forever a student. I tell my students that if you finish a study where you started, you are subject to the worst criticism that is possible in our genre of research—you have learned nothing: nothing that would change the way you started; nothing that would alter the way you originally conceived of your study; nothing that would change the trajectory of your methodology. The student that is the ethnographer must forever be willing to learn, must expect to learn, and must expect, therefore, to be forever ignorant. Ethnographic learning is at best conditional. Some of my students complain that asking me a question gets an answer that almost always has the form "It depends." While I hope I do not always answer every question in this form, whatever wisdom I have gained from others tells me it *does* depend. It depends on conditions, on the scene, on the people you are with, on what you want to try to achieve, on how you understand the problem, and so on. The wisdom that can come from being forever a student is the wisdom of conditional understanding, and the realization that any understanding is partial.

Finally, I think we must commit to being an advocate. When you understand people, when you have committed to them, and when you have learned from them, you advocate for them. This does not mean that you will be uncritical, nor does it mean that you will advocate in the ways they necessarily would prefer you to advocate for them. For, you are not they. You can become similar in the struggle to understand, but you will never be they. Advocating may come in various forms. It may come in the form of direct political action. An injustice so incenses us that we begin to try to effect political change, to alter the injustice we have seen. Often, however, it will come in more subtle forms, where advocating means trying to promote their world view as reasonable. Advocating may also take the form of simply putting people's views into play. I often think the role of writing for publication is not so much to change the way others work but to create a way for readers to realize that their perspective is not the only one. The commitment to documenting people's lives advocates the form, the meaning, and the value of their lives. When we ignore this, we are advocating for the dominant world view.

Committing, however, does not have to be reciprocal. I have been fired for doing fieldwork that I thought was competent and accurate. By representing the views of teachers, I taught school administrators there was resistance to their efforts. The administrators decided suppression of our study was the first step needed. Being fired, of course, is an ignoble result of fieldwork. Yet it does signify to me that committing to be with others does not always solve any moral problems. Rather it generates moral problems. We all know that field-workers are not neutral influences on the field. So committing is a dangerous act. It invites relationships that are wonderful and rewarding. It invites relationships that thwart, relationships that hurt you, and relationships that leave you wondering why you had bothered to commit anyway.

Working

One of my former students, Brian McCadden, was team-teaching a fieldwork class with me one night. I had been talking about working-class culture and how in some working-class cultures the value of hard work was attached to achievement: If one worked hard enough, achievement would naturally follow. The class took a break and I left the room. Brian taught next, and he was explaining something about the projects they would be working on when I returned. I walked into the room as he was saying "You'll find that George values hard work." It is true that in the culture in which I was raised, hard work is largely equivalent to achievement. It is both the mechanism and the end result of your efforts. Working, for me, in the context of ethnographic research, means more than hard work. Working means attending to all the details of things that need to be done in order for you to know and for people to believe that you are sincere in coming to know about their lives. Part of working is technique. While I teach a lot of research technique, I do not care about technique in the end. For me, it is important for novice ethnographers to know the technical aspects of how to interview, how to observe, etc. But through working, they should learn how to go beyond the technical: how to eschew method in the pursuit of understanding—how to alter what seems to be good practice for what seems to be good reasoning.

Working, for me, is a relationship. I always think of my studies as being my working with others. Working with them is a way of demonstrating my concern for their lives. I attend to them earnestly. I pay attention. I laugh. I cry. I am as emotional as they are. I am by nature gregarious and probably more than a bit obnoxious. All the interactional details of fieldwork are energizing and engaging for me. Yet, as I tell my students, the thing that I notice most when I am working is the loneliness. Ultimately, the pursuit of understanding is a lonely task. The people you are working with usually understand what they are doing in taken-for-granted ways. Only you are trying to understand something that you do not understand. It is only you that wants to get beyond the taken-for-granteds. Even research techniques promote loneliness: the pursuit of a good interview, listening to others, and asking questions to keep them talking. They separate you even as you use them to get inside someone's perspective.

Working also means being with other researchers. I construct the ethnographic endeavor as a team enterprise. It is always better to have more than one ethnographer at work. First, another ethnographer allows a different perspective, a different way of viewing. Someone may tell him or her something different, or he or she may understand in a different way the same thing told to both of us. So working, for me, involves not only the people whose culture you wish to understand, but someone who is in pursuit of understanding that culture with you. It means that you must maintain relationships with your coresearchers in ways that make them wish to continue the ethnographic enterprise. For some people there are different rewards for ethnography. Some find it tedious work and need downtime away from you. Some find it exhilarating and want to spend a lot of time with their coresearchers talking about it, understanding it, etc. The successful ethnographer who works with teams must learn to recognize the different ways people need to be with one another as coresearchers.

For me, the primary rule of field etiquette is respect. It is important to me to convey to people that I respect their lives. I must respect my coresearchers too. Actually, it is harder for me to respect a coresearcher than a person whose life is very different from mine. It is probably an irony of my work, but I have a love-hate relationship with the academy. Academics are trained to be solitary experts. When I am working in the field, the differences between coresearchers are always apparent to me. I have to work against myself continuously to truly understand what others see in a scene and to respect it as equal to what I see in a scene.

Finally, working is a commitment to working through. On the one hand, you have to work through an entire study. One has to understand everything one can about the work and the scene that is being studied. Yet working through for me means carrying out the human commitments that you began with. One of the rules of thumb that I work with is that the people with whom I am studying deserve the first product. When I am working, I must find a way to prepare what they want before I prepare what I want out of the study. I have created a celebratory history of a school, a play for the schoolchildren to perform about the school, a videotape about educational value shown in the churches, and an oral storytelling that dramatizes what a group has been through.

Only after completing these products am I free to write my articles and book. In my life, there is a half-life to ethnographic commitment. There is a point at which people no longer care to have you around. For my work, a project seems to have a three- or four-year duration. By the end of the project, everyone is ready for it to come to an end. Yet I am less ready than the others. For me, the loneliness of being the field-worker is only matched by the loneliness of walking away. I feel as though the committing I have done is being negated. I am not sure others view it this way. They probably view their commitment to any project as being temporal and limited. It is I who want a larger commitment. It is my needs and wants that make working through such a sad endeavor. I, of course, do not simply walk away at the end. I try to make sure there are ways that we can be together: subsequent phone calls, an occasional letter, stopping by. My relationship with the people I work with does not end abruptly. It still is available should anyone wish to reactivate it. I would like to say I remain friends with the people I work with, but of course that is not always the case. Many of them are friends, and we have found a profound respect for each other. It is also true that some people found the research an imposing situation, found my presence disrupting, or simply did not like me. These situations make me even lonelier.

Theorizing

I spend a lot of time reading social theory. For me it is important to understand how my colleagues view the world and how that view changes over time. I want to understand the interplay of social theory and history, to understand how ideas are grounded in the conditions of the theorists' lives. Theory for me is historicism. Theory is not truth. Rather theory represents a set of ideas that seem to make sense to people in a specific historical context. What appears to be grand theory is particularistic in its own way. Theory is no more special a product than people's own beliefs about their own lives. I use an analogy that not all of my colleagues like. I liken theory to pottery. Pottery can be grand and elegant, or it can be simple and rough. Pottery can be finished, glazed, and colorful, or it can be unfinished and drab. Pottery can be beautiful, a supreme expression of artistic ability, or it can be primarily functional. But ultimately, pottery is made by humans and will ultimately crack, break, and dissolve back to dust. Theory is just like pottery. Like pottery, it can be elegant or glazed or finished or artistic. Like pottery, it can be drab, functional, and broken. Theory is what is produced by humans who call themselves theorists. This is not to devalue theory but to place it in its particular historical and social context. As a result, theory is something to be studied, to be watched, to be ethnographically understood.

More important to me is theorizing. Theorizing is what I do as part of my work, as I think through what people have told me and think of what questions to ask next. Theorizing is thinking through the conclusions I draw from different sets of information so that I may try to understand how things go together or do not. Theorizing is a process of trying out ideas. I prefer emic ideas: Words that the people use to characterize their own lives. I search assiduously through my field notes, through their documents, and through their lives for metaphors, phrases, and tropes. While people use the emic terms in a matter-of-fact way, such terms give me purchase on the uniqueness and the wonder of their lives.

Sometimes people's speech does not come in phrases, themes, or metaphors that allow me to understand it so that I can communicate it well to another audience. I often find it necessary to turn to social thought, to the emic terms of theorists, as a way to communicate the particular to my colleagues. Sometimes I have to make up my own terms. These situations worry me even more. They require me to assume that I understand what is going on in ways that other people do not. I find this hard to believe. The ethnographer may lay bare the reifications of everyday life. Yet I am always leery when I make up the metaphors that characterize someone else's way of life.

My students in qualitative methods classes like the idea of metaphors. They run the common ones: circuses, carnivals, and the like. Thankfully, teaching students and seeing them rush to their own metaphors is a good therapy for me. It reminds me of how I am likely to proceed when I do not understand someone's life. It forces me to research emic metaphors once again.

Theorizing is also a connective endeavor. For me, the unique contribution of ethnographic research is showing how things are connected to other things. Qualitative researchers can specify the mechanisms between proceeding events and following events. They can show how multiple prospectives interact and play out. This kind of theorizing is the ultimate ethnographic work. It is making sense of lived experiences.

Reading

> Books are to be called for, and supplied, on the assumption that the process of reading is not half-sleep, but, in the highest sense, an exercise, a gymnast's struggle; that the reader is to do something for himself, must be on the alert, must himself or herself construct indeed the poem, argument, history, metaphysical essay—the text furnishing the hints, the clue, the start of framework. Not the book needs so much to be the complete thing, but the reader of the book does. That were to make a nation of supple and athletic minds, well-trained, intuitive, used to depend on themselves, and not a few coteries of writers. (Walt Whitman, 1892)

Educational ethnography is an arena of discovery and controversy. The closer we look at schools, the more we discover our own perspectives. As Peshkin (1988) recounts, the discovery of our own subjectivity gives us new insights into that which we are studying. This is why we do this kind of research. We want to know them and we want them to know us. This connects us to human life in ways denied us in other modes of research. Perhaps because our research is so personal, we have had a methodological fetish. We have concentrated so much on *how* we know that we have largely forgotten our purpose. Our purpose, to paraphrase Geertz (1973, 1988), is to enlarge the human discourse. This requires us not only to get our "interpretations of interpretations" (Geertz, 1973) straight, but to have others participate in the act of interpretation. To foster human discourse, we must get people to read our accounts and to make interpretations of their own. Reading an interpretive account is not like reading a positivistic study. It requires that the reader participate in making sense of the account. Reading ethnography is not a passive activity. It is a social construction involving the reader, the ethnographer's account, and the text the reader evokes.

A Methodological Fetish

It is a source of amazement to anthropologists and sociologists that fieldwork, in its application in education, has resulted in a plethora of works on methodology. In my own discipline of sociology, fieldwork is more a craft (and often denigrated as such) than a set of techniques and methods, and this is more true in anthropology. Nonetheless, there has emerged an extensive literature on ethnographic and qualitative research methods in education. Indeed, we have seen attempts to translate what we do into the terms of positivists. Probably the most stark of these attempts involves concepts of reliability and validity (e.g. Goetz & LeCompte, 1984; Kirk & Miller, 1985). It is, of course, not wrong to try to be understood by those who do not share our view of research, but it is problematic to alter our discourse to do so.

There are those who are aware of the distortion that the fetish brings. Wolcott (1980, p. 56) has argued:

> One could do a participant-observer study from now to doomsday and never come up with a sliver of ethnography. . . . We are fast losing sight of the fact that the essential ethnographic contribution is interpretive rather that methodological.

The point is that research techniques and methods in qualitative research are incidental to the central act of interpretation. We employ them so that we can make sense of some social scene, but they have no significance independent of the interpretation and the context in which they are used.

The more recent aspect of the fetish, and I see this as a sign of the demise of the methodological fetish, is the focus on how to write ethnographic accounts. Becker (1986), Clifford and Marcus (1986), and even Geertz (1988) have tried to give us a new understanding of how one should write when the intent is to be interpretive. Brodkey (1987a, 1987b) has examined ethnographic, critical ethnographic, and modernistic writing. Van Maanen (1988), Richardson (1990), and Wolcott (1990) all offer good advice. The point of each of these authors is that the process of interpreting the meaning of social life and expressing it to others is likely to involve writing, and writing is not the mechanical act we are so often taught in school. Writing is inextricably an act of making sense of some social and cultural scene.

The emphasis on writing I take as a positive indicator that we are transcending the methodological fetish, but I also see elements of it that continue the fetish. If we learn to write in the "correct" way, then ethnography will automatically deliver what it promises. To be fair, each of the above authors is careful to avoid this type of pronouncement. Yet the point of my argument is that readers can evoke whatever meaning they see in the writing. There is no way to stop readers from evoking the methodological fetish if that is part of their thought pattern, and current training in educational research seems to promise this thought pattern. Even worse, it is clear that we teach people to read educational research in terms of methods and techniques. Vierra and Pollock (1988) portray the reading of research, quantitative and qualitative, as simply involving the reader's understanding how researchers do their work. Their reader is passive, trying to discern the author's words not the reader's own thoughts. What we need is an alternative way to think about reading educational research, especially ethnographic research.

There is a larger reason to be concerned about how people read our writing. Clearly, there is a crisis in social science. Marcus and Fischer (1986) depict a "crisis of representation" and a "loss of encompassing theory" (p. 71). The popularity of ethnography in education is a response to this. However, it is also true that there is a crisis in meaning in the larger society. This seems to be related to the gradual withdrawal of intellectuals from the public discourse, an abandonment of the goal of ethnographic research. As Jacoby (1987, p. ix) argues:

> Intellectuals who write with vigor and clarity may be as scarce as low rents in New York or San Francisco. Raised in city streets and cafes before the age of massive universities, the "last" generation of intellectuals wrote for the educated reader. They have been supplanted by high-tech intellectuals, consultants and professors—anonymous souls, who may be competent, and more than competent, but who do not enrich public life. Younger intellectuals, whose lives have unfolded almost entirely on campuses, direct themselves to professional colleagues but are inaccessible and unknown to others. This is the danger and the threat; the public culture relies on a dwindling band of older intellectuals who command the vernacular that is slipping out of reach of their successors.

We hope that educational ethnography will be able to reestablish the public discourse that is being lost. This requires that we not only write and publish so that others have access to our work, but also that the "publics" are able to read what we write.

Participative Reading
Educators are all too imbued with the notions that expression involves a set of skills, and if we teach these skills and students learn them, then reading, writing, and mathematics will no longer be problematic.

Yet each of these methods of expression involves more than skills. Each involves people employing skills to create expressions. Even if we are less than sure that reading is on par with writing and mathematics, yet it is true that reading is a method of expression also. We take what is printed on a page and from it create a new understanding. Reading is participative, not passive (Atkinson, 1992).

To some, what the reader is to express is the meaning the author intended. Mortimer Adler (1940, p. 124) exemplified this:

> The process of understanding can be further divided. To understand a book, you must approach it, first, as a whole, having a unity and a structure of parts; and, second, in terms of its elements, its units of language and thought.

In literary criticism, New Criticism paralleled the approach that Adler was recommending. Brooks (1974) characterizes New Criticism by its focus on the literary object itself—its structure, the words in context of the whole work, its contextual unity—and on distinguishing literature from religion and morality. This approach, and Adler's, has been soundly rebuked on a number of fronts. Many of these critics simply wish to express another way to look at the author's intention and execution in a work. One school of thought has attempted, however, to conceive of reading as a participative act. Pater (1910, p. viii) foreshadowed this when he wrote:

> What is this song or picture . . . to me? What effect does it really produce on me? And if so, what sort or degree or pleasure? The answers to these questions are the original facts with which the aesthetic critic has to do; and, as in the study of light, of morals, of number, one must realize such primary data for one's self, or not at all.

Pater foreshadowed reader-response criticism, but not entirely. His approach was not fully developed in the role the reader plays in evoking meaning from a text. Rosenblatt (1978) was one of the early proponents of a more transactional understanding of reading. She argues that in much writing and literary criticism the reader was seen as an "invisible eavesdropper" (p. 2). In her view the reader is active. A piece of writing becomes a text only when it is read. An ethnographic account, viewed this way, is "a stimulus activating elements of the reader's past experience" and a blueprint, "a guide for selecting, rejecting, and ordering of what is being called forth" (p. 11). It becomes a text only when the symbols (words, structures, etc.) are given meaning by a reader.

Rosenblatt (1978) distinguishes two types of reading: efferent and aesthetic. Efferent reading focuses on the concepts, ideas, and facts to be retained, and the actions to be performed as a result of reading some work. Aesthetic reading focuses on what happens during the reading of the work; "the reader's attention is centered directly on what he is living through during his relationship with that particular text" (p. 25). Clearly, aesthetic reading involves what ethnographers normally refer to as interpretation. Efferent reading is what positivists would see as more appropriate.

To read ethnographies, one must be a participant in interpretation. It is not enough to read the "facts" and consider the evidence and methods before coming to some decision about the worthiness of the text. Ethnographies are constructions designed to persuade (Geertz, 1988). However, the value of an account is not contained within the words, but within the reader's conversion of the account into an interpretive text. The reader must be prepared to make meaning as he or she reads, putting something into the account and doing something with it. While there may be few "rules" like those of Adler to guide participative reading, it is possible to talk about how one might go about making sense of an ethnographic account.

How to Read an Ethnography
Stanley Fish (1980, p. 347) points out that in a text "[w]hat is noticeable has been made noticeable . . . by an interpretive strategy." Given our methodological fetish in educational ethnography, we know more about how to analyze qualitative data than how to interpret it. In part this is because there is little that is mechanical to the process of interpretation. The process of interpretation is simply the making sense of a phenomenon. Merleau-Ponty (1962) conceives of interpretation as discerning the "essence" of some phenomenon. Taylor (1982) views it as understanding the "sense" of things. Yet we should be clear that the sense or essence is not independent of the perceiver. It is difficult to distinguish the knower from the known. Indeed, in reading an ethnography, I create a new web of significance (Geertz, 1973) around my own life, even as I come to understand the author's interpretations of the interpretations present in the school, classroom, or community.

In a more direct sense, it is the reader who evokes a meaning from an account. This involves a process of thinking and comparing. As Rosenblatt (1978, p. 54) describes:

In the broadest terms, then, the basic paradigm of the reading process consists in the response to cues; the adoption of an efferent or aesthetic stance;
the development of a tentative framework or guiding principle of organization; the arousal of expectations that influence the selection and synthesis of
further responses; the fulfillment or reinforcement of expectations, or their
frustration, sometimes leading to revision of the framework, and sometimes,
if necessary, to re-reading; the arousal of further expectations; until, if all
goes well, with the completed decoding of the text, the final synthesis or
organization is achieved.

The reader is in an analogous position to the ethnographer. Geertz
(1988) argues that the writer's central issue is to create a connection
between "being there" and "being here," to somehow persuade the
reader that the account being written is an accurate portrayal of what
was witnessed. The reader is one more step removed, and has a more
involved, though analogous, task. "Here" is the reader's perspective;
"there" is the writer's "here" and "there" in conjunction. The participative reader may well decide that the conjunction is problematic, as
did both Everhart (1985a, 1985b) and Cusick (1985a, 1985b) in their
exchange of critiques. Each argued the other's account of "there" (the
school studied) was plausible, but that the other's interpretation was
less so. This exchange also highlights that the participative reader is
working on his or her own interpretation when reading another's.
Everhart and Cusick were each experiencing a frustration with the
organizing framework of the other and, in the end, constructed a rejection of the other's while reinforcing her or his own.

Reading an educational ethnography can be seen as a successive
situating of the work. I originally situate it in selecting it to read. I then
respond to the cues it gives me by situating it again and again and so
on. In doing so, I (re)situate my own ideas and others to which I have
been exposed. I impute meaning into the account, and into my perspective. I critique my understanding and the understandings that others have offered. In doing so, I critique my culture (Marcus & Fischer,
1986).

The cues that sponsor situating are many. Rosenblatt (1978, p. 54)
argues that for the "aesthetic" reader "while holding on to the sound
and primary reference of the words, he must pay attention to the
shimmering interplay of meanings, associations, feeling-tones." My
own approach (Noblit & Hare, 1988) is to focus on what I consider to
be the metaphors or tropes that ethnographers use to interpret their
accounts. I consciously treat what others might call themes, organiz-

ers, or theoretical constructs as metaphors to remind myself that these are imperfect renditions of what happened. Themes, organizers, or theoretical constructs are best understood as having the "as if" status of metaphors. Thinking of these cues as metaphors frees me to the "apparency," the making apparent of multiple connotations that Martin (1975) sees as the unique power of metaphors. I read the interpretive metaphors of an ethnography as having these multiple connotations, giving me new possibilities for my interpretation of the study. The words and phrases, and their relationships to each other cue me to evoke a text from the words.

Geertz (1988), while conceiving of his account to be of the writing of ethnographies, can be read as a way to think about other cues than the interpretive metaphors. He examines the writings of four major figures in anthropology: Levi-Strauss, Evans-Pritchard, Malinowski, and Benedict. As noted above, Geertz sees the essential issue in ethnographic writing as creating a "textual connection of the Being Here and Being There" (p. 144). Each of the authors he considers makes sense of the comparison of the home culture of their audience and themselves and the culture they are interpreting. Levi-Strauss's strategy, according to Geertz, is to overlay a travel guide, an ethnographic report, a philosophical discourse, a reformist tract and a literary work. The result, is a "myth about myths" (p. 45); that to get close to another culture one must create abstract representations of it and our relationship to it. Evans-Pritchard constructs visual representations, demonstrating that his audience's usual frames of social perception are fully adequate even if what is seen by them is a bit odd. Malinowski constructs an "I-witnessing" account that relies heavily on the confessional establishment of the I that is the witness. Ruth Benedict's strategy is to portray the alien ways as reasonable and, in juxtaposition, our ways as strange.

Each of these strategies serve as a cue to the reader. Geertz evokes an understanding of the essential problems in ethnographic writing. Another reader situated in a different biography and perspective will evoke something quite different. There are of course a range of cues in any work. We can find literary devices such as allegory, irony, farce, and so on to be cues, and I will return to these later in considering how we might write to be read. Cues can be systematic or incidental, but nonetheless are noticed because the reader has an interpretive strategy of his or her own.

Some may see this as a relativistic position, but I do not. The evoking of a text from an ethnographic account may vary by reader, but cues are interpreted by contextualizing them, as best the reader is able. In this sense, reading is cumulative: All prior reading gives a context to all future reading. Moreover, one's perspective is not simply one's own. It derives from one's biography and community.

As Fish (1980) argues, there is no way to determine a correct way of reading. The only determination is from which perspective the reading will proceed. One's reading of a work is affected by the interpretive community of which one is a part. This is to say that reading is not only an interpretive act, it also is fundamentally social. We recognize cues because they refer to the assumptions, practices, purposes, and goals that exist in the contexts we have experienced, and we make sense of cues out of these contexts. Rosenblatt's (1978) notion of a text as a blueprint also contains some tempering of relativism. A blueprint constrains as it guides. The text we construct from a piece of writing delimits our interpretation even as we create the interpretation.

Reading an ethnography is an involved task. It requires us to be active. We take the cues a study provides us and make more of them than is in the written words. We use the words, author's strategies, literary devices, tone, and whatever else we recognize to create a text, a new signification. In doing so, we construct our perspective even as we express the perspectives available to us in our interpretive communities. We create and reproduce in the same moment.

Reading as a Beginning

Reading an educational ethnography is, for students, often an assignment, either an end in itself or a means to the end of satisfying the professor. Even those who teach educational ethnography tend to send students out to find the facts in the study, an efferent reading. Once we have the facts, we do not need to read further or deeper. It is another end to interpretation. Aesthetic reading, or participative reading, or whatever we wish to call it, is not an ending, but a beginning. It is the beginning of interpretation. Students can practice interpretation by reading as well as by researching and writing. Moreover, it is through reading and evoking a text that readers begin to recognize their interpretive communities, the contexts in which their work makes sense. Reading is the beginning of interpretation and the end goal of all ethnographic writing. Through it we enlarge and enrich the human discourse.

Writing[1]

Ethnographies, however, are rarely written to be read in the ways I have discussed above. They are usually written as an author's representation of a cultural scene. Writing to be read requires conscious consideration of the construction of the written account. Authors who wish to be read are aware that they are doing more than writing; they are creating. Writing is an act of cultural construction. In writing, we make something that did not exist before. The written text is new and therefore was not available to human discourses in this form. Further, even the characterization of a particular social/cultural scene did not exist. As our writing characterizes a scene, the scene keeps on going. Yet we "fix" its meaning in our act of qualitative writing, by describing and interpreting it. Regardless of qualitative researchers' intent to be emic and to generate a text that represents the voices and lives studied, ultimately a qualitative paper, article, or book is the writer's construction. As Clifford (1988) has argued, we "inscribe" our interpretation of a social scene.

Inscription refers to the notion that the act of writing renders what is learned in doing a qualitative study into a form that others can use in their construction of meaning. We offer our interpretation. The readers consider our offering and make their own interpretations. Their interpretations, however, are not based on the social scene studied but rather on our inscription of it.

Our inscription is also a form of translation (Turner, 1980) where we examine a scene for its meaning, we translate it into our meaning system, and thus we actually inscribe a translation. The form of such a translation is essentially the construction of analogies (Turner, 1980) between two or more "interpretive communities" (Fish, 1980). There are two forms of translation to consider when writing: literal and idiomatic. Literal translations involve word-for-word and concept-for-concept transpositions. This form of translation assumes that two scenes share semantic logic and structural logic. Literal translation should be used only when this assumption seems reasonable. Since qualitative research often reveals the differences between semantic logic and structural logic even in the same culture, this form of translation is of limited use in qualitative writing.

Qualitative writing is more likely to involve the construction and inscription of an idiomatic translation. Our goal is to translate the meaning of that studied into the meaning system of an audience, constructing an analogy between the meaning systems. We attempt to maintain the key concepts of those studied as we use the language and concepts of our audience to explain the scene to them. This is what Geertz (1988) means when he says writing is the bridge between "being there" and "writing here."

Constructing analogies is another way to think of "making sense" (Taylor, 1982) and revealing the "essence" (Merleau-Ponty, 1962) of a social/cultural scene. In this we can accomplish three things (Schlechty & Noblit, 1982). We can make *the hidden obvious*. In doing this we usually reveal the taken-for-granted assumptions of a scene. These assumptions are implicit, not explicit, and order lives in ways often hidden to participants. We can make *the obvious dubious*. In so doing, we reveal how what seems to be a normal and straightforward way of understanding lacks veracity when looking at life in greater detail. We can also make *the obvious obvious*. Qualitative research may simply confirm what people assumed all along. The act of doing this has important implications. Such a study confirms a cultural view and may potentially reify it, giving it a status of being unquestionably true.

Authors usually inscribe their interpretations, translations, and/or analogies in one of three ways: (1) detailed description; (2) use of theory, and (3) figure/ground reversal. Again each of these is used to construct idiomatic translations.

Detailed Description. Geertz (1973) has argued that interpretations involve thick description. In cross-cultural studies, this is a way of ensuring emic portraits and revealing the subtleties of cultural dynamics and differences. This is also true in qualitative research of our own culture. Detailed descriptions ground the interpretations in the scene studied. Detailed descriptions of our culture also serve to defamiliarize. Attention to detail allows readers to see more deeply into their own actions and beliefs by comparing their ways of knowing with those of others.

As Turner (1980) argues, the reader must experience a breakdown in the presumption that the cultural practice described is the cultural practice with which he or she is familiar. Extensive use of transcripts and a focus on semantics, language, and actions slow the reader's presumptiveness and prepare him or her for the breakdown Turner discusses. Detailed descriptions of our own culture both ground and defamiliarize the culture scenes, but not alone. Theory can also prove useful in this regard.

Use of Theory. The use of theory as a part of writing attempts to strategically defamiliarize a scene for the audience while at the same time grounding it in an interpretive community. Using theory is a strategic choice. Theory is a *preference* not an *obligation,* and in many ways represents the author's statement of value explicitness. The use of a known theoretical model is a structure for inscribing a scene in a way that is culturally familiar to the audience.

Berger (1981) sees interpretation of one's own culture as "transposition" of a naturally occurring scene into a recognizable genre of social science. That is to say, any interpretation involves some re-arranging of that studied into such a genre. In choosing a theory, the author is able to reexamine the detailed description and reveal how it could be conceptualized. This once again defamiliarizes the text for the reader, and deeper understandings are generated. On the other hand, the use of known theoretical models grounds the study for the reader. The reader is reassured that even the defamiliarized will eventually be made understandable.

Figure/Ground Reversal. We also may use figure/ground reversal to create our idiomatic translation. A figure/ground reversal involves revealing commonplace understanding, which masks a deeper understanding of the phenomena under study (McLuhan et al., 1980).

Figure/ground reversals, of course, are powerful examples of how cultural grounding and strategic defamiliarization can be accomplished at the same time. We write a scene so that the culturally familiar figure is highlighted. Then, in our interpretation we reveal that the important meanings are contained in the ground around the figure. This invites the audience to consider their own interpretive frames as a problem for understanding another social scene.

To me, then, the act of writing is not a technical accomplishment but a highly substantive enterprise of inscribing translations. It is qualitative theorizing personified—an iterative process of making sense and inscribing a translation of our understanding to an audience. In each iteration, we also must make choices about how we *represent* our translations: The forms of our representations are as powerful as the substance of our interpretive translations.

Making Text
By engaging in the writing, we rarely are writing for the mere pleasure of putting pen to paper. We have some intention of producing a text to which our audience can respond. This text is some form of representation.

I prefer to conceive of the term as *re-present*. In a sense, we are re-presenting in some altered form what we have learned. Representing involves several considerations: those whom we study, what we saw and heard, and the meaning that we, as the authors, make of what we experienced in the field. Equally as important is the audience we have chosen to include in this particular translation. I believe that concern for audience pushes us beyond our normal understanding of ethnographic writing.

Writing as representation, as with translation, requires us to be qualitative researchers of our audience or audiences. We need to know our audiences as well as the study participants in order for our representation to be understandable and meaningful to those audiences. This requires us to understand at least three things about the chosen audience: what they value, how they speak, and perhaps most importantly what they expect in a written text. Knowing these three things is essential if one wants to write to be aesthetically read.

Yet how do we know exactly what words to write to portray *the right meaning* to those readers? Some might be daunted by this slippery question, but it is in fact liberating. Our job is not in any way to provide readers with *the complete text* but rather to issue them an invitation in the form of *an account*. We invite our audience to interpret our interpretations of the interpretations of those we studied.

Writing to be read presumes an audience of meaning makers who read "aesthetically." Clearly, such is not the case for many readers, particularly those in the academic audiences for whom we usually write. Our readers are, many times, those who are the efferent readers, the readers who read for "facts" rather than for the meanings that it is possible to construct from the author's written cues. Given an emphasis on reading for facts or truth, it is efferent reading that makes the writing of qualitative studies problematic. Efferent reading is from a positivist paradigm that acknowledges *only one possible* text. Moreover, given the legacy of scientific positivism, we have often constructed our own representations along the lines of this legacy: the introduction, problem statement, literature review, methods, findings, discussion, and conclusions. In so doing, we have done ourselves, our participants, and our readers a disservice. If we wish readers to read aesthetically, then we must invite their participation in meaning making. One way to accomplish this is to eschew qualitative writing as a form of science, and to embrace ethnography as literature.

Ethnography as Literature

I want to be clear about my intentions. Many ethnographers will quail at exchanging science for literature. I, personally, would be happy to rewrite the concept of science to include literary forms, but the first step is to break the habits of how we think about the concept of science. As Geertz (1973; p. 212) has argued, we ethnographers are well advised to reconsider our "vehicles of conception." Schrag (1981) has argued that practice (even ethnographic practice) is most informed by *invalid* ideas and theories. These, he argues, enable us to fully reconsider the assumptions upon which we base our practices. Here the *invalid* idea I want to explore is that ethnography is best considered as literature. This, I believe, will allow us to reconsider the vehicles of conception we use in educational ethnography. The result may be a redefinition of science, an embracing of ethnography as literature, or a rejection of my attempt here. I have, however, just completed reading a draft of Robert Everhart's ethnographic novel and am convinced that thinking of ethnography as literature is one valuable way to write to be read. Literary devices will help ethnographers create more holistic and symbolic accounts. They are a set of tools that invite in readers the empathic understanding Weber (1949) saw as essential. In this, I propose writing against ethnography itself.

In what follows, I will discuss seven literary devices: metaphor, irony, tragedy, comedy, satire, farce, and allegory. Each of these devices enables a "sense of things" that literal texts are unable to render. This "sense of things" is largely what empirical and literal accounts of social and cultural scenes miss. Unfortunately, there has been little discussion of literary devices in qualitative research, something I will attempt to redress here.

Metaphor

In a sense, all qualitative research is metaphoric. On the one hand, metaphors are often interpretively employed in qualitative accounts and on the other hand, the accounts are often metaphors for what was studied. Brown (1977, p. 77) has argued: "In the broadest sense, metaphor is seeing something from the viewpoint of something else, which means . . . that all knowledge is metaphoric." Metaphors are involved in "the fundamental questions of similarity, identity, and difference. This is not only because metaphors are employed in every realm of knowledge; it is also because metaphors are our principal instruments for integrating diverse phenomena and viewpoints without destroying their differences" (Brown 1977, p. 79).

Metaphors are in essence "as if" characterizations. "As if" statements are essential in constructing the idiomatic translations. Brown (1977), Martin (1975), and House (1979) have all considered what criteria there are for adequacy of metaphors. Brown (1977) argues that there are three basic criteria: economy, cogency, and range. For economy, a metaphor is adequate when it is the most simplistic concept that accounts for the phenomena and has a superior "ease of representation and manipulation" (p. 104). For cogency, an "elegantly efficient integration" without "redundancy, ambiguity, and contradiction" (p. 106) is the criterion. Range refers to the "power of incorporating other symbolic domains" (p. 105): Adequate metaphors enable the incorporation of multiple symbolic domains. Martin (1975) suggests an additional criterion, apparency. He writes: "[T]he ability of language to (seemingly) 'show' us experience rather than 'refer' to it—I shall term 'Apparency'" (p. 168; parentheses and emphases in the original). For Martin, an adequate metaphor is one that is successful in "the making apparent of connotations" (p. 208). A final criterion, credibility, is suggested by House (1979). That is to say, while adequate metaphors are consciously "as if" and involve a transference between a literal sense and an absurd sense of a word or phrase (Brown, 1977), adequate metaphors also must be credible to, and understood by, the audience(s) of the study.

In considering metaphor, it is "apparent" that qualitative writing, when considered as a form of literature, can be informed on many levels. First, we construct our interpretations, wholly, as overarching metaphors, as many qualitative researchers do, to render the salient themes of the situation in an understandable way to an audience. Second, we can use metaphors, as many qualitative researchers do, to render the salient, discrete themes of the situation in order to reveal the complexity of the situation for an audience. Third, we can use emic metaphors: the words and/or concepts of the people studied. This enables readers to make a direct search of the similarities and differences between their culture and that of the others.

Irony

"Irony is a metaphor of opposites, a seeing of something from the viewpoint of its antithesis" (Brown, 1977, p. 172). Brown goes on to argue that irony, to be fully developed, depends on the interaction of incongruity and inevitability. Irony requires that an incongruity of opposites, that in itself is unstable, be developed. This must be coupled with an unexpected result that is established as inevitable.

Irony then, gives a drama to qualitative accounts: "a man sayth one and gyveth to understande the contraye" (Sedgewick, 1935, p. 5). Irony includes "in a general sense the shocks and clashes between one aspect and another of some double situation, the whole grasped by the spectator, only part known to some at least of the personages in the scene" (Moulton, 1903, pp. 209-210). In short, irony, to be effective, must not only establish an incongruity of instable opposites and the inevitability of an expected result, but must also invite the audience on a dramatic journey, revealing the holism of the incongruity and anticipating the inevitable and unexpected.

Irony can serve qualitative writers in at least two ways (Brown, 1977, pp. 172–173). It is a device that we can use to promote a critical self-awareness on the part of the audience: It admonishes them to look deeper and to search for the taken-for-granteds. In doing so, it also creates an audience for the holistic and comparative accounts of qualitative researchers. Irony is an ideal literary device to use to represent scenes where good intentions unintendedly create negative consequences. It also serves to foster critical self-awareness on the part of ethnographers who by understanding the irony of methodological fetishism may create an ethnography worthy of being read.

Tragedy

Lucas (1927, p. 58) argues that "tragedy . . . is a representation of human unhappiness which pleases us notwithstanding, by the truth with which it is seen and the skill with which it is communicated." Like irony, tragedy involves aspects of the incongruity of opposites and inevitability. The opposites are in the form of a "mortal will engaged in an unequal struggle with destiny" (Butcher, 1951, pp. 311–312). The inevitability is that "the opposite is grafted into the action from the very beginning" (Mandel, 1961, p. 24).

McCollum (1957, pp. 15–16) argues that there are two "validity" tests of a particular tragedy: "(a) Is the view or attitude believable in its main outlines? (b) Does it permit true action without underestimating the hindrances in the way of human activity and accomplishment?" Mandel provides the following characterization of tragedy:

> A protagonist who commands our earnest good will is impelled in a given world by a purpose, or undertakes an action, of certain seriousness and magnitude; and by that very purpose or action, subject to that same given world, necessarily and inevitably meets with grave spiritual or physical suffering (1961, p. 20).

While tragedies do rely on human agency and moral action, they also demonstrate an overpowering determinism. Thus, tragedy may well be the literary device of choice to represent how forces cause the demise of moral agents and actions. The message of a tragedy is powerful. It reinforces idealistic values while portraying their inevitable demise to more powerful social forces. This would be an ideal literary device to use to represent the power of educational institutions over attempts to reform them.

Comedy

Comedy is very similar to tragedy in form but rather different in its meaning. Tragedy, in portraying the powerful forces, affirms this power. Comedy, on the other hand, depends on "an insufficient compromise under *any* given conditions" (Feibleman, 1970, p. 176; emphasis in original). Comedy is one kind of exemplification of the proposition that "nothing actual is wholly logical" (Feibleman, 1970, p. 178). Those who study literature are quick to point out that it is incorrect to equate laughter with comedy (Grawe, 1983). Comedy, as a genre, reveals the ludicrous or ridiculous and, in some or many instances, laughter on the part of the audience will result. As Grawe explains:

> Laughter in comedy serves as a highlighting device. If properly handled, laughter creates memorable high points in the redundant pattern of the play, often the most memorable aspects of that patterning. But such technical importance does not make laughter fundamentally important to either the formal or the emotional definition of tragedy (Grawe, 1983, p. 65).

Comedy gives us hope for tomorrow. In tragedy, the hero or heroine has character traits that are as deterministic as the forces of destiny. The steadfastness of these traits leads to the downfall. In comedy, the hero or heroine is more adaptable, flaws are modified by experience, and creation of a harmonious ending occurs. Grawe (1983) explains:

> [C]omedy as seen from a formal perspective is the representation of life patterned to demonstrate or to assert a faith in human survival, often including or emphasizing how that survival is possible or under what conditions that survival takes place (p. 17).

He goes on to argue a few key principles of comedy:

> First, comedy is a representation of life, not the representation of action (p. 17).
> Second, comedy's assertion is a faith, not a fact (p. 18).
> [Third,] comedy depends upon a certain kind of patterning . . . any conscious repetition of material in juxtaposition with intervening, contrastive material (p. 18).

It is in this patterning that the assertion of faith is revealed. The ludicrous or ridiculous juxtaposition serves to underscore the faith in human survival.

Comedy, then, may enable qualitative writers to better represent situations involving insufficient compromises, unsatisfactory trade-offs, and unresolvable dilemmas. Yet it is also the story of human agency, the indeterminacy of forces, and the faith in the perseverance of people over the forces. Comedy would be an ideal form for telling many of our stories of educators trying to reform the organizations or systems in which they work, and failing to achieve that reform, while revealing the valiant, moral commitments of teachers that persist regardless of the seeming inevitability of the failure of educational reform.

Satire
Worchester (1940) writes of satire:

> It has an aim, a preconceived purpose: to instill a given set of emotions or opinions into its reader. To succeed, it must practice the art of persuasion and become proficient with the tools of that art (pp. 8–9).

He goes on to argue that there are two steps in forming a satire. First, the author establishes a criticism of human (or divine) conduct. Second, the author "contrives ways of making his readers comprehend and remember that criticism and adopt it as their own" (p. 13). The satirist is a "guardian of ideas," ever "conscious of the differences between what things are and what they ought to be" (Pollard, 1970, p. 3). Yet the satirist, in many ways, depends on false virtue and is "able to exploit more fully the differences between appearance and reality and especially to expose hypocrisy" (p. 3). Satire "deflates" but "does not exalt" (p. 7): "Protest becomes art" (Jack, 1954, p. 17). Successful satire has dual effects: it angers the victims and amuses the audiences.

Satire involves a characterization of people as having only "limited independence" (Pollard, 1970, p. 54). The character serves only to illustrate the author's satiric position, which is established early in the work. Further, satire is often accomplished by an allusion or a pun in the form of an innuendo (Pollard, 1970). In the end, however, the satirist makes an appeal "to common sense and reason" by using the tools of comedy to expose a reality that is so different from appearances (Worchester, 1940, p. 36). The imagery is always denigratory, but the author escapes being seen as merely malicious by efforts to "allege the magnitude of the need for satire and the satirist's role as a public benefactor" and by moving the audience "from laughter through ridicule, contempt and anger to hate" (Worchester, 1940, pp. 73–74).

Many would argue that qualitative research should reveal the myths, the taken-for-granteds, and I would argue, satire is a means to do this. Yet satire may be too personal in revealing a character. Thus, our norms of anonymity and value expression may make satire appear to be inappropriate. It is also true that satire as a literary device may well be the best way to reveal hypocrisy when we find it and thus serve as a "regulating force in society" (Worchester, 1940, p. 10). This may require qualitative researchers to be truly value-explicit and to "go native," choosing a side to stand with. For satire to be used effectively, we must find justification to lampoon those who say one thing and do another such as when governments pass legislation requiring action but decline to fund the action required.

Farce

Farce as a literary device reflects opposition to the order of things (Davis, 1978). Bernel (1982, p. 14) argues that farce is a "negating force." It does not create order anew, but rather leaves disorder in place. Shaw (1932) despised farce for its lack of social conscience. Indeed, some governments have censored farce. Farce as opposition, however, also stands for something. It is a celebration of foolery: In the face of ambiguities and misunderstandings, aspirations are a joke. Some versions of postmodernity are termed "ludic" for precisely this reason (Kinchloe & McLaren, 1994).

Farce provokes laughter because it reveals a fundamental human predicament. Davis (1978) writes:

> Their fun is derived from the way in which the normal train of domestic events is transformed into a whirlwind of confusions and mistaken identities (p. 20).

A farce requires the characterizations of "types" of people whom the actors represent by masking themselves in various ways. This mimicry takes place in a physically active and usually imaginative setting portraying the "eternal comic conflict between forces of conventional authority and the forces of rebellion" (Davis, 1978, p. 24). Yet it stops short of open rebellion and/or satire by being indulgent of the foibles of humans.

Horace Miner's account (1981) of the "body ritual among the Nacirema" is clearly an example of ethnographic farce. He gives us an autobiographical account of Americans (*Nacirema* is *American* spelled backwards), "a magic ridden people" (p. 30), whose "fundamental belief . . . appears to be that the human body is ugly and that its natural tendency is to debility and disease" (p. 26). The account itself is of an anthropologist looking at a primitive people—their rituals and myths, their temples and their medicine men—and describing how they are all implicated in this fundamental belief. Miner is the indulgent observer. The mistaken identity in Miner's farcical account is our own culture. Our conventional beliefs are revealed in their ridiculousness. The mimicry is a reminder not to take ourselves, our research, or our professional practices too seriously.

Farce may be consistent with the qualitative researcher's understanding of the interaction between agency and structure. First, humans struggle to create an identity in the face of strong social and cultural forces. Second, understanding this struggle and understanding that agency and structure are inseparable (Giddens, 1979), each being implicated in the other, the qualitative researcher's mood is often indulgent. We may see elements of education as farcical, but ethnographers seem reluctant to portray that. In this, ethnographers reveal their commitments to order and/or resistance over ludic understandings of our social world.

Allegory

Allegory is commonly referred to as an "extended metaphor" in that it involves an "as if" interpretation. However, allegory in itself is a form that originated in the expression of myths (McQueen, 1970). Allegory is distinguished from metaphor by the fact that the reader is placed in the position of being the producer of meaning (Quilligan, 1979) and that language and symbolism are chosen to cue the meanings the readers produce (Clifford, 1974). The images, language, and symbols are purposively separated from their contexts and new meanings connoted. "The worlds of allegory are only half-familiar and they are rarely safe" (Clifford, 1974, p. 3). Allegories are also essentially concerned with revealing the interaction of forces so that often the allegory takes the form of a journey, quest, or pursuit.

Clifford (1974) summarizes the aims of the allegorist:

> First, he is concerned with abstractions, with universals, which by their linguistic nature must be comprehensible in so diverse a range of context as almost to give objective status. Second, he is concerned to demonstrate these in terms accessible to any number of interested readers: the truth may be difficult to access but it cannot be inaccessible. Finally, since he is generally interested in a complicated process, he needs an immense range of material to offer the expressive terms for the naked abstraction (pp. 122–123).

In a sense, all qualitative interpretation is allegorical. Our interpretation of a culture invites readers to find the universal lessons of a particular, yet "strange," culture.

Formal allegories are rare in qualitative research, yet allegory is an appropriate literary device when the concern is to express the interaction of forces in some social or cultural process. This requires an abstraction. But, qualitative research, like allegory, has abstraction embedded in "thick description" (Geertz, 1973). Studies of organizational change and program implementation seem to be appropriate for allegory. Moreover, allegory may be particularly useful when the purpose of the qualitative research is to have the participants reflect on their condition, as in many evaluation situations. I have used allegory in the form of storytelling to people whose revered program lost funding for political reasons. The story as an allegory helped them understand their experience in a different way. It is also useful for educational purposes in general, providing direction as to what is to be learned while giving the lesson a concrete manifestation.

The Ends of Writing

I have attempted to portray an image of qualitative writing quite different from the scientific and technical writing typical of ethnography and educational research in general. The scientific image of writing treats what should be discussed and how as relatively unproblematic. Qualitative writing, however, is problematic. Like our data collection methods, our writing must be strategic and purposive. Good writing is that which speaks to the audience and allows them to engage the text and create their own translations, analogies, and interpretations. Ethnographers should make strategic decisions about how we write based on this goal. Our writing is purposive in that what we wish readers to engage is a text that represents those and that being written about. We must both characterize the situation fully and represent it in a manner that gives the audience the opportunity and wish to engage it.

Our decisions about which literary devices to use and when these should be used are dependent on the nature of the scene we studied, the audience for whom we wish to write, and the substance of the translation necessary to link the two. Literary devices can be employed in many different types of qualitative tales. They are the essence of qualitative writing and what makes it both hard work and an act of cultural construction.

However, we must remember that the literary devices I have discussed are also cultural constructions. They have a long history in Western cultures and are appropriate for Western audiences. Other cultures have other devices that help with aesthetic reading. Again, the point is to know your audience and write appropriately for that audience. This means the ethnographer who writes of cultures quite different from the audience for the writing is always charged with creating an analogy, a translation, of the culture of those studied to the culture of the audience. This is why ethnography is always partial and why we are always writing against culture, against ourselves, and ultimately against ethnography itself.

This Book

I have tried to collect in this volume two sets of my work: essays on the ethnographic endeavor in education and a set of ethnographies that concern education and race. The chapters that follow will demonstrate two of my beliefs. First, each piece emerges from the particularities of time, place and relationship. I will discuss each chapter below in these terms. Second, this collection should also dispel the all-too-common belief that scholarship is the result of some singular genius. This is not my story. My writing is a collective project. Those who teach me—teachers, students, parents, administrators, and others—are the geniuses. My writing is best seen as testimony to their genius. Further, I rarely do studies, think, or write alone. My coauthors, in the words of one of my former students and coauthor, "make me look good." Indeed, what saddens me most is that I must leave out some of those who lent me their genius.

PART 1 includes five chapters of my thinking about ethnography in education. Chapter 1 is a product of the paradigm wars over research on ethnography. I wrote it after I had moved from a sociology department to a school of education and I found myself continuously engaged in explicating my view of qualitative research to students and faculty who were interested but had little background in this way of thinking. I quote Mannheim in the piece, but a close reader will find that the chapter itself is a play on his work. Chapter 2 I wrote much later and with a good friend. John Engel is a qualitative researcher in medical education, a field I dabbled in for a number of years. He and I wanted to write against the increasing focus on qualitative technique, and about reclaiming holism and seeing ethnography as a humanistic and moral enterprise. Chapter 3 was written with Deborah Eaker. She is certainly at the top of the list of those "who make me look good." She and I worked together a number of years and wrote many pieces together. In this piece, we take seriously the adage that all knowledge is political. We consider a range of evaluation research methods, including ethnography, and describe the political strategy that each represents. I am second author on Chapter 4. The first author, Dwight Rogers, is a colleague who dragged me into the world of action research and, in doing so, taught me that the usual ways of doing ethnography were too circumscribed. Phyllis Ferrell, the third author, demonstrated to me that a powerful use of an ethnographic approach is by people who want to better understand their own practice. The final chapter in Part 1 involves thinking about how to synthesize multiple qualitative studies. I wrote this with Dwight Hare, a friend who helped me become both a professor of education and a better teacher of qualitative methods.

PART 2 includes a set of ethnographic studies concerned with education and race. Chapters 6, 7, and 8 are from my first ethnography, funded by Ray Rist, then at the National Institute of Education. They are written with Thomas Collins, an anthropologist, who in many ways taught me this craft. The student, faculty, and parents of the school we studied as it was desegregating taught both of us more than we were ready to learn. Chapters 6 and 7 taken together are meant to show both that white is as much a racial construct as black and how whites maintain race advantage over African Americans. Chapter 8 focuses on the politics of race and leadership in a highly political context. In terms of literary devices, this chapter is a double tragedy even though it is written as a realist ethnography. I am second author on Chapter 9. The chapter is an earlier analysis of the data that resulted in the book Van Dempsey and I wrote, *The Social Construction of Virtue* (Noblit & Dempsey, 1996). This chapter and the book emerged from a four-year study by a large team of people that wrote the ethnohistory of two elementary schools joined by school desegregation. In this chapter, Van and I are writing a narrative and breaking from a more realistic ethnography. Again, it is a tragedy. Chapter 10 I believe is my best article to date. It is an example of self-reflective ethnography. Here I am subjected to the same lens that I turn on the teacher. The story incorporates elements of both irony and comedy, but it is a comedy that makes me cry every time I read it.

Please remember I do not want you to read the following efferently, for the facts. Rather, I hope you will read it aesthetically, making your meaning as you go.

Note

1   Deborah Eaker is coauthor of an earlier draft of this section of the
    introduction.

References

Abu-Lughod, L. (1991). Writing against culture. In R. Fox (Ed.), *Recapturing anthropology* (pp. 120–142). Santa Fe, NM: School of American Research Press.

Adler, M. (1940). *How to read a book*. New York: Simon and Schuster.

Atkinson, P. (1992). *Understanding ethnographic texts*. Thousand Oaks, CA: Sage.

Becker, H. (1986). *Writing for social scientists*. Chicago: University of Chicago Press.

Berger, P., & Luckmann, T. (1967). *The social construction of reality*. Garden City, NJ: Doubleday.

Berger, P. (1981). *Sociology reinterpreted*. Garden City, NJ: Doubleday.

Bernel, A. (1982). *Farce*. New York: Simon & Schuster.

Brodkey, L. (1987a). Writing ethnographic narratives. *Written Communication,* 4, (1), 25–50.

————. (1987b). Modernism and the scene(s) of writing. *College English*, 49 (4), 396–418.

Brooks, C. (1974). New Criticism. In A. Preminger et al., *Princeton encyclopedia of poetry and poetics*. Princeton: Princeton University Press.

Brown, R. (1977). *A poetic for sociology*. Cambridge: Cambridge University Press.

Butcher, S. H. (1951). *Aristotle's theory of poetry and fine art*. 4th. ed. New York: Dover Publications.

Cizek, G. (1995). Crunchy granola and the hegemony of narrative. *Educational Researcher, 24*(3), 26–28.

Clifford, G. (1974). *The transformations of allegory*. Boston: Routledge & Kegan Paul.

Clifford, J. (Ed.) (1988). *The predicament of culture*. Cambridge, MA: Harvard University Press.

Clifford, J., & Marcus, G. (Eds.) (1986). *Writing culture*. Berkeley: University of California Press.

Cusick, P. (1985a). Review of *Reading, writing, and resistance. Anthropology and Education Quarterly, 16*, 269–272.

————. (1985b). Comment on the Everhart/Cusick reviews. *Anthropology and Education Quarterly, 16*, 246–247.

Davis, J. (1978). *Farce*. London: Methuen & Co.

Everhart, R. (1985a). Review of *The egalitarian ideal and the American high school*. *Anthropology and Education Quarterly, 16*, 73–77.

———. (1985b). Comment on the Cusick/Everhart reviews. *Anthropology and Education Quarterly, 16*, 247–248.

Feibleman, J. (1970). *In praise of comedy*. New York: Horizon Press.

Fish, S. E. (1980). *Is there a text in this class? The authority of interpretive communities*. Cambridge, MA: Harvard University Press.

Geertz, C. (1973). *The interpretation of cultures*. New York: Basic Books.

———. (1988). *Works and lives*. Stanford, CA: Stanford University Press.

Giddens, A. (1979). *Central problems in social theory*. London: Macmillan.

Goetz, J. P., & LeCompte, M. D. (1984). *Ethnography and qualitative design in educational research*. Orlando, FL: Academic Press.

Grawe, P. (1983). *Comedy in space, time, and the imagination*. Chicago: Nelson-Hall.

House, E. (1979). Coherence and credibility: The aesthetics of evaluation. *Educational Evaluation and Policy Analysis, 1* (5), 5–17.

Jack, I. (1954). *Pope*. New York: Longmans Green.

Jacoby, R. (1987). *The last intellectuals*. New York: Basic Books.

Kincheloe, J., and McLaren, P. (1994). Rethinking critical theory and qualitative research. In N. Denzin & Y. Lincoln (Eds.), *Handbook of Qualitative Research*. Thousand Oaks, CA: Sage, 138–157.

Kirk, J., & Miller, M. (1985). *Reliability and validity in qualitative research*. Beverly Hills, CA: Sage.

Lucas, F. (1927). *Tragedy in relation to Aristotle's "Poetics."* Oxford: Oxford University Press.

Mandel, O. (1961). *A definition of tragedy*. New York: New York University Press.

Marcus, G. & Fischer, M. (1986). *Anthropology as cultural critique*. Chicago: University of Chicago Press.

Martin, G. (1975). *Language, truth, and poetry*. Edinburgh: Edinburgh University Press.

McCollum, W. (1957). *Tragedy*. New York: Macmillan.

McLuhan, M., Hutchon, K., & McLuhan, E. (1980). Training perception. In *Media messages and language: The world as your classroom*. Skokie, IL: National Textbook Co.

McQueen, J. (1970). *Allegory*. London: Methuen.

Merleau-Ponty, M. (1962). *Phenomenology of perception.* (C. Smith, Trans.). London: Routledge & Kegan Paul.

Mills, C. (1959). *The sociological imagination.* New York: Oxford Press.

Miner, H. (1981). Body ritual among the nacirema. In J.M. Henslin (Ed.), *Down to earth sociology.* (3rd ed.) (pp. 25–30). New York: The Free Press.

Moulton, R. (1903). *The moral system of Shakespere.* London: Macmillan.

Noblit, G. W. (1995). Review of *Handbook of qualitative research* and *The handbook of qualitative research in education. Qualitative Health Research, 5* (2), 401–404.

Noblit, G. W. & Dempsey, V. (1996). *The social construction of virtue.* Albany, NY: SUNY Press.

Noblit, G.W. & Hare, R. D. (1988). *Meta-ethnography: Synthesizing qualitative studies.* Newbury Park, CA: Sage.

Pater, W. (1910). *The renaissance.* London: New Library Edition.

Peshkin, A. (1988). In search of subjectivity—One's own. *Educational Researcher,* 17 (7), 17–21.

Pollard, A. (1970). *Satire.* London: Methuen.

Quilligan, M. (1979). *The language of allegory.* Ithaca, NY: Cornell University Press.

Richardson, L. (1990). *Writing strategies.* Thousand Oaks, CA: Sage.

Rosenblatt, L. (1978). *The reader, the text, the poem.* Carbondale, IL: Southern Illinois University Press.

Schlechty, D. & Noblit, G. W. (1982). Some uses of sociological theory in educational evaluation. In R. Corwin (Ed.), *Policy research* (pp. 283–306). Greenwich, CT: JAI Press.

Schrag, F. (1981). Knowing and doing. *American Journal of Education,* 89 (3), 253–262.

Sedgewick, G. (1935). *Of irony: Especially in drama.* Toronto: University of Toronto Press.

Shaw, G. B. (1932). *Our theatre in the nineties,* Vol. II. London: Constable & Co., Ltd.

Taylor, C. (1982). Interpretation and the sciences of man. In E. Bredo and W. Feinberg (Eds.), *Knowledge and values in social and educational research.* Philadelphia: Temple University Press.

Turner, S. (1980). *Sociological explanations as translations.* New York: Cambridge University Press.

Van Galen, J., & Eaker, D. (1995). Beyond setting for scholarship. In W. Pink and G. W. Noblit (Eds.), *Continuity and contradiction* (pp. 113–132). Cresskill, NJ: Hampton Press.

Van Maanen, J. (1988). *Tales of the field.* Chicago: University of Chicago Press.

Vierra, A., & Pollock, J. (1988). *Reading educational research.* Scottsdale, AZ: Gorsuch Scarisvrick.

Weber, M. (1949). *The methodology of the social sciences.* (E. Shils & H. Finch, Trans. & Eds.), Glencoe, IL: Free Press.

Whitman, W. (1892). Democratic Vistas. In F. Stovall (Ed.), *Prose works 1892.* (1964). New York: New York University Press.

Wolcott, H. (1980). How to look like an anthropologist without really being one. *Practicing Anthropology,* 3 (1), 67, 56–59.

————. (1990). *Writing up qualitative research.* Thousand Oaks, CA: Sage.

Worchester, D. (1940). *The art of satire.* Cambridge, MA: Harvard University Press.

Part 1

THINKING ABOUT
ETHNOGRAPHY AND EDUCATION

Chapter 1

The Prospects of an Applied Ethnography for Education: A Sociology of Knowledge Interpretation

George W. Noblit

Ethnography as an approach to apprehending and ultimately comprehending social reality no doubt has proven itself to be useful in anthro
pology and sociology. In many ways, it was the original way of knowing in social science. Based on qualitative methods, inductive logic,
and holistic explanation, the approach predated the deductive logic,
reductionistic explanation, and quantitative methods of positivism and
as such has often suffered degradation by positivists as an outmoded
and inadequate method. To those of us, however, who are concerned
with the social, cultural, political, and even technological worlds that
humans create, reify, and institutionalize, any critique of the approach
as outmoded and/or inadequate indicates not the laudable advancement of social science but the almost laughable paradox of humans
seeking social understanding. That is, understanding is necessarily
unique, but it must be shared. In the process of sharing, the unique
interpretations are rendered forth for judgment and some are judged
more worthy than others. Because judgments can have various bases,
humans disagree; and to the extent that both particular judgments
and disagreements threaten the interests of some and advantage others, there may be an attempt to change the basis of judgment to benefit ourselves or to seek a basis that is universal, if not universally fair
and just. Positivism is predicated on the belief that such universal bases
are attainable; and our problem is that, as humans and social scientists, we have not reevaluated this premise of positivism and as a result have reified and institutionalized the approach beyond any assessments of its usefulness to human understanding.

Social scientists who use the ethnographic approach continually remind positivists of this and in doing so focus on the social bases of understanding and knowledge: a sociology of knowledge interpretation. Ethnographers, of course, are as human as positivists and can be guilty of similar offenses. We can be so convinced of our way of knowing that we fail to consider the social context in which we employ an ethnographic approach. I believe that this is the case with "applied ethnography," where we employ our approach not only to seek understanding but to guide decisions.

It is, of course, foolish to distinguish between "basic" research and "applied" research without extreme care. Knowledge is always potentially useful. All that is required is that humans find it sufficiently convincing to incorporate it into their personal modes of knowing and valuing. Normatively, knowledge can be judged useful because it "works" in some way or another, but, of course, such an assessment is fatally flawed because as reflective and reflexive beings we can create the belief that it does work when other forces may be responsible. Thus applied research is not different from basic research in terms of its usefulness. Rather, it is distinguishable because of its intent to be useful: The manifest purpose of the understanding to be gained is that someone may be guided by it. In some ways, applied research is impatient. It does not want to wait for someone to find the results convincing; it wants someone to be convinced from the outset. It is inherently political because it wishes to establish the bases of judgment for others and moreover to replace those that might otherwise be employed. The social scientist who ventures into applied research can make no claim to value neutrality. Although value neutrality is also problematic for the social scientist engaged in basic research, this does not excuse the applied researcher. The applied researcher intends to adjudicate values using logic, data, and argumentation, and never should be allowed to escape the responsibility that this entails.

This responsibility is involved because simply employing scientific approaches confuses issues of the appropriateness of ways of knowing with the legitimacy commonly assigned to systematic pursuit of knowledge and understanding. We may "convince" appropriately according to the norms of the academy or not, but nevertheless persons not of the academy are little able to critique or challenge the norms. To them "science" is a legitimate source of authority. Further, even when the applied researcher is careful to be explicit in his or her values and the limitations of his or her approach, there is the problem of the researcher, intentionally or not, defining the medium that is to be convincing. It is our turf: We know it and the lay person does not. The lay person almost invariably will be a second-class citizen in our context, as we, unfortunately, are all too often in the context of everyday life and its emotion and uncertainty (Merton, 1957).

Applied research will not be stopped, nor probably should it. I believe that applied research is, or at least has the potential to be, the most honest form of social science when, without pretense, it seeks to maximize the reflective capacity of humans concerning their own thought and action. This potential is conditional, however, on our own care and concern to reflect on that which we attempt to do. It is my intent here to facilitate that reflectivity. I will not consider applied research generically because that is too ambitious and outside my concerns. I have little interest in positivism except as an intriguing case of a scientific paradigm awaiting the revolution (Kuhn, 1962). I have great interest in ethnography as part of a past paradigm and as part of a future paradigm. It is applied ethnography that must not lose an understanding of its own context since it contextualizes human experience. The popularity of ethnography in educational research and evaluation is to me both the promise and the peril. Rist (1980) pointed to the peril that this popularity poses to the rigor and capability of the approach: It threatens to trivialize it. I would like to consider if ethnography is the appropriate approach to practical understanding and knowledge in education, and, if so, what are the threats to its capability. Given this, I will speculate what might be required of us for an applied ethnography.

The Prospects for Practical Ethnography

Any assessment such as the one I will attempt here must be done cautiously. It must include not only a search of the history of knowledge but also a conceptualization of varieties in the nature of knowledge with which we should be concerned. For some, an applied social science simply replaces the interests and theories of scholarly knowledge with the interests of policy (Coleman, 1972), assuming that these are similar. Yet they may not be. Mannheim (1936) proposes a distinction in the realm of the practical that researchers often do not make. He argues that one must distinguish between "administration" and "politics." Administration is concerned with "a series of social events which have acquired a set pattern and recur regularly," whereas politics is concerned with "those events which are still in the process of becoming, in which, in individual cases, decisions have to be made that give rise to new and unique situations" (p. 112). By distinguishing between the rationalized world and that not rationalized, it is apparent that applied social science is called upon to satisfy two different types of questions, to provide two different kinds of knowledge. On the one hand, we may be asked to assist in further rationalizing the social world so that administration of it is more feasible, efficient, or appropriate, while, on the other hand, we may be called upon to clarify the emergent and to assist in comprehending what is going on and what might be done with it or, more usually, about it. Mannheim (1936) specifies the issues that administration and politics are concerned with:

> There is no question that we do have some knowledge concerning that part of social life in which everything and life itself has already been rationalized and ordered. Here the conflict between theory and practice does not become an issue because, as a matter of fact, the mere treatment of an individual case by subjecting it to a generally existing law can hardly be designated as political practice. Rationalized as our life may seem to have become, all the rationalizations that have taken place so far are merely partial since the most important realms of our social life are even now anchored in the irrational. Our economic life, although extensively rationalized on the technical side and in some limited connections calculable, does not, as a whole, constitute a planned economy. In spite of all tendencies toward trustification and organization, free competition still plays a decisive role. Our social structure is built along class lines, which means that not objective tests but irrational forces of social competition and struggle decide the place and function of the individual in society. Dominance in national and international life is achieved through struggle, in itself irrational, in which chance plays an important part. These irrational forces in society form that sphere of social life which is unorganized and unrationalized, and in which conduct and politics become necessary. The two main sources of irrationalism in the social structure (uncontrolled competition and domination of force) constitute the realm of social life which is still unorganized and where politics becomes necessary. Around these two centers there accumulate those other more profound irrational elements, which we call emotions (pp. 115–116).

Administration and applied positivism emerge from the same historical roots, and both tend "to include as much as possible in the realm of the rational and to bring it under administrative control" (Mannheim, 1936, p. 114). Politics however, is quite different and requires a different approach to applied research. Mannheim (1936) reveals the difference when he asks, "Is there a science of becoming, a science of creative activity?" (p. 112). Shackle (1966) provides more definition:

In everyday language and in that of the policy sciences, decision includes two quite contrasted meanings. Two contrasting psychic activities, two attitudes to life and two different types of mind are involved. There are truth-seekers and truth-makers. On the one hand, the pure scientist deems himself to be typically faced with a problem which has one right answer. His business is, in the map-maker's language, to get a fix on that problem, to take bearings from opposite ends of a base-line and plot them to converge upon the solution, the truth to-be-found. On the other hand, the poet-architect-adventurer sees before him a landscape inexhaustibly rich in suggestions and materials for making things, for making works of literature or art or technology, for making policies and history itself, or perhaps for making the complex, delicate, existential system called a business (p. 767).

In applied research and particularly in an applied ethnography of "politics," the gap between theory and practice is a gap in orientation and conceptualization. The truth-makers are engaging in "originative" acts: creating the social worlds in which they will live. The truth-seekers are finding that which already exists. Bridging the gap is, I believe, the responsibility of the applied researcher and is not, as is so often argued, the result of undereducated or unconvinced practitioners. They would believe in science if only we could show how science might help them. Applied ethnography may be well served if it can transform itself into a "science of becoming" and replace the notion of prediction with the notion of anticipation, which may be best understood as the creative construction of possibilities. Prediction is limited by known events and patterns and by nonuniformity of social life. Anticipation takes these into account but is not limited to only what they suggest. Anticipation, although obviously less precise, is the requisite for politics much as prediction is for administration.

There is another way in which applied ethnography may be able to bridge the gap between theory and practice, and that is to rethink the questions to which we seek answers. Although obviously the researcher is often only a technician to the policymaker, we must be careful to know what the appropriate questions are because the policymaker may simply be seeking a rationalistic solution to problems that appropriately are in the realm of the irrational. Again Shackle (1966) may be of assistance as he reconsiders the questions of decision:

My first proposition is that decision is choice amongst the products of imagination. All we know or can know concerns what is past. . . . Everything we know about the future is an inference, the end of a reasoning process, whether or not the reasoning is sound. But *decision* is wholly concerned with the future. Decision is choice of future action aimed at results which we look for in the further future. Thus, decision cannot be the choice of facts. We do not find displayed before us a range of entities which, at one and the same time, are facts already realized and therefore, observable, and are also hypotheses, figments, imaginations of what might come true in some future remote or immediate. The questions for the investigator of decision are: (1) Does the past repeat itself? In what sense, and in what circumstances does it do so? How can we feel whether it will repeat itself? For to know that the past is going, in known respects, to repeat itself, is to know some part of the future in those respects. (2) When the kind or degree of repetition that we can rely on are only sufficient to circumscribe, and not to *describe* with precision and certainty, those aspects of the consequences of present action which concern us, how can we adapt our policy-decision to this lack of knowledge? (p. 758)

The gap between theory and practice then can be solved by an applied, practical ethnography. It can use history; it can distinguish between kind and degree; it can place knowledge in context; and it can capture how humans adapt to and make use of uncertainty.

The prospects of an applied, practical ethnography, then, are quite encouraging. Its strengths are in areas that vitally need research and will inform us in areas where rationalism and positivism cannot. Further, applied ethnography can be a "science of becoming" even though I believe we have yet to fully understand what this might entail. Certainly, Shackle's formulation of the questions of decision are a start. They need the holism, the perspectives of the participants (emic), the history, and the comparisons that are the strengths of applied ethnography (Spicer, 1976).

I would be remiss, however, if I did not point out that although the intellectual prospects are good, there are threats to these prospects rooted in some of the same issues that we have discussed already.

Utilitarian Culture

As we have noted, Mannheim believed that administration (and rationalism) has a tendency to encroach on the irrational: to apply their approach inappropriately. This involves not only the definition of the problems with which applied ethnography might be concerned but also the role the researcher is called upon to assume.

In applied research that threat to the researcher is that of conversion from intellectual to technician. Merton (1957) succinctly formulates the problem:

From all this arises the dilemma facing the intellectual who is actively concerned with furthering social innovations. Not too inaccurately, this may be expressed as a slogan: he who innovates is not heard; he who is heard does

not innovate. If the intellectual is to play an effective role in putting his knowledge to work, it is increasingly necessary that he become a part of a bureaucratic power-structure. This, however, often requires him to abdicate his privilege of exploring policy-possibilities which he regards as significant. If, on the
other hand, he remains unattached in order to preserve full opportunity of
choice, he characteristically has neither the resources to carry through his
investigations on an appropriate scale nor any strong likelihood of having his
findings accepted by policy-makers as a basis for action (p. 217).

The dilemma, however, is clearly more involved. The applied researcher
borders on classic alienation, separating thought from action, as he or
she serves the interests of the powerful in the "policy space" (Rossi,
1980) which is allowed. The researcher surrenders substantive discussion of goals for detailed study of means. As Rossi (1980) warns,

It should be kept in mind, however, that applied social research is no occupa-
tion for would-be philosopher kings. The applied researcher ordinarily does
not get very close to the seats of decision making and policy formation
(p. 897).

The threat to the researcher, unfortunately, is second to the threat
to knowledge. Tailoring research to the interests of the powerful will
do little to advance knowledge and understanding. At best the result
would be a prototheory having all the trappings of theory but lacking
one fundamental aspect-perspective. Such prototheory transforms our
understanding of the social meaning and multiperspectival realities
(Douglas, 1976) that humans attach to everyday life. Further, it requires that knowledge be useful to the powerful. Knowledge is produced to fit the characteristics of the demand, including limits on perspective, time, and funds and thus approach to be used. Utilitarian
culture is an enemy of applied ethnography (Rist, 1980). The limits
placed on it may mitigate its ability to comprehend the social realities
at issue. More important, however, utilitarianism engenders a substantive theory that research will not be able to critique. A utilitarian
culture implies an appropriate interpretation to events:

Utilitarian culture also has consequences of considerable importance for social theory. Most particularly, it entails a shift from the traditional definitions
of the object-world in which the moral dimension (the "goodness-badness"
dimension . . .) becomes increasingly salient. Utilitarianism's focus on consequences engenders an increased concern with the sheer potency of objects
as a way of achieving desired outcomes, independent of the moral dimension. It is thus not simply that utilitarianism fosters a concern with cognitive
judgments as distinct from moral evaluations, but that cognitive judgments

themselves come to center on judgments of potency. In this view, to know what is, is to know what is powerful; knowledge is power, when knowledge becomes a knowledge of power (Gouldner, 1970, p. 84).

Utilitarian culture attempts to redefine the nature of social research and even the meaning of the variables or factors that we identify. Further, it will select, because of the interest in power, deterministic causal chains as the subjects of interest. It will discover a deterministic social reality because that is what it seeks. The threat of utilitarian culture, then, is its reification of rationalistic models that seek to explain struggle, power, and emotion as technical problems in prediction and control, and thus propose administrative solutions over political ones: It attempts to transform political problems into technical, administrative problems.

Gouldner's and Mannheim's critiques also engender at least four other threats to an applied ethnography in education. First is the threat to holism and history. Utilitarian culture focuses on the immediate and seeks discrete facts. As a result, process, context, and multiperspectival realities are not viewed as significant. Second, and related to the first threat, there is a press toward viewing society and culture as autonomous, rather than as symbolic realities created by humans and obviously used by humans in various, and even insidious, ways. These two threats are not limited to concerns with perspective and theory. They influence method. The third threat is to specify criteria for research and research procedure and thus promote a "control" of knowledge through technical judgments rather than "disciplining" it by observation, reason, and argument. The fourth threat is that all this may render applied ethnography useful only to those who have power. Rossi (1980) writes,

Applied social research tends to be conservative, devoted mainly to the examination of policy alternatives that are not radically different from existing social policies. Fine tuning, rather than revolution, is on the political agenda. At best, applied social research is politically congenial both to those who are liberals and to the right of liberals (p. 897).

Some Suggestions for an Applied Ethnography

No doubt, some may think I have overstated the case, and some may argue that I have confused the functions of basic social research with those of applied research. Obviously, I do not think so. Applied research itself is purposive, although possibly unspecific, political action. The key in my way of thinking is to keep explicit the political, to not render it technical. I concede I believe that this requires applied ethnography to hold sacred its concern with holism, history, comparison, and emic understandings, and thus to serve equally well those who wish to make policy and those who wish to resist it. Only in this way can a value-expressive, applied ethnography be value-neutral. It would express the various interests and sentiments and uncover the dynamics of struggle and power.

This is not to say, however, that all ethnographic research that meets only these criteria will be practical. Much educational ethnography, whether it be the sociolinguistic studies of Gumperz and Hymes (1972), the microethnographies of Mehan (1979), the ethnographics of schooling (Spindler, 1982), or the more macroethnographies of Ogbu (1978), is often better understood as basic research that tests and/or elaborates theory than as applied research which invites anticipatory and originative thought. Basic ethnography is often in the language of truth-seeking and not in the language of truth-making.

Thus I argue for a kind of conservation in applied ethnography. It should remain true to an emphasis on synthesis, even as it concentrates on politics. It should only carefully and reasonably emphasize analysis: Analytic thought is easily transformed into technical thought. It should remain concerned with the creation of everyday life rather than judging the veracity of theory. It should specify technique only so far as to make intelligible what was attempted and what was learned and to facilitate argument-after all, that is what evaluation is about (House, 1977).

Finally, an applied ethnography that is truly practical must incorporate two ideas:

> Those who demand of politics as a science that it teach norms and ends should consider that this demand implies actually the denial of the reality of politics. The only thing we can demand of politics as a science is that it see reality with the eyes of acting human beings, and that it teach men, in action, to understand even their opponents in the light of their actual motives and their position in the historical-social situation (Mannheim, 1936, pp. 163–164).

And,

> Syntheses in thought styles are not made only by those who are primarily synthesists, and who more or less consciously attempt to comprehend a whole epoch in their thinking. They are achieved also by contending groups in so far as they try to unify and reconcile at least all those conflicting currents which they encounter in their own limited sphere (Mannheim, 1936, pp. 152–153).

References

Coleman, J. S. (1972). *Policy research in the social sciences.* Morristown, NJ: General Learning Press Module.

Douglas, J. D. (1976). *Investigative social research.* Beverly Hills, CA: Sage Publications.

Gouldner, A. W. (1970). *The coming crisis of western sociology.* New York: Basic Books.

Gumperz, J., & Hymes, D. (1972). *Directions in sociolinguistics: Ethnography of communications.* New York: Holt, Rinehart and Winston.

House, E. (1977). *The logic of evaluative argument.* Los Angeles: Center for the Study of Evaluation at the University of California at Los Angeles.

Kuhn, T. S. (1962). *The structure of scientific revolutions.* Chicago: University of Chicago Press.

Mannheim, K. (1936). *Ideology and utopia.* New York: Harcourt, Brace and World.

Mehan, H. (1979). *Learning lessons: Social organization in the classroom.* Cambridge: Harvard University Press.

Merton, R. K. (1957). *Social theory and social structure.* Glencoe, IL: Free Press.

Ogbu, J. (1978). *Minority education and caste: The American system in cross-cultural perspective.* New York: Academic Press.

Rist, R. C. (1980). Blitzkrieg ethnography: On the transformation of a method into a movement. *Educational Researcher, 9*(2), 8–10.

Rossi, P. H. (1980). The challenge and opportunities of applied social research. *American Sociological Review, 45*(6), 889–904.

Shackle, G. L. S. (1966). Policy, poetry, and success. *The Economic Journal* (December), 755–767.

Spicer, E. (1976). Beyond analysis and explanation. *Human Organization, 35*(4), 335–343.

Spindler, G. (Ed.). (1982). *Doing the ethnography of schooling.* New York: Holt, Rinehart, and Winston.

Chapter 2

The Holistic Injunction: An Ideal and a Moral Imperative for Qualitative Research

George W. Noblit and John D. Engel

Qualitative researchers are constantly involved in synthesis. We describe, we compare, and we demonstrate cases (Patton, 1980), all in the service of making something larger: an interpretation of what we have seen. All of this activity revolves around what may be called a *holistic injunction* in qualitative research. This injunction requires us to learn all, to take all into account, and to tell all. Holism is, of course, an *ideal*, for the world works against it on every level. It also carries a moral imperative for the research-it is what we ought to do!

Every project is constrained by practical issues-time, money, energy, commitments, and intellectual issues (e.g., ideologies and methodologies). Without the ideal (i.e., the holistic injunction), we could easily fall prey to analytic or systems thought (technical rationality), focusing solely on key pieces and their relations. We would miss the totality of relations, their significance to the participants, and their meaning in the wider human discourse. Further, without this injunction we would not need to be as concerned with how we synthesize our accounts and interpretations.

In this article, we examine the holistic injunction, the programs that it creates for qualitative research, and how we normally go about moving toward holism. In the end, we believe that this requires understanding the nature of synthesis.

The Holistic Injunction

To be sure, qualitative research is about many things. Spicer (1976) and Marcus (1988), among others, noted that qualitative work is emic, comparative, historical, holistic. In being emic, we must understand the multiple perspectives, the competing beliefs, the ways lives are lived, and their implications for social relations. In being comparative, we seek not only to contrast but to combine. We ask, What is the meaning of all perspectives taken together as well as in contrast to one another? In being historical, we not only put events and interpretations into sequence but try to discern how this history and other histories are implicated in present action and what this means for those involved. In all of these, we attend to the fourth criterion, holism. We are emic, comparative, and historical so that we may be holistic.

Holism, of course, is a difficult injunction. Marcus and Fischer (1986) saw it as "an unattainable idea. . . . not to be taken literally" (p. 188). It purposely lacks some overall structure and may be understood in a variety of ways. Patton (1980) wrote:

> This holistic approach assumes that the whole is greater than the sum of the parts; it also assumes that a description and understanding of a program's context is essential for understanding the program (p. 40).

In many ways, it is Patton's latter statement that gives meaning to his first. The key holism test is: Does the qualitative account allow the reader to understand the difference between "surface data and deep structure"? (Light, 1983, p. 57). Marcus and Fischer (1986) wrote:

> The essence of holistic representation in modern ethnography has not been to produce a catalog or an encyclopedia (although the classic assumption supporting the authority of the ethnographic writer is that he commands this sort of background knowledge), but to contextualize elements of culture and to make systematic connections among them (p. 23).

Understanding holism as contextualization does not give more clarity as Marcus and Fischer (1986) went on to explain:

> How to present rich views of the meaning systems of a delimited set of subjects and also to represent the broader system of political economy that links them to other subjects, who are also richly portrayed in their own world, is an experimental ideal (p. 91).

The moral force of the holistic injunction admonishes us to be ambitious, to try to learn all, to take all into account, and to tell all.

Learning All

To learn all, we consciously search for all the variations in language, belief, social relations, events, and action. The holistic injunction is usually responded to by planning an early "mapping" phase in the research that involves searching for and documenting this variation. In mapping, we create the feature of a local terrain—a social and cultural topography. In developing these local features, we observe, and talk to those involved, using informants to validate what we think we know, and searching for disconfirming as well as confirming evidence. Learning all is an exhausting process of eagerly pursuing leads which all too often turn out to be false, then deciding which of all the possibilities to pursue next, and always checking against yourself and your perceptions.

Qualitative researchers check themselves in many ways. In both fieldwork and analysis, multiple approaches are pursued. This strategy can operate at several levels. Denzin (1978) identified four:

1. *Data triangulation* has three subtypes: (a) time, (b) space, and (c) person.
   Person analysis, in turn, has three levels: (a) aggregate, (b) interactive, and (c) collectively.
2. *Investigator triangulation* consists of using multiple rather than single observers of the same object.
3. *Theory triangulation* consists of using multiple rather than single perspectives in relation to the same set of objects.
4. *Methodological triangulation* can entail within-method triangulation and between-method triangulation (p. 295).

When data from triangulation activities stop yielding new insights (a traditional sign that we have learned all), we begin to worry if it is us and not the evidence that is not yielding insights. We then try to take all into account as a way of checking our perspective.

Taking All Into Account

Learning all is essentially naturalistic: You know what you have experienced, seen, been told, and sought out. Taking all into account is, in some sense, contextualizing the naturalistic understanding. Usually, this begins in the later phases of fieldwork, where events are being compared and the scholar's understanding of the local terrain is being elaborated through strategic studies. As Asad (1986) and Turner (1980) suggested, taking all into account involves moving beyond point-by-point comparisons to translations.

Translations try to preserve the completeness and complexity of each event as they are compared. Turner (1980) saw translations as essentially creating analogies, the simplest form being *This is like that except. . . .* Of course, in practice, the analogies created by translating all 'of one scene into another are considerably more involved.

In fieldwork, taking all into account involves not just focusing on a few aspects of social and cultural relations but putting all the relations into their salient contexts. These contexts may involve larger belief systems and social trends or an established pattern of small-group relations. To the qualitative researcher, the sense of things is often understood in terms of all the contexts to things taken together. We find the meaning of particular events in their myriad social and cultural contexts. We then translate the contexts and events into one another and develop an analogy that takes all into account.

The inexperienced field researcher often expresses concern over the perpetual motion possibility of infinite egress. There are so many contexts to be contextualized that taking all into account may never come to an end. The more experienced field researcher sees the process as iterative-working backward and forward until no new interpretations emerge (Glaser & Strauss, 1967).

Telling All

The holistic injunction, finally, requires us to tell all.[1] In practice, we must "tell all" with some real constraints. We have come to think of these constraints collectively as "the audience" for our interpretation. Moreover, we think the audience is primary in that we always "tell all" to someone, real or imagined. This "someone" gives us a referent around which to organize our interpretation. Our interpretations are translations of what we understand into what we believe to be someone else's understanding.

For a translation to approximate holism, it must be "idiomatic," (Barnwell, 1980) in that the meaning of what is studied must be translated into the meaning system of the audience. Of course, some social and cultural scenes and meaning systems may not be directly intelligible to an audience. In this situation, the holistic injunction leaves us with three possibilities (Barnwell, 1980). First, we may use a broadly descriptive account so that the general meaning is conveyed. Second, we may use emic characterizations from the participant, while contextualizing as much as possible. This keeps the strange familiar. Third, we may use emic characterizations from the audience's meaning system, making the familiar strange. This obviously requires the qualitative researcher to be as much a student of human discourse as of the particular scene studied.

Clifford (1986) argued that in constructing this dialogue we are creating an "ethnographic fiction" (p. 6). The *fiction* must speak to how we make sense of anything, and we are keenly aware that the instrument affects the reading (Geertz, 1973). We use our own values as a template for this, often choosing to write our studies as journeys or quests, and may write in the first-person present tense to keep human authorship (Bowers, 1984) and the evolving nature of our understanding in the reader's mind.

Berger (1981) saw this issue as one of transposition. In telling all, we reorganize and reposition the elements of the fiction in the frame of the audience while discussing the problems of doing so. There are dual goals in this fiction making. The first is to "enlarge human discourse" (Geertz, 1973). The second is to defamiliarize so as to allow cultural critique (Marcus & Fischer, 1986) to take place. We will use what is taken to be conventional knowledge about the scene under study and reveal how incomplete and misguided this knowledge is to the comprehension of the scene. By giving the "sense" (Taylor, 1982) and "essence" (Merleau-Ponty, 1962), we defamiliarize our common understandings by comparing them with different conceptions of things. The holistic injunction engages the readers' critical conscience about the scene studied but more important about their own ways of being and thinking.

Conclusion

The holistic injunction in qualitative research leads to all kinds of trouble in everyday practice. Every time you create an interpretation, compare cases, or consider interpretations, you are driven by injunction to be more inclusive, more intelligible, and more complete. Without this injunction, we could simply look at something and express our opinion about it. We could selectively seek and report evidence. We could favor one world view over another. With it, the scholar must come forth, for it is the scholar who learns all, takes all into account, and tells all; it is the scholar who pursues a holistic description, an exhaustive interpretation, and takes the role of representing the particular to the universal and vice versa. The holistic injunction is not a technique or a standard but an ethic that is pursued by individual scholars in real-world contexts. Without the scholars, there is no ethic, no injunction. But without the holistic injunction, there is little value to qualitative research.

Note

1. Our discussion here is from the perspective or constructivist accounts of "telling all." We recognize the active debate regarding types of telling; however, space does not allow us to adequately explore this important issue. We suggest that the interested reader refer to Van Maanen (1988), Geertz (1988), and Clifford & Marcus (1986).

References

Asad, T. (1986). The concept of cultural translation in British social anthropology. In J. Clifford & C. Marcus (Eds.), *Writing culture*. Berkeley: University of California Press.

Barnwell, K. (1980). *Introduction to semantics and translation*. Horsleys Green, UK: Summer Institute of Linguistics.

Berger, P., with Keller, H. (1981). *Sociology reinterpreted*. Garden City, NY: Doubleday.

Bowers, C. (1984). *The promise of theory*. New York: Longman.

Clifford, J. (1986). One ethnographic allegory. In J. Clifford & G. Marcus (Eds.), *Writing culture*. Berkeley: University of California Press.

Clifford, J., & Marcus, G. E. (1986). *Writing culture: The poetics and politics of ethnography*. Berkeley: University of California Press.

Denzin, N. (1978). *The research act: A theoretical introduction to sociological methods*. New York: McGraw-Hill.

Geertz, C. (1973). The interpretation of cultures. New York: Basic Books.

———. (1988). *Works and lives: The anthropologist as author*. Stanford, CA: Stanford University Press.

Glaser, B., & Strauss, A. (1967). *The discovery of grounded theory*. New York: Aldine.

Light, D., Jr. (1983). Surface data and deep structure. In J. Van Maanen (Ed.), *Qualitative methodology* (pp, 57–69). Beverly Hills, CA: Sage.

Marcus, G. (1988). *Imagining the whole: Ethnography's contemporary efforts to situate itself*. Paper presented at the Ethnography in Education Forum, University of Pennsylvania.

Marcus, G., & Fischer, M. (1986). *Anthropology as cultural critique*. Chicago: University of Chicago Press.

Merleau-Ponty, M. (1962). *Phenomenology of perception*. (C. Smith, Trans.). London: Routledge & Kegan Paul.

Patton, M. (1980). *Qualitative evaluation methods*. Beverly Hills, CA: Sage.

Spicer, E. (1976). Beyond analysis and explanation. *Human Organization, 35*, 335–343.

Taylor, C. (1982). Interpretation and the sciences of man. In E. Bredo & W. Feinberg (Eds.), *Knowledge and values in social and educational research*. Philadelphia: Temple University Press.

Turner, S. (1980). *Sociological explanation as translation*. New York: Cambridge University Press.

Van Maanen, J. (1988). *Tales of the field: On writing ethnography*. Chicago: University of Chicago Press.

Chapter 3

Evaluation Designs as Political Strategies

George W. Noblit and Deborah J. Eaker

Evaluation flourishes in eras of accountability such as that reflected by the recent reform movement in education. As the Fuhrman (1988) and Gutmann (1988) chapters in this volume reveal, the school reform agenda is organized around the evaluation of the effectiveness of public education. And, as Corbett and Wilson (1988) show, school reform has intensified the evaluation of individual student, school, and district performance. In many ways, the reformers make the presumption that an evaluation process itself is objective and that its effects are direct and simple, rather than being a political act.

A similar notion is apparent in a recent article by Eleanor Chelimsky (of the General Accounting Office) in which she reviews the recent history of the politics of program evaluation. She speaks of the "very difficult program of *integrating* the *disparate* worlds of politics and evaluation research" (Chelimsky, 1987, p. 200, emphasis added). We disagree and will show that politics and evaluation research, although giving the impression of disparate worlds, are instead inextricably linked. We argue that not only the outcomes of evaluation, but the evaluation process itself is political and the decision to subject a program and its participants to evaluation is a policy decision.

Policymakers and evaluators alike take a number of things for granted in evaluation. First, they assume that evaluation research does not have the characteristics of other social situations. That is, they assume that all parties involved in an evaluation will suspend any vested interests and accord special status to the evaluation. As a result, they assume that the only salient outcome of the evaluation will be a report upon which they can base future actions. They seem to ignore the potential consequences of the evaluation for the parties involved. We suggest that these taken-for-granted assumptions of policymakers and evaluators have consequences which are in fact inherent in evaluation designs.

In this chapter, we examine evaluation designs and identify the inherent political strategy in each. Evaluation, as with any applied research, is "inherently political because it wishes to establish the bases of judgement for others and moreover to replace those that might otherwise be employed" (Noblit, 1984, p. 96). Corbett and Wilson (1988), for example, show how minimum competency testing changes social (and political) relations. We argue that all evaluation designs have the potential of realigning political power and redefining what is credible knowledge. The choice of evaluation design, then, is more than a technical issue. To this end, we examine the alignment of political power and definitions of credible knowledge inherent in six evaluation approaches or designs; positivism, interpretivism, critical theory, aesthetics, collaborative research, and action research. We believe that the issues of political power and credible knowledge take different forms in each of these evaluation designs. The power and credibility of those in charge (or the sponsor), the evaluator-researcher, the evaluatees, and even the evaluation design itself are all at issue. We assert that each evaluation design implicitly presupposes and promotes patterns of social relations and particular knowledge bases and assumptions that facilitate the evaluator's access to the evaluation situation, develop commitment of participants to the evaluation, and thereby enable the evaluation to be politically salient.

Nature of Knowledge and Social Relations

The examination of evaluation designs as political strategies is appropriately a sociology-of-knowledge problem. The sociology of knowledge concerns itself with the social bases, construction, and effects of forms of knowledge such as evaluations (Berger and Luckmann, 1967). As Berger and Luckmann write:

> It is our contention, then, that the sociology of knowledge must concern itself with whatever passes for "knowledge" in a society regardless of the ultimate validity or invalidity. And insofar as all human knowledge is developed, transmitted and maintained in social situations, the sociology of knowledge must seek to understand the processes by which this is done in such a way that a taken-for-granted "reality" congeals for the man in the street (p. 3).

The relative credibility of knowledge is evidenced in belief systems, variously conceptualized as culture, values, ideology, and the like. This set of beliefs is what Collins (1982) refers to as the Durkheimian notion of "precontractual basis of solidarity" inherent in social contracts. Durkheim has posited that every social contract, in this case that of evaluation, actually entails two contracts. The first is the agreed-upon contract, that of engaging in an evaluation using a particular approach. The second is the "hidden contract" that rests on the implicit assumption that all participants agree to the rules of the first contract (Collins, 1982). Thus, because of the political nature of evaluation, the hidden contract brings the belief systems of the various parties to the evaluation into question.

Likewise, the social relations among the evaluation parties are also called into question. Evaluation situations generally involve relations among three parties: the evaluators, the evaluatees, and the sponsors to the evaluation, although in some designs the sponsors may be the evaluatees. To examine the social relations of evaluation design, we use ideas from social network theory, particularly "political clientelism" (Schmidt et al., 1977) In its briefest form, political clientelism posits that networks are maintained by exchange of favors in such a way that an obligation to reciprocate is engendered. Some (horizontal) networks can be more or less equal in power and status, and network relations maintain that equality. Other (vertical) networks consist of patrons and clients. In these networks, clients typically exchange deference and loyalty to the patron for the patron's protection and support. Again, network relations maintain this essential inequality.

Clearly, knowledge and social relations are interactive in evaluation as in all social processes. Evaluation designs are intended to establish the credibility of the knowledge the evaluation generates (House, 1980). In so doing, evaluation challenges the belief systems of some parties and seeks to establish the dominance of the belief systems of others. As we will argue, some evaluation designs establish the credibility of local knowledge (Geertz, 1983), although we use this in a more particularistic sense than Geertz. Local knowledge, as we use it, is simply the knowledge which considers the beliefs of *all* parties to the evaluation as credible. Alternatively, externally legitimated knowledge establishes the dominance of *one* set of beliefs, usually that of the sponsor or evaluator.

In what follows, we reconsider the evaluation designs of positivism, interpretivism, critical theory, aesthetics, collaborative research, and action research as political strategies according to the nature of the knowledge and social relations each implies. The six designs are not always distinct. Collaborative researchers may employ interpretivist ideas, as may aesthetics. Action researchers may be rather positivistic. Critical theory is maintained to encompass and go beyond interpretivism and positivism. Research projects may be both collaborative and action research. Yet, since each evaluation design seeks to create a distinct set of social relations and beliefs, it is useful to examine the six approaches as discrete entities.

Evaluation Designs: The Meaning of "Policy"

Positivism

Knowledge discovered through a positivistic evaluation model is in the service of patrons rather than that of clients, with the design serving to promote the authority of scientific knowledge. Positivism extolls science as the superior way of knowing and the scientist as the expert, or credible agent. Knowledge is discovered through a reductionistic epistemology using a traditional scientific methodology. Human events are seen as part of the natural world and, therefore, as lawful. Smith argues that "these laws describe in neutral scientific language how . . . independently existing reality really operates" (1983, p. 11). As applied to educational evaluation, a positivistic design provides a utilitarian approach to solving evaluation issues "to explain, and by extension to be able to predict, the relationship between or the invariant succession of educational objects and events" (see figure 1).

The evaluator-scientist role in this approach is one of the credible expert. His or her scientific expertise is used to legitimate this status as well as the evaluation design itself. Interpersonal skills are only minimally required, and the relationship between the evaluator and evaluatees is often distant in the pursuit of objectivity. The evaluator-scientist relies on the authoritarian relations between the sponsor and the evaluatees to gain access to and maintain relations with the evaluatees.

The implementation of a positivistic evaluation design clearly assumes social relations that are defined according to carefully delimited patron-client networks. Initially, the evaluator-scientist is client to the patron-sponsor. He or she must show deference and loyalty during the careful negotiation of contract domains to gain access to the evaluatees and to assure power and credibility during the evaluation process. As this juncture, the evaluator-scientist theoretically becomes a competing patron to the sponsor. While the sponsor may maintain

	Positivism	Interpretivism	Critical Theory	Aesthetics	Collaborative Research	Action Research
Credible knowledge	Science	Negotiated	Dialogue and critique	Connoisseurship and Criticism	Joint construction	Practitioner expertise
Network relations	Sponsor as patron	Evaluator as broker	Evaluator as patron	Altruism	Relative equality	Evaluatee as patron
Political result	Evaluator as co-patron	Multiple perspectives	Sponsor "disappears"	Sponsor "disappears"	Reification of collaboration	Sponsor "disappears"

Figure 1 Evaluation designs

certain aspects of patronage, the evaluatees become clients to the evaluator-patron. This patron status is largely based in technical expertise and is reinforced by the access given to the evaluator by the sponsor.

The sponsor in this design is, in the end, also a client to the patron-scientist while continuing to be a patron to the evaluatees. If weak horizontal networks are present among the evaluatees, as might be expected in loosely coupled educational organizations (Weick, 1982), evaluatee clientelism is maintained by authoritarian relations previously established between the evaluatees and sponsor. However, if strong horizontal evaluatee networks exist or develop during the evaluation process, and these networks have an ongoing basis of exchange, the evaluatee client networks can gain power and undermine the evaluation by playing off one patron against the other (i.e. the sponsor and the evaluator).

The belief system required by the positivistic design is one of reification of science. Credibility rests on the hidden contract by all parties that science is indeed an appropriate basis upon which to evaluate and make decisions. The utilitarian nature inherent in this model would seem to demand that knowledge gained would be instrumental or "practical," presumably for the evaluatees. However, such knowledge may be instrumental only in terms of assuring a justification for sponsor decisions and reinforcement of science and the scientific method as the appropriate way to know (House, 1980).

Interpretivism

Interpretivist evaluations are constructive of both belief systems and patron-client relations. They give "voice" to the multiple perspectives revealed in the evaluation. Interpretivism, Patton (1980) has argued, is a dramatic alternative to positivism that focuses on putting the meaning of social situations into relevant contexts (Mishler, 1979). In interpretive evaluations, the evaluator typically observes and interviews the parties to the evaluation to construct a "reading" (Geertz, 1973) of the "multiperspectival realities" (Douglas, 1976) of the situation being evaluated. While interpretivists often view their role as ending with the completion of the research endeavor and its sharing, they will often propose that taking action based on the evaluation is not as straightforward as the sponsor or evaluatees may believe. As interpretivists will argue, the source of problems in an educational program may largely be the assumptions involved in creating the situation, and less so in technical deficiencies in program design or implementation.

Interpretivists see their evaluator role as one of revealing such taken-for-granted assumptions. Since interpretivists are cautious about proposing an instrumental value to their evaluations, they focus more on developing relationships that first provide access to the situation and, over time, create trust in the evaluator. For interpretivists, though, the question "whose side are we on?" (Becker, 1967) looms throughout the evaluation. This question is resolved either by consciously "going native" (Wolcott, 1977) or by providing a descriptive account that puts the case of each "side" into an understandable context.

The social relations of an interpretive evaluation, thus, are complex and changing. The interpretivist usually negotiates for the unique status of a "voyeur," a person who is able to watch universally but reserves the right to decide when participation is appropriate. In doing so, the interpretive evaluator maintains a distance from the normal authority structures present in the situation, carefully avoiding becoming an exclusive member of any network. The role, then, is like that of a broker between social networks. Yet, this broker, unlike most, withholds transmitting messages or facilitating social exchanges until the end of the evaluation, when credible knowledge is revealed in the words of those evaluated.

The evaluatees in an interpretive evaluation are expected to grant access of various sorts to the evaluator. However, they are not assumed to trust the evaluator or the evaluation, as interpretivists view trust as being earned through ongoing social interaction. In granting access, the sponsor-evaluatees in many ways are behaving altruistically. Access, then, comes from a sponsor with sufficient authority and/or patron status vis-à-vis the evaluatee's clientelism, or of existing inter-network relations that include the evaluator prior to the evaluation. In any case, the evaluator avoids being either a patron or a client, while the evaluatee becomes dependent on the good faith of the evaluator. In our experience, both sponsors and evaluatees resolve this issue by coming to believe that the evaluator's account will vindicate their position and actions (cf. Collins & Noblit 1978).

Unlike the other evaluation designs discussed here, interpretivism does not entail a prior belief concerning the legitimacy of the approach; rather only access is required. Interpretivists disavow the usual bases of legitimacy such as content expertise, instrumental utility, or authority. Yet it is expected that over time both trust and the legitimacy of the evaluation will be negotiated. That is to say, interpretivists seek to create a belief in the legitimacy of the evaluation in question, and interpretivism in general. In this way, intepretivists seek converts, and if the conversion is complete, assume the role of a compassionate and evenhanded patron to the evaluatees and sponsor. Loyalty and deference may be exchanged for the protection of a "democratic" multiperspectival reality and the support of the evaluator-patron. If the interpretivist-evaluator cannot achieve this patron status, the evaluation may be rejected as biased and/or not useful.

Critical Theory

Critical theory as a mode of evaluation, is not as popular as the other approaches we discuss here (Bredo & Feinburg, 1982). Yet we have seen its popularity increase in education in recent years (cf. Giroux, 1981). An evaluation that uses the critical theory approach legitimates critique as the form of credible knowledge and the critical theorist as the expert patron. Nonetheless, the beliefs of the critical theorist-evaluator are potentially subject to the same critique as the beliefs of all other parties to the evaluation. Critical theory is essentially the critique of ideologies that justify domination. In Habermas' formulation, ideology distorts communication by masking social contradictions. Such distortion makes it difficult for individuals to discern the ideological content of the beliefs that structure their lives and their consciousness (Geuss, 1981). The critical theorist would have people emancipated from ideological domination through a program of dialogue and discourse (dialogue about the nature of communication itself) designed to promote self-reflection and, consequently, enlightenment or emancipation. Such an evaluation program requires, however, that the evaluator be able to create an approximation of an "ideal speech situation" which allows free and uncoerced discussion (Habermas, 1970).

An evaluation based in critical theory is largely participative, trying to facilitate the evaluatees' free and uncoerced discussion of their situation. Yet, we see that the role of the evaluator-critical theorist is one of first among equals. The evaluator-critical theorist has expertise in critique as a genre as well as in the process of facilitating the ideal speech situation and the dialogue and discourse that ensue. Further, to the extent that such discourse must be based in evidence about social conditions, intersubjective meanings, and the connections between the two, the evaluator-critical theorist also may have roles approximating those of the positivist or interpretivist.

The social relations involved in a critical theory are obviously delicate. The evaluator-critical theorist is in many ways a supreme patron, providing both content and process direction in the service of free and uncoerced dialogue. The evaluator-critical theorist must continually legitimate critique as a genre and reassure the evaluatees of the value of shedding their false consciousness. The evaluatees, at least initially, are clientele to the critical theorist's patronage, in the sense that they must commit to following the patron to some enticing, yet unspecified, and in many ways, unpredictable end. They engage in the approximation of the ideal speech situation as equals among themselves, free to discern ideological distortions as they see them, and free even to decide not to proceed with a course of action once ideologies are revealed (Geuss, 1981). Yet they are not equal to the evaluator-critical theorist in creating the content and process through which this occurs. An evaluation based in critical theory would be wary of an outside sponsor, since the interests of a sponsor may well perpetuate ideological distortions. Any outside sponsor would, of necessity, be more of a philanthropist, providing resources for others to do with as they wish.

A critical theory evaluation requires a set of prior beliefs to be credible. In critical theory, the agreed-upon contract about what is credible knowledge includes agreement concerning the need to shed delusions, a predisposition to critique as the genre in which to do so, and an interest in emancipation. Beliefs in the instrumental or technical value of the evaluation are not required and indeed may be exposed as ideology in the process. What is intriguing about the critical theory approach is that, while the evaluator is a strong patron, there is no suspension of belief in the vested interests of the evaluator-critical theorist. Indeed, since to critical theorists all knowledge has interests (Habermas, 1971), the interests of the evaluator, as well as those of evaluatees, are subject to examination and reflection. Nevertheless, as part of the hidden contract, a critical theory evaluation in the end requires that the evaluatees believe the evaluator is serving their best interests.

Aesthetics

Aesthetic evaluations require that the evaluation be not a goal but an expression of key values that in the end reinforce the altruistic belief in aesthetics. Aesthetics is another type of qualitative approach to evaluation (Eisner, 1979; House 1980). In Eisner's formulation, aesthetic evaluation involves both "connoisseurship" and "criticism." Connoisseurship is the "art of appreciation" (p. 14). The evaluator must have "developed a highly differentiated array of anticipatory schema that enable one to discern qualities and relationships that others, less differentiated, are less likely to see" (p. 14). Connoisseurship is necessary to aesthetic evaluations in that "it provides that content for our knowing. It makes possible the stuff we use for reflection" (p. 15). Yet to Eisner, connoisseurship is private, not public. To make it public, it must be transformed into a form that others can understand. This is the role of criticism. Criticism entails first creating an artistic description so that others may "vicariously participate" (p. 15) in the events at issue. Second, criticism includes rendering an interpretation by "applying theoretical ideas to explain the conditions that have been described" (p. 16). Third, criticism involves an appraisal. This appraisal is not in the form of an outcome-based evaluation. Rather it is to provide constructive criticism, "providing the conditions that lead to the improvement of the educational process" (p. 16).

Eisner and his students have conceived of the role of the evaluator as one that provides "a fresh eye" (p. 17). To do so, he argues that interpersonal skills and trust are essential between the critic and evaluatee: "The teacher must be willing to have a critic in the classroom and must be willing to listen to (but not necessarily heed) what the critic says" (p. 17). In Eisner's view, this relationship is one of a dialogue between friends.

Yet on closer analysis, the social basis of aesthetics involves social relations that are not typically friendship relations. The evaluator-critic must have considerable expertise to be recognized as a source of credible knowledge, yet also be sufficiently independent of other power and authority relations so that the evaluatee is willing to participate in good faith and trust the evaluator-critic. The evaluatee must believe that improvement is so desirable as to seek "a fresh eye." Nevertheless, the evaluatee is dependent on the critic for insight and direction. Eisner argues that schools should provide "structures" (p. 17) for observation and reflection; however, he is clear that connoisseurship and criticism concern that particular, not the universal, rendering aesthetic evaluation not amenable to bureaucratic ends.

The social relations between evaluator-critic and evaluatee involve a subtle dependency of the evaluatee on the expertise of the evaluator-critic without requiring compliance, much like the ideal speech situation in critical theory. Any sponsors outside of this dyadic relationship are simply to provide the opportunity for the evaluation, with the faith that improvement will occur. Intriguingly, the evaluator-critic is not in a patron status as he or she is unable to provide protection and support within the authority of the educational organization. The sponsor, on the other hand, is more like a patron of the arts than a direct supervisor to either party. He or she must believe in the value of aesthetics and sponsor its practice, but not assured of any instrumental gain for the organization, except possibly in social status or in the evaluatee's internal motivations.

Aesthetics, like other designs, seems to involve a precontractual basis of solidarity (Collins, 1982). The conscious contract is an expression of belief in the legitimacy of art criticism as applied to educational practice. Parties must believe that the pursuit of creative expression and its critique is valuable. On the other hand, the hidden contract requires a suspension of belief on the part of the evaluatee in the vested interests of the evaluator-critic and sponsor. Altruism for all parties is assumed. Trust and skills in interpersonal relations are to hold the relationships and beliefs together.

Collaborative Research

There are not real "results" in a collaborative evaluation, as these evaluations can be considered ongoing "experiments in practice" (Torbet, 1981, p. 147). Certainly, there is no search for instrumental knowledge. Rather, Torbet (1981, p. 151) states that collaborative inquiry is a seeking of "valid social knowledge" for the participants to develop and apply to their everyday lives. Collaborative research assumes that research and action are inseparable, except in any analytic sense, and that knowledge comes through and for action. Collaborative inquiry diminishes some of the substantive differences that can be present among practitioners, sponsors, and evaluatees (Schlechty & Noblit, 1982). In collaborative evaluation, all aspects are negotiated—the research design, the roles of all participants, and the issues. The design of collaborative inquiry, then, is not pre-defined nor necessarily stable but is an evolutionary, developmental process (Torbet, 1981).

The evaluator in collaborative inquiry must develop a "shared reality" with all other participants in terms of belief in the collaborative process, role domains, and evaluation issues. Thus, the evaluator's role must be or must become one of an interested agent within the evaluation process.

Collaborative inquiry in its "purest" form requires relative equality of power. This requirement presupposes that social relations are in place prior to the evaluation and that socially enforced equality is maintained through negotiation and active bargaining. Networks within a collaborative design are, in essence, an alliance based on mutual trust and belief rather than one of patrons or clients. Thus, whether the participants are technically evaluator, sponsor, or evaluatee, they must operate as a horizontal network, with the interests of all parties given equal consideration. Yet if collaboration is to achieve an evaluation or a reevaluation of a setting, it must avoid "group think" characteristics of groups together over time. This typically is the job of the evaluator (Schlechty & Noblit, 1982; Newman & Noblit, 1982), who takes the role of representative. The evaluator in the collaborative endeavor represents perspectives from outside the evaluation situation as well as representing the collaboration's perspectives to wider audiences. The evaluator thus assumes an instrumental expertise as a translator. In social networks, this is akin to the role of a "broker" who, in transmitting a message, also invariably alters its content (Lande, 1977). Collaborative research creates a horizontal network and ideally avoids creating patrons. Yet the evaluator-as-broker is a boundary-spanning member of the social network and thus has a subtle, manipulative power upon which the fruits of collaboration are dependent.

It is also true that evaluations using a collaborative design require a precontractual basis of solidarity (Collins, 1982). Legitimate knowledge is process knowledge, not substantive knowledge. The reification of this collaborative process is the basis of the conscious contract. In practice, however, the hidden contract requires a prior trust in the other participants that the negotiated social contract will not be violated. This social contract is definitive only in requiring collaboration and not in specifying a substantive knowledge base as credible.

Action Research

Action research is as technical as positivism for it reifies practical knowledge. Unlike positivism, however, it does so in the service of the interests of the usual underdog in evaluations, the practitioner. Action research has several commonalities with collaborative research and, in fact, differences in the two may be virtually nondiscernible in actual practice. However, we believe theoretically there are differences worth examining in the context of evaluation as political strategy.

Action research insists that the interests of the *practitioner* be primary. The particular method of the evaluation is not as important as its appropriateness to the environment, problem, and participants (Nixon, 1981). The action research approach is being adopted as a mode of evaluation and supervision in many situations, perhaps because it attempts to fill the gap between research and practice through a practice emphasis. In fact, action research uses the evaluatee or practitioner world view as the most credible knowledge base.

The role of the evaluator within action research requires that he or she suspend all personal and professional beliefs about the evaluation issues and setting and believe single-mindedly in the priorities of the practitioner. The evaluator must establish himself or herself as a credible technician to the practitioner as well as a trusted reporter at the conclusion of the evaluation.

This evaluation design is the only one in which the evaluator is ultimately the client to the evaluatees. Although this evaluator clientelism changes somewhat from the initiation to the conclusion of the process, the social networks remain relatively intact. Initially, the evaluator evidences deference and loyalty to the patron-evaluatee through his or her total attention to practitioner-defined issues. The evaluator may prompt action, but it must be justified in terms of practical knowledge as defined by the participants. At the conclusion of the process, the evaluator assumes a representative role, being charged with reporting the results obtained. However, any evaluation results would have been previously created and approved by the evaluatees (Sanford,

1981, p. 178), reinforcing their patron status. Evaluatees would not feel the need to fulfill a clientele role of deference and loyalty to the evaluator since sponsor and evaluator power and authority do not exist within this design. Should a sponsor have a role in the process, generally in the initiation phases, the sponsor essentially "disappears" as is the case in the aesthetic and critical theory designs.

The precontractual basis of solidarity (Collins, 1982) in action research is predicted on a prior agreed-upon contract that the practitioner is the expert and that the process and results of action research are legitimate and credible. Practitioner knowledge, or local knowledge, is the credible knowledge base. The knowledge gained is considered authentic *and* instrumental, unlike the more formal knowledge bases of positivism, interpretivism, and critical theory. Like the aesthetic designs, the hidden contract in action research necessitates the suspension of belief by the evaluatees concerning the vested interests of the sponsors and/or the evaluator. Any sponsor operates under the altruistic belief that the process and results will be valuable for the practitioner evaluatees and, therefore, that the action research evaluation is justified.

The Political Strategy of Evaluation

We have made the case that evaluation is a socially created "reality" that alters social relations and beliefs. In this way, evaluation designs are actually political strategies. Corbett and Wilson (1988) show how relations among teachers, students, and what is taught have changed in the recent reform agenda. Johnson's (1988) chapter argues that teachers have not been empowered by this movement. As Fuhrman (1988) shows, the evaluation upon which the reform agenda has been based produced a new coalition of federal and state actors overcoming prior political coalitions. The essence of the political strategies of evaluation is to fashion a dominant coalition (Benson, 1975). If we look at figure 1, we see that different evaluation designs result in dominant coalitions of rather different forms.

Positivism establishes a dominant coalition of co-patrons, the sponsor, and the evaluator, enabling the evaluatees to, at best, play the co-patrons off against each other (Lande, 1977). In any case, positivistic evaluation designs institutionalize the evaluatee's client status to some patron or patrons. Interpretivism negotiates a local definition of credible knowledge. The evaluator spans network boundaries between sponsor and evaluatee. The political result is less determinant than with positivism. However, an interpretivist evaluation that develops new understandings of what is credible knowledge through a broker role allows for considerable political bargaining. The political strategy of collaborative research, by comparison, is based in relatively equal political power between the parties. This reification of collaborative social relations also allows for considerable bargaining. Without a broker, however, the possibilities for new understandings of what is credible knowledge are considerably fewer than with interpretivism.

Critical theory, aesthetics, and action research all result in a curious "disappearance" of the sponsor from the dominant coalition that results from the evaluation design. Moreover, each has the sense that the sponsor "volunteers" to disappear. What the disappearance means for the sponsor, however, varies. In aesthetic designs, the sponsor disappears because of an altruistic belief that the artistic is a valuable perspective to add to more instrumental perspectives on education. Critical theory designs consider the sponsor's position to be (potentially) an ideological masking of raw power relations, undercutting any claims by the sponsor to legitimate and/or patron status. Inasmuch as the method is critique, the basis of new coalitions is in opposition to externally legitimated belief systems and patterns of social relations. As Everhart (1983) argues, however, opposition may well be reproductive of hegemonic social relations. Practical knowledge is reified in action research. The sponsor "disappears" because this knowledge is the product of the practitioner. This reification of practical knowledge also reduces the creditability of evaluator to that of a technician. The dominant coalition in action research has the practitioners as the patrons.

If we combine this analysis of the six designs along the dimensions of relative power, and credibility of knowledge systems, the resulting table (see figure 2) suggests the conditions under which each of the six evaluation approaches would be successful as a political strategy to fashion a dominant coalition (Benson, 1975).

When there is a high power imbalance in favor of those in authority and an externally legitimated belief in science as a credible way to know, positivistic evaluation designs are most likely to fashion a dominant coalition. Under similar conditions, except that the externally legitimated knowledge base involves the process and substance of critique, critical theory is the effective strategy to achieve a dominant coalition. A high power imbalance (toward the evaluatees) and locally

	High Power Imbalance		Low Power Imbalance	
	Externally legitimated knowledge	Local knowledge	Externally legitimated knowledge	Local knowledge
Appropriate evaluation designs	Positivism Critical theory	Action research	Aesthetics	Interpretivism Collaborative research

Figure 2 Fashioning a dominant coalition by evaluation

legitimated knowledge are the conditions under which action research is an effective political strategy.

Under the conditions of a low power imbalance and an externally limited knowledge base that is personified in experts, aesthetic designs seem to be the appropriate mechanism by which to fashion a dominant coalition. Low power imbalance and a belief in locally legitimated knowledge indicate two appropriate designs. When multiple knowledge bases are legitimated, collaborative research is the political strategy leading to a dominant coalition. When the legitimated local knowledge is based less in practitioner expertise and more in a belief that what takes place "here" is more worthy than knowledge based externally to the evaluation situation, interpretivism is the political strategy of choice.

In the final analysis, however, it would be a mistake to consider the conditions and the resulting appropriate design as absolute. In practice, the choice of an evaluation design is recognized, we would argue, as a political strategy and, as much, the choice may alter the conditions themselves. We expect that politically successful evaluations (i.e., those fashioning a dominant coalition) are an iterative process, a series of moves and countermoves that, in the end, produce a design or series of designs. This seems to require evaluators that are politically adept and methodologically flexible.

Conclusions

It is apparent from our analysis that the sociology-of-knowledge approach exposes many of the take-for-granted assumptions in evaluation research. Evaluators seem to take a number of things for granted. First, regardless of the design they employ, they take for granted that evaluation research does not have the characteristics of other social situations. Our analysis shows that this is not fully the case. Evaluation situations have the same bases in patterns of social relations and beliefs as any other social endeavor. Not only are evaluation designs political strategies, but they must be considered as political as any other social design, plan, or program. Second and related, (specific) evaluators take for granted that the evaluatees will suspend a belief in the vested interests of the parties to the evaluation. This is, they assume that evaluatees will accord evaluation a special status and treat it as an unusual social situation. Third, many evaluators take for granted a precontractual basis of solidarity (Collins, 1982) in an evaluation situation. Positivists assume it emerges from the legitimacy of science. Action researchers, collaborative researchers, critical theorists, and aesthetic evaluators all also argue that trust is a precondition. Only the interpretivists, as is consistent with their approach, view trust as something to be developed through the usual processes of social interaction. Fourth, evaluation researchers seem to take for granted that the salient outcome of the evaluation situation is a factual report or a set of values upon which future actions can be based or both. Our analysis suggests that another salient outcome is a new political arrangement between the parties to the evaluation situation. Further, we would argue that this arrangement may well be the primary basis of future action.

This reconsideration of evaluation should not be taken to imply that we believe evaluations designs are *only* political strategies; but we would argue that *at their base* they are political strategies. Further, it should not be inferred that, because we see evaluations as political, evaluations are not worthy social processes. If anything, our analysis establishes that evaluations are recognizable processes through which values and, thus, worthiness are created.

Similarly, we can reconsider the recent reform movement as an attempt to improve American education through a political realignment. The "crisis" evaluations made in the report *Nation at Risk* and elsewhere politically galvanized, as Fuhrman argues, state leadership and redefined state political contexts. As Corbett and Wilson demonstrate, the "game" has changed for local systems. State responsibility to a national norm was established by the various reform reports. Local districts and teachers have been undercut in the process. This evaluation, like all evaluations, is well understood as a political strategy.

References

Becker, H. (1967). Whose side are we on? *Social Problems, 14*, pp. 239–247.

Benson, J. K. (1975). The interorganizational network as a political economy, *Administrative Science Quarterly, 20*, pp. 229–248.

Berger, P., & Luckmann, T. (1967). *The social construction of reality: A treatise in the sociology of knowledge.* Garden City, NY: Doubleday.

Bredo, E., & Feinberg, W. (1982). *Knowledge and values in social and educational research.* Philadelphia: Temple University Press.

Chelimsky, E. (1987). What have we learned about the politics of program evaluation? *Educational Evaluation and Policy Analysis, 9* (3), pp. 199–213.

Collins, R. (1982) *Sociological insight.* New York: Oxford University Press.

Collins, T., & Noblit, G. W. (1978). Stratification and resegregation: The case of Crossover High School. Final report of NIE Contract 400-76-009.

Corbett, R., & Wilson. B. L. (1988). Raising the stakes in statewide mandatory minimum competency testing. In J. Hannaway and R. Crowson (Eds.), *The politics of reforming school administration.* London: Falmer Press.

Douglas, J. D. (1976). *Investigative social research.* Beverly Hills, CA: Sage.

Eisner, E. (1979). The use of qualitative forms of evaluation for improving educational practice. *Educational Evaluation and Policy Analysis, 6* (1), pp. 11–19.

Everhart, R. (1983). *Reading, writing and resistance.* Boston: Routledge & Kegan Paul.

Fuhrman, S. (1988). State politics and education reform. In J. Hannaway & R. Crowson (Eds.), *The politics of reforming school administration.* London: Falmer Press.

Geertz, C. (1973). *The interpretation of cultures.* New York: Basic Books.

———. (1983). *Local knowledge.* New York: Basic Books.

Geuss, R. (1981). *The idea of a critical theory: Habermas and the Frankfurt school.* New York: Cambridge University Press.

Giroux, H. (1981). *Ideology, culture, and the process of schooling.* Philadelphia: Temple University Press.

Gutmann, A. (1988). Democratic theory and the role of teachers in democratic education. In J. Hannaway & R. Crowson (Eds.), *The politics of reforming social administration.* London: Falmer Press.

Habermas, J. (1970). Toward a theory of communicative competence. In H. P. Dreitzel (Ed.), *Recent sociology no. 2: Patterns of communicative behavior.* Basingstoke: Macmillan.

————. (1971). *Knowledge and human interests.* Boston: Beacon Press.

House, E. R. (1980). *Evaluating with validity.* Beverly Hills, CA: Sage.

Johnson, S. M. (1988). Schoolwork and its reform. In J. Hannaway and R. Crowson (Eds.), *The politics of reforming school administration.* London: Falmer Press.

Lande, C. H. (1977). Introduction: the dyadic basis of clientelism. In S. W. Schmidt et al. (eds.) *Friends, Followers and Factions.* (Berkeley, CA: University of California Press).

Mishler, E. (1979). Meaning in context, *Harvard Educational Review, 49,* pp. 1–19.

National Commission on Excellence in Education, The. (April,1983). *A Nation At Risk: The Imperative for Educational Reform* (ED1.2:N21). Washington, DC: US Government Printing Office.

Newman, C., & Noblit, G. W. (1982). Collaborative research: A staff development experience, *The Journal of Staff Development, 3*(2), pp. 119–129.

Nixon, J. (Ed.). (1981). *A teachers' guide to action research: Evaluation, enquiry, and development in the classroom.* London: Grant McIntyre.

Noblit, G. W. (1984). The prospects of an applied ethnography for education: a sociology of knowledge interpretation, *Education Evaluation and Policy Analysis, 6*(1), pp. 95–101.

Patton, M. Q. (1980). *Qualitative evaluation methods.* Beverly Hills, CA: Sage.

Sanford, N. (1981). A model for actions research. In P. Reason and J. Rowan (Eds.), *Human inquiry: A sourcebook of new paradigm research.* New York: Wiley.

Schlechty P., & Noblit, G. W. (1982). Some uses of sociological theory in educational evaluation. *Research in Sociology of Education and Socialization, 3,* pp. 283–306.

Schmidt, S. W., et al. (Eds.). *Friends, followers, and factions.* Berkeley, CA: University of California Press.

Smith, J. K. (1983). Quantitative versus qualitative research: An attempt to clarify the issue, *Educational Researcher, 12*(3), pp. 6–13.

Torbet, W. R. (1981). Why educational research has been so uneducational: The case of a new model of social science based on collaborative inquiry. In P. Reason & J. Rowan (Eds.), *Human Inquiry: A sourcebook of new paradigm research.* New York: Wiley.

Weick, K. E. (1982). Administering education in loosely coupled schools. *Phi Delta Kappan, 63*(10), pp. 673–676.

Wolcott, H. (1977). *Teachers versus technocrats: An educational innovation in anthropological perspective.* Eugene, OR: Center for Educational Policy and Management at the University of Oregon.

Chapter 4

Action Research as an Agent for Developing Teachers' Communicative Competence

Dwight L. Rogers
George W. Noblit
Phyllis Ferrell

Action research is a vehicle to put teachers in charge of their craft and its improvement. Yet there is considerable variation in what people see action research accomplishing for teachers. These variations range from mundane technical improvement in classrooms to transforming a teacher's identity (Oberg & McCutcheon, 1987).

Some see these variations as a problem (Holly, 1987). We do not. It appears to us that what is changed through a teacher's involvement in action research is the ability to participate in the culture, to decide what will be maintained and what will be altered. Different teachers and action research groups create different types of changes because teachers become empowered to decide what they wish to change and what they do not.

In a close look at individual teachers, both change and maintenance can be seen to occur. This is often missed because university faculty sponsors of action research groups may be vested in a particular type of change, whether it be improving classroom teaching, advancing social justice, or empowering teachers. Many of these sponsors may not have fully considered the complex nature of change in general and for the individual teacher in particular. We reconsider this simplistic notion of change by (A) exploring how one teacher described what action research did for her; (B) examining our naive view of change; and (C) proposing an explanation for the variability in change that results from action research.

We begin below with a story of the involvement of one third-grade teacher (Fig Ferrell[1]) in action research. This account is compiled from excerpts from a number of "research reports" written by Fig between September 1988 and June 1989.

Fig's Story

Over the years, my teaching style has changed. After being chosen "outstanding future educator" by my college professors, I began my teaching life realizing my hopes and dreams for providing my children with a stimulating, holistic learning environment. The children and I sang, played soccer, learned to do primitive firings in pottery, and also learned the "core curriculum."

Now, eight years later, the types of activities I most wanted to do are performed by "specialists." I have become consumed with making absolutely certain that all of the curricular objectives mandated by our state are drilled into the minds of twenty-five third-grade students. I have become obsessed with the performance of the duties I consider to be the necessary components of "teaching." Each day is an attempt to have the perfect program-classes begin on time, transitions are smooth and quick, lessons follow the seven-step plan, all students are "on task," and procedures are established and evident in the function of the class.

The change in my teaching began about four years ago. I lost my vision of teaching. My brain was taken over by a notebook full of learning objectives and by numbers that appeared on labels each spring that were supposed to measure how effective an educator I was.

I have always received great evaluations. Nonetheless, I felt uncomfortable about what was happening in my class. The children were performing well, but I felt the atmosphere was not right. Still, I continued teaching in the same manner, knowing that something would have to give or I would be looking into another profession very soon.

This past year I enrolled in a university action research class. It is a course designed for active educators who want to take a close look at what they are doing in their classrooms, evaluate it, alter it, evaluate it again, and determine its effectiveness given their goals.

My original goal was to spend more time with my children. It soon became clear that I first needed to know how much individual time I spent with children during the instructional part of the day. I already spent time with them at lunch, while walking in lines, and after school.

My goal was to somehow spend more time with them so that the teachable moment was once again possible and so that they could have a chance to share their lives with me.

I tried several methods of collecting data about how much time I spent with each child. Recording in a nightly journal was not effective because I could not remember all of the interactions. I asked the children to keep a record on a special form. We discussed my goal as a class and what they should consider an interaction to be, but the children never could remember to mark their forms or agree on just what constituted an interaction. I tried wearing a form on my back for children to mark immediately after having an interaction. This worked well at first. They loved writing on my back. The excitement soon faded, however, and I was spending valuable time tracking down someone who had not marked his form.

I decided to try one more method. I made a large wall chart with all the children's names on it. Each time I interacted with a child, I would hand out a sticker for the child to place on the chart. I scribbled a few words on each sticker about the nature of the interaction. This lasted about a week. Writing down what the interaction was became distracting to me. However, the chart was revealing. For the first time I had devised a method that was cumulative. Over the course of a week, some children had accumulated twenty or more stickers, while some children had only one, or none.

It was during this time I sent Jessica's parents a note indicating that her work was careless, incomplete, and not up to her potential. The next morning I received a phone call requesting a conference for that day. I was not prepared for what I heard. The conference went smoothly until Jessica's mother said her daughter did not feel that I spent enough time with her. It was then I realized that Jessica was responding to the chart. I mentioned my research project to her mother, and she said that when she asked Jessica what the problem was in school, Jessica had broken down and cried and mumbled something about only one sticker and a tornado.

I was devastated. I knew immediately what Jessica was talking about. There had been a tornado in a nearby city a week earlier, and Jessica's grandmother's house had been partially destroyed. The next morning, Jessica had talked to me about it, and I had given her a sticker with the word tornado on it to place on the chart.

I had only used the wall chart for one week, and it was still up on the wall at the time of the conference a week later. Jessica sat directly across from the chart. Every day she was looking at it, seeing that some children had many stickers, while she had only that one about the tornado. She felt that I didn't care. I was crushed for not foreseeing the consequences of displaying the chart.

To end the conference, I tried to comfort her mother by explaining why some children had so many stickers while others had none. This child does not read, this child has attention deficit problems, this child is learning disabled. . . . I told her mother that I would have lunch with Jessica the next day to discuss concerns and to explain my side of the situation. Her mother left feeling as though I did care and confident that I would deal with the situation.

Jessica and I did have lunch. We discussed my time limitations and her needs. I told her to be sure to seek me out first thing in the morning if she had something to share and to please sit with me at lunch a couple of days a week. She seemed satisfied and I felt better, but I also knew that Jessica was just one symptom of a larger problem. What about the others in my class who had undoubtedly felt similar feelings?

I am still driven by the curriculum notebook and test scores, but not as much. It is an addiction that is hard to break. Most of the time I feel schizophrenic: one part of me driven to teach those objectives and the other begging to engage in meaningful learning and interaction with the children. I have learned there are more important issues in our children's lives than learning letter sounds and parts of speech. Tornadoes are important and so is communication with others.

My research question has been answered. How much time do I spend with my children? Not enough. I did not find that answer directly through my research. A child has told me that she needs me more than I give of myself.

I have come to feel better concerning my own ideas about teaching, but I am still not satisfied. I know more about what teaching should be, but there is still a part of me that believes I will never really understand teaching. As changing social and economic forces within our society influence the school's role in helping our children learn to lead healthy, responsible, and enriched lives, I think I will have to be comfortable with a continual questioning of my own values and decisions concerning just what teaching is in order to be the best I can be.

Action Research and Change

As Fig's story illustrates, action research provides teachers with a personal and meaningful way to thoughtfully investigate their own practice. Unlike "traditional" educational research, action research is interwoven with change and "takes place in direct cooperation with the educational practice the research seeks to serve" (Brock-Utne, 1980, p. 10).

The primary assumption behind encouraging teachers to engage in action research is that through careful study of their practice they will improve their teaching (Winter, 1987). Advocates of action research claim it has a transformative effect and leads teachers to gain a new perspective and an enriched understanding of the classroom (McCutcheon, 1981; Mohr, 1987; Nixon, 1981). Teacher researchers "testify to the power of their own research to help them better understand and ultimately to transform their teaching practices" (Cochran-Smith & Lytle, 1988, p. 13).

Stenhouse (1975) argues action research is the "route to teachers' emancipation" and that through action research teachers can strengthen their judgments and improve their classroom practices. Evans and colleagues (Evans et al., 1987) contend that generating and conducting their own research can "lead teachers to improve their practice and to develop a new vision of their role within the profession so that they come to see themselves as able to contribute to the improvement of educational practice more broadly" (pp. 1–2).

Action research seems promising. If we believe the literature, it may be even a little too promising. As illustrated above, action research appears to lead to understanding, improvement, empowerment, and even transformation. Yet our experience working with Fig and other teacher researchers tempers this a bit. While some individual teachers may improve their practice, become empowered, and even transform themselves or their teaching, not all do.

We agree with Cochran-Smith and Lytle (1988) who point out, "This view of the transformative power of teacher research is probably naive; not only does it once again put the onus of school reform on the teachers, but also it does not acknowledge the many structural features of school systems that constrain bottom-up, inside-out reform" (p. 14). When an emphasis is placed on the power of action research to improve teaching and bring about change, action research is assigned the role of "change agent." As a change agent, action research is presumed to be something that helps teachers to improve their practice.

Those writing about the value of action research may have placed too much emphasis on its power to change (Winter, 1987). Change is not always what we have taken it to be. The concept of change in education is permeated with a technological rationality (Kemmis & DiChiro, 1987), with change understood as an intentional effect of a planned intervention. Change is seen as part of improvement that in turn is defined as doing one's job better (Kyle & Hovda, 1987).

Giddens (1979) notes that change is not a linear process whereby what is planned becomes rationally and systematically linked to outcomes. He believes that part of any change is the unacknowledged conditions carried with it. According to Giddens, change often generates not what was intended but unanticipated consequences. It is the complex nature of change that keeps society from being fully deterministic. For educators, this is why policies and what happens in classrooms seem quite different.

Our understanding of change through action research is naive in other ways. Our society has come to assume that change is necessary, natural, and good (Bowers, 1984). This view of change is part of our notion of progress. According to Bowers this belief about change disempowers the masses of our society because it leads them to believe that cultural and social practices are created and altered by some unknown force and not by them.

Communicative Competence

Although teachers' involvement in action research may result in validation and in such various personal changes as empowerment, improvement, and transformation, its power to facilitate "communicative competence" (Bowers, 1984, p. 2) is what makes action research so valuable to teachers. Communicative competence is the ability to participate in the discussion about what should be maintained and what should be changed in our culture. A communicatively competent person can negotiate the meanings that are attached to the events and purposes of social practices instead of simply accepting them as given.

For example, in our action research class, we start by reviewing how others have defined action research. If we stopped here, accepting others' definitions as the "correct" way to think of action research, we would inhibit communicative competence. We do not. We use these definitions as a place to start and have our teachers create and then negotiate their own definitions with one another. Action research becomes something they control and can change, should they see the need.

We see this in Fig's account, when she defines action research as repeated evaluation of her effectiveness given *her* goals, not someone else's. Fig exhibits her communicative competence when she states, "I will have to be comfortable with a continual questioning of my own values and decisions concerning just what teaching is in order to be the best I can be."

Communicative competence in teaching is also revealed by the following statement of a fifth-grade teacher-researcher: "Since my involvement in the action research group I have begun to feel more in control of what I teach and how I teach it. I can change and improve with the knowledge that I have studied the situation and I know which changes are necessary and will improve my classroom" (Fleming et al., 1988, p. 8).

As illustrated by these examples, the importance of action research is not that it will facilitate change but that it creates conditions for developing communicative competence and provides the opportunity for teachers to better understand themselves, their colleagues, and their practice. Nixon (1981) argues, "Action research serves primarily to sharpen perceptions, stimulate discussion and encourage questions" (p. 9).

Teachers' participation in dialogue about their classroom practices is a critical part of their process of searching for meaning in their teaching. Action research groups establish a forum where teachers can talk candidly and openly about their classrooms and thus themselves. Another teacher-researcher, Margaret Mason, has told us in a personal communication that it is "the stimulation of sharing with other teachers and the support we get from each other; the opportunity to talk seriously about what we are doing in education, to ask questions, explore ideas, and think, that is so very important to me."

Like Kemmis and DiChiro (1987), we believe the communal search for meaning is central to the action research process and crucial for the development of communicative competence. As the teacher-researchers from our first action research class assert, it was their participation in and commitment to the action research group that brought "significance to our views of our classrooms and the children in them. Overall, the group has led us to think in greater depth about our teaching, helped us to crystallize new insights, and provided us with the incentive and confidence to make changes in our classrooms" (Fleming et al., 1988, p. 4).

It was through their involvement with action research and the support and stimulation of fellow teacher-researchers that Fig and the other teachers became communicatively competent and changed not only their classrooms but also their stance concerning change. Instead of simply responding to the cultural forces, they began to create culture themselves. They became cultural participants in ways they were not before.

Communicative Competence and Change Agentry

Communicative competence begins with the recognition of the taken-for-granteds in teaching, a dereification of knowledge (Bowers, 1984). The range of changes promoted by action research is an indication of teachers' becoming communicatively competent. The teacher who is a cultural participant can decide to conserve as well as change.

In Fig's case, she altered some of her practices and beliefs about teaching while retaining others. It was, however, the dereification of knowledge triggered by her awareness of the impact of outside forces (e.g., mandated skills, teacher effectiveness research, teaching evaluations, parents) on her teaching that first encouraged her to act on her concern that she was not spending enough time with the children. As she said, "They say you can never lick a problem until you realize you have one. I know I need to exorcise from my soul that obsession which began four years ago-that driving, never-let-up, stressful manner which I have allowed to take over my conscience and dominate my teaching."

Fig claimed that the action research class and Jessica helped her recognize the problem that had been plaguing her for the past few years. It required her to reconsider and dereify what counts as knowledge and good practice in education today. In doing so, she became aware that the increased technological rationality was interfering with her values about her involvement with the children. After she identified the problem, she was able to try to do something about it. This action took the form of her research project. As Bowers (1984) and Giddens (1979) have warned, changing a teaching situation is not as simple or straightforward as we have portrayed it to be.

Fig's story and her comments below show how her new understanding of the taken-for-granteds in her classroom made it possible for her to realize her own "power" to change plus the "trade-offs" she must make in altering and maintaining her classroom processes (Bowers, 1984). As Fig explains, "I'm struggling and scared. If I change my style, I'm worried that those little scores will fall and my performance will be questioned. But I'm giving in. I have changed my style a little bit so far, and I feel better about the atmosphere of my classroom already."

Communicative competence gives one the "ability to read or decode the taken-for-granted assumptions and conceptional categories that underlie the individual's world of experience" (Bowers, 1984, p. 2). We believe communicative competence is the product of teachers' self-study, reflection, and dialogue about their work. As Bowers suggests, the development of communicative competence occurs through the process of negotiating a new basis for understanding, which in turn helps expand teachers' knowledge in a way that makes informed choice possible. Through creating an arena that promotes honest, thoughtful, serious dialogue about teaching, action research encourages communicative competence, which in turn gives teachers a voice and a chance to participate in the discussions about what to change and what not to change in their classrooms.

Conclusion

Many authors see action research as an agent or mechanism for changing teachers. Certainly, some change results from action research. But not all teachers make the same changes (Oberg & McCutcheon, 1987). All of the teacher-researchers we have worked with *both* changed and remained the same. The point is that teachers are the agents, not action research. As the agents, teachers can choose what to change or not to change at all.

Fig, for all her communicative competence, still is "driven" by the curriculum and test scores, even if less so. She still believes that accomplishing curriculum objectives is important. Moreover, she is now more able to culturally negotiate and create that belief in others in the action research class and through her writings. The crucial issue is the extent to which action research promotes communicative competence and cultural participation, and enables teachers to better promote whatever values they hold.

Being communicatively competent does not mean that teachers will inevitably adopt critical social science perspectives or transform their identities (Kemmis & DiChiro, 1987; Oberg & McCutcheon, 1987). They are unlikely to change their classrooms in ways we might wish because they now are better able to create their classrooms as they would wish them to be. An indeterminacy is created in this process. Teachers, empowered to both change and stay the same, negotiate these meanings with other teachers through the dialogue over action research projects. Their voice and participation in the cultural discourse about education are vital as they create and reproduce their cultural beliefs in action research classes as well as in their own schools and classrooms.

Note

1. Fig Ferrell is Phyliis Ferrell, one of the authors of this article.

References

Bowers, C. (1984). *The promise of theory*. New York: Longman.

Brock-Utne, B. (1980). What is educational action research? In J. Elliott & D. White-head (Eds.), *Classroom action research network: The Theory and practice of educational action research* (Bulletin No. 4, pp. 10–15). Cambridge, UK: Cambridge Institute of Education.

Cochran-Smith, M., & Lytle, S. L. (1988, February). *Teacher research: Contrasting perspectives on collaboration and critique*. Paper presented at the Ethnography and Education Forum, University of Pennsylvania, Philadelphia.

Evans, C. L., et al. (1987). *Educational practitioners: Absent voices in the building of educational theory*. Wellesley, MA: Working Paper No. 170, Wellesley College Center for Research on Women.

Fleming, J. et al. (1988). *Talking seriously about teaching: Empowerment through enforced reflection*. Unpublished manuscript, University of North Carolina at Chapel Hill.

Giddens, A. (1979). *Control problems of social theory*. Berkeley: University of California Press.

Holly, P. (1987). Action research: Cul-de-sac or turnpike? *Peabody Journal of Education, 64*(3), 71–99.

Kemmis, S., & DiChiro, G. (1987). Emerging and evolving issues of action research praxis: An Australian perspective. *Peabody Journal of Education, 64*(3), 101–130.

Kyle, D. W., & Hovda, R. A. (1987). Action research: Comments on current trends and future possibilities. *Peabody Journal of Education, 64*(3), 170–175.

McCutcheon, G. (1981). The impact of the insider. In J. Nixon (Ed.), *A teachers' guide to action research* (pp. 186–193). London: Grant McIntyre.

Mohr, M. (1987). Teacher-researchers and the study of the writing process. In D. Goswami & P. R. Stillman (Eds.), *Reclaiming the classroom: Teacher research as an agency for change* (pp. 94–106). Upper Montclair, NJ: Boynton/Cook.

Nixon, J. (1981). *A teachers' guide to action research*. London: Grant McIntyre.

Oberg, A., & McCutcheon, G. (1987). Teachers' experience doing action research, *Peabody Journal of Education, 64*(2), 116–127.

Stenhouse, L. (1975). *An introduction to curriculum research and development*. London: Heinemann.

Winter, R. (1987). *Action-research and the nature of social inquiry: Professional innovation and educational work*. Aldershot, UK: Avebury.

Chapter 5

Meta-Ethnography:
Synthesizing Qualitative Studies

George W. Noblit and R. Dwight Hare

Introduction

In what follows, we present an argument concerning how qualitative researchers ought to think about interpretive explanation and practice the synthesizing of multiple studies. Our approach to synthesizing qualitative studies has two primary applications. First, students and researchers are perennially involved in conducting and writing literature reviews. Our meta-ethnographic approach enables a rigorous procedure for deriving substantive interpretations about any set of ethnographic or interpretive studies. Like the quantitative counterparts of meta-analysis (Glass et al., 1981; Hunter et al., 1982) and the integrative research review (Cooper, 1984), a meta-ethnography can be considered a complete study in itself. It compares and analyzes texts, creating new interpretations in the process. It is much more than what we usually mean by a literature review. Second, qualitative researchers in the process of analyzing data create various texts: notes, matrices, preliminary descriptions, and analyses. We compare these texts as we create a holistic interpretation. Our approach suggests a way to approach this comparative and interpretive task. As will become evident, synthesizing qualitative research is no simple task. It requires a sophisticated understanding of the nature of comparison and interpretation, a meticulous yet creative rendering of the texts to be synthesized, and reciprocal translations of the meanings of one case into the meanings of another.

While interpretivists are reluctant to define things in the abstract, we will venture what we mean by the term *meta-ethnography*. Meta-ethnography is the synthesis of interpretive research. To preserve the uniqueness and holism that characterize qualitative studies, we argue that one form of meta-ethnography involves the translation of studies into one another. The translation of studies takes the form of an analogy between and/or among the studies. Further explanation and elaboration follow.

The Idea of a Meta-Ethnography

Meta-ethnography is a term we use to characterize our approach to synthesizing understanding from ethnographic accounts. Our analogy here is obviously to meta-analysis (see Glass et al., 1981; Hunter et al., 1982). Any similarity lies only in a shared interest in synthesizing empirical studies. What follows is our idea about how qualitative researchers ought to think about this task. This book is not for everyone. It will be of most interest to social scientists who struggle to "put together" the many qualitative studies now being produced, to the researcher or student who wishes to construct interpretivist literature reviews, to policy researchers and policymakers who wish to use humanistic research in their deliberations but who are at a loss about how to "reduce" it, and to qualitative researchers concerned with interpreting multiple cases and/or alternative lines of argument.

We argue that a meta-ethnography should be interpretive rather than aggregative. We make the case that it should take the form of reciprocal translations of studies into one another. The need for this type of discourse is based on a concrete example of a synthesis attempt that failed. The example itself reveals why this type of discourse is needed. As argued elsewhere (Noblit, 1981), utilitarian culture places unique demands on qualitative evaluation research. Since research and evaluation funding are tied to improvement of practice, it is especially important that interpretivists discuss how they construct explanations, how interpretive explanations are different from other ways of constructing explanations, and what can reasonably be said about some sets of studies. Despite our utilitarian culture, a meta-ethnography cannot be driven by technical interests (Habermas, 1971). Instead, meta-ethnography must be driven by the desire to construct adequate interpretive explanations. As the range of interpretive, qualitative social research expands, we will need to focus our discourse on how we might compare our accounts. This focus must occur even if, as Geertz (1973) argues, there is little prospect of creating a general theory of interpretivism. The more formal qualitative researchers (e.g., Miles & Huberman, 1984) see the issue of comparing studies as one of explicitness about the processes we use to analyze our data. We tend to agree with Marshall's assessment (1985) that this is the "bureaucratization" of data analysis. The meta-ethnographic approach we develop here takes a different tack: We focus on constructing interpretations not analyses. To our way of thinking, the synthesis of qualitative research should be as interpretive as any ethnographic account.

The Paradigm Problem

Our notion of meta-ethnography is firmly based in the interpretive paradigm. It is an alternative to developed approaches in the positivist paradigm. *Paradigm*, as Kuhn (1970) uses the term, refers to both "the entire constellation of beliefs, values, techniques, and so on shared by the member of a given community" (p. 175) and the exemplary but "concrete puzzle-solutions" (p. 175) of the scientific community. In the social sciences, the two major paradigms are interpretivism and positivism.

The interpretivist paradigm includes research that is termed *ethnographic, interactive, qualitative, naturalistic, hermeneutic,* or *phenomenological*. All these types of research are interpretive in that they seek an explanation for social or cultural events based upon the perspectives and experiences of the people being studied. In this way, all interpretive research is "grounded" in the everyday lives of people. In doing so, interpretivists seek "to make sense of an object of study . . . to bring to light an underlying coherence" (Taylor, 1982, p. 153).

Interpretivist studies usually rely on "thick description" (Geertz, 1973), the detailed reporting of social or cultural events that focuses on the "webs of significance" (Geertz, 1973) evident in the lives of the people being studied. Since these studies reveal that context affects the meaning of events, interpretivists are dubious about the prospects of developing natural science-type theories or laws for social and cultural affairs.

The positivist paradigm is optimistic about the prospects for general theories or laws and largely seeks to develop them. Some positivists insist on a strict deductive logic-stating theory, deducing hypotheses, and testing the hypotheses. Others are less strict, arguing that the causal laws of social affairs can be discovered through empirical study, and through the accumulation of such studies. In general, however, positivists quantify social events and assess the statistical relationships between variables in the service of constructing an abstract theory.

Explanation in the positivist paradigm is causal and predictive (Bredo & Feinberg, 1982, p. 19). Positivists seek cause-and-effect laws that are sufficiently generalizable to ensure that a knowledge of prior events enables a reasonable prediction of subsequent events.

Because the positivists see knowledge as accumulating, they have been more interested in developing approaches to research synthesis than have interpretivists. A meta-ethnography fills this void by proposing a uniquely interpretive approach to research synthesis.

The Meaning of Meta-Ethnography

The intent of this book is to provide one way for interpretivists to derive understanding from multiple cases, accounts, narratives, or studies. A meta-ethnography is intended to enable:

1. More interpretive literature reviews
2. Critical examination of multiple accounts of an event, situation, and so forth
3. Systematic comparison of case studies to draw cross-case conclusions
4. A way of talking about our work and comparing it to the works of others
5. Synthesis of ethnographic studies

The type of thinking we propose is useful to the researchers trying to compare across case studies within a single study as well as to someone wishing to review the ethnographic literature on some area of interest. We will focus more on the latter in this book, demonstrating how interpretive studies may be reduced, compared, and translated as a way of synthesizing the studies. We use the prefix *meta* to indicate our intent to focus on the synthesis enterprise. A meta-ethnography seeks to go beyond single accounts to reveal the analogies between the accounts. It reduces the accounts while preserving the sense of the account through the selection of key metaphors and organizers. The "senses" of different accounts are then translated into one another. The analogies revealed in these translations are the form of the meta-ethnographic synthesis.

What this synthesis entails will be explained in the following chapters. In constructing these explanations, we rely on a set of terms that need some definition. Of most concern is how we distinguish among *interpretive, qualitative,* and *ethnographic.* For us, *interpretive* refers to the larger paradigm we have just discussed. *Qualitative,* for us, refers to the range of approaches practiced within the interpretive paradigm, including ethnography, case study research, intensive interviewing studies, and discourse analysis, among others. *Ethnographic* refers to a basic approach within interpretivism that is common to anthropologists and sociologists. Our focus here is largely on studies that define themselves as ethnographic. By this we usually mean long term, intensive studies involving observation, interviewing, and document review (as well as review of other human products). However, in defining ethnography, we agree with Wolcott (1980, p. 56):

> One could do a participant-observer study from now to doomsday and never come up with a sliver of ethnography. . . . We are fast losing sight of the fact that the essential ethnographic contribution is interpretive rather than methodological.

We refer to the texts of studies created by interpretivists in various ways. Since we focus on the synthesis of ethnographic studies, we refer to these alternatively as accounts, studies, and ethnographies. Others may wish to distinguish between them, but we do not do so here.

Metaphor is a term that we develop in some detail. For now, it is important to know that when we talk about the key metaphors of a study, we are referring to what others may call the themes, perspectives, organizers, and/or concepts revealed by qualitative studies. Further, while we discuss criteria for adequate metaphors and the appropriate form of translations, we wish to be clear that, in the interpretive paradigm, any interpretation, metaphor, or translation is only one possible reading of that studied. Other investigations will have other readings.

In many ways, a meta-ethnographic synthesis reveals as much about the perspective of the synthesizer as it does about the substance of the synthesis. This idea is reflected in several ways in what follows. First, we are concerned with an aspect of practice within the interpretive paradigm. Our audience, then, is interpretivists and students of interpretivism. Second, we are educational ethnographers. We want to know what interpretivism, ethnography, and qualitative research can reveal about the social institution of education. Third, we are interested in understanding education in our own society. Cross-cultural and cross-national studies are amenable to the same approach we develop here. However, it is clear that cross-cultural studies involve translation at another level (Asad, 1986). Such translation needs more consideration than we can provide in this volume, but we encourage those who conduct cross-cultural studies to undertake this task.

The meaning of meta-ethnography for us is as a form of synthesis for ethnographic or other interpretive studies. It enables us to talk to each other about our studies; to communicate to policy makers, concerned citizens, and scholars what interpretive research reveals; and to reflect on our collective craft and the place of our own studies within it.

Knowledge Synthesis

The synthesis of research for many is, no doubt, equated with doing literature reviews. Positivists and interpretivists alike find literature reviews as usually practiced to be of little value. The study-by-study presentation of questions, methods, limitations, findings, and conclusions lacks some way to make sense of what the *collection* of studies is saying. As a result, literature reviews in practice are more rituals than substantive accomplishments.

Positivists have had more interest in knowledge synthesis than *interpretives*. For them, knowledge accumulates. The problem has been how best to accomplish that accumulation. Positivists have had major advances in this area in recent years. [For examples, see works on meta-analysis (Glass, 1977; Hunter et al., 1982) and integrative research reviews (Cooper, 1984).] This emphasis on accumulation of data is not an accident. Meta-analysis was designed with the presumption that there were many small-scale studies, chiefly evaluations, that gathered some common data; however, these individual studies were too limited for reliable generalizations. Driven by a wish to overcome this problem, integrative reviews and meta-analysis guide the pooling of data from the studies, and its subsequent statistical analysis.

In applied research, *meta-analysis* has come to refer to a specific technique. Glass et al. (1981, p. 21) write:

> The approach to research integration referred to as "meta-analysis" is nothing more than the attitude of data analysis applied to quantitative summaries of individual experiments. By recording the properties of studies and their findings in quantitative terms, the meta-analysis of research invites one who would integrate numerous and diverse findings to apply the full power of statistical methods to the task. Thus it is not a technique, rather it is a perspective that uses many techniques of measurement and statistical analysis.

Glass et al. (1981) move beyond assessing the properties of studies to considering how the data can be integrated, given those properties. Even in their positivism, they give us hope for the analogy between meta-analysis and meta-ethnography. First, they denote meta-analysis as an "attitude" and "perspective," reinforcing the idea that the concept is not limited to statistical applications. Second, they promote some humility, saying it is "nothing more than the attitude." They suggest that the concept, while important, is not a paradigm shift, but rather an elaboration of existing understandings about data analysis.

Hunter et al. (1982) elaborate the general approach used by Glass et al. of "averaging results across studies" (p. 11). While they continue to include only quantitative studies, they highlight the essentially interpretive nature of meta-analysis. They argue, for example, that "restriction of scope should be topical rather than methodological" (p. 166). Further, they point to the inductive nature of all synthesis activities in arguing against exclusion of studies with "methodological deficiencies since 'deficiency' is usually based on a theory that is itself not empirically tested" (p. 186). The worth of studies, in their view and in ours, is determined in the process of achieving a synthesis.

As valuable as meta-analysis and integrative research reviews are as extensions of positivism, the synthesis enterprise itself is essentially an interpretive endeavor. As Ward (1983) argues: "'synthesis' can be used to refer to all efforts to relate knowledge, including previously unrelated or contradictory knowledge, and to show it is relevant to a specific situation or topic" (p. 26). Certainly, the accumulation of data may proceed by positivistic assumptions. Nonetheless, relating knowledge and showing its relevance is establishing its meaning: It is an interpretation (see Strike & Posner, 1983a).

Strike and Posner (1983b) extend the definition of synthesis along this line. They argue that

> synthesis is usually held to be activity or the product of activity where some set of parts is combined or integrated into a whole. . . . [Synthesis] involves some degree of conceptual innovation, or employment of concepts not found in the characterization of the parts as means of creating the whole (p. 346).

Knowledge syntheses, to Strike and Posner, may take a number of forms. All forms are inductive: Based on the evidence, some interpretation is proposed. Further, these interpretations are judged by three criteria: whether they "clarify and resolve, rather than observe, inconsistencies or tensions between material synthesized"; whether a "progressive problem shift results"; and "whether or not the synthesis is

extreme or excessive

consistent, parsimonious, elegant, fruitful, and useful" (Strike & Posner, 1983b, pp. 356–357).

These criteria are all essentially interpretive, inquiring about the quality of the interpretation of various studies. It is indeed curious that, although the synthesis of knowledge has been conceived of as inductive and interpretive, the most-developed approaches are inductive and positivistic. As Mills (1959) suggests, this may be the result of an "abstracted empiricism" that relies on quantification more than on the testing of theoretically deduced hypotheses. The approach we call meta-ethnography is an attempt to develop an *inductive and interpretive* form of knowledge synthesis.

Synthesizing Understanding

We assert that the business of synthesis is essentially interpretive and inductive. However, no one has developed a description of what this interpretive synthesis involves. We believe it involves understanding the nature of interpretive explanation. As Spicer (1976, p. 341) writes:

> In the study there should be use of the emic approach, that is, the gathering of data on attitudes and values orientations and social relations directly from people engaged in the making of a given policy and those on whom the policy impinges. It should be holistic, that is, include placement of the policy decision in the context of the competing or cooperating interests, with their value orientations, out of which the policy formulation emerged; this requires relating it to the economic, political, and other contexts identifiable as relevant in the sociocultural system. It should include historical study, that is, some diachronic acquaintance with the policy and policies giving rise to it. Finally, it should include consideration of conceivable alternatives and of how other varieties of this class of policy have been applied with what results, in short, comparative understanding.

Qualitative research focuses on "meaning in context" (Mishler, 1979) and thus captures a uniqueness that more deductive approaches cannot. Meta-analysis and integrative reviews, as quantitative approaches, require a determination of a basic comparability between phenomena so that the data can be aggregated for the analysis. This is the crux of the problem with a meta-analysis analogy for a meta-ethnography. As will be seen in the failed synthesis of the desegregation ethnographies, the assumption of comparability stripped these studies of their interpretive merit and worth (Lincoln & Guba, 1980). Comparison became aggregating; holism became analysis; etic (the imposition of an outside frame of reference) became preferred over emic; and history became confounding.

Interpretive explanation does not yield knowledge in the same sense as qualitative explanation. Taylor (1982, p. 153) argues that interpretation in qualitative research "is an attempt to make clear, to make sense of an object of study. . . . The interpretation aims to bring to light an underlying coherence of sense." Schlechty and Noblit (1982) conclude that an interpretation may take one of three forms: (1) making the obvious obvious, (2) making the obvious dubious, and (3) making the hidden obvious. An interpretation that makes the "obvious obvious" is Geertz's study (1973) of the Bali cockfight, in which the meaning of the games, Geertz found, was essentially an expression of the culture and had no other function. Bossert's study (1979) of task organization in classrooms revealed that the obvious explanation that differences in individual characteristics of teachers was dubious; differences in task organization was a better explanation. Everhart's interpretation (1983) of student culture reveals the hidden meaning of schooling and of resistance to schooling in terms of social reproduction of society, he makes the hidden obvious. Each of these studies makes clear both what the "sense of things" was and what implications that sense of things has for the human discourse.

Interpretive explanations are narratives through which the meanings of social phenomena are revealed. They represent "multiperspectival reality" (Douglas, 1976) of any social event and the holistic meaning of these multiple perspectives. They teach an understanding of the meaning of a particular event in dialogue with a more universal audience (Schlechty & Noblit, 1982). They enable us not to predict but to "anticipate" (Geertz, 1973) what might be involved in analogous situations; they help us understand how things might connect and interact. An interpretation enables the reader to translate the case studied into his or her own social understanding: Interpretive accounts, above all, provide a perspective and, in doing so, achieve the goal of enhancing human discourse.

To appropriately synthesize understanding from qualitative studies, we must hold to the essential task of synthesis using both induction and interpretation. The nature of interpretive explanation is such that we need to construct an alternative to the aggregative theory of synthesis entailed in integrative research reviews and meta-analysis and be explicit about it. The influence of positivistic thinking is pervasive, yet subtle. An example will reveal how subtle and how dramatic this influence can be.

Not Seeing the Forest for the Tree: The Failure of Synthesis for the Desegregation Ethnographies

In 1975, the National Institute of Education (NIE) awarded six contracts for ethnographic field studies in urban desegregated schools. The decision to make the awards was controversial. However, in the end, Ray Rist was able to convince other NIE officials that such studies were appropriate to inform the research agenda of the newly formed Desegregation Studies Team which he headed. For NIE, studies that focused on the process of interracial schooling promised to generate new insights. The resulting studies accomplished this objective. Later, Rist (1979, p. 7) was to write:

> Despite the pressing need to learn more of the political and social dynamics of school desegregation, of the interactions within multiracial student populations, and of how schools learn to cope with new discipline and community relations matters, the research has been extremely limited. The very large majority of studies has not been grounded in the analysis of the day-to-day working out of school desegregation.

Almost three years later, detailed analyses of the schools were submitted to NIE, and NIE reviewers dubbed them successful studies but "gloomy" in terms of the outlook for school desegregation. The schools studied had initially been chosen because they were reputed to be good examples of desegregated schools within their respective school districts. The research teams found that, even in these "good" schools, desegregation was not smoothly implemented and had encountered significant resistance on many fronts. The schools even had considerable difficulty in defining the appropriate meaning of desegregation. Further, in the absence of such agreement, "business as usual" (Sagar & Schofield, 1979) was the reaction of schools. As a result, resegregation of the schools and classrooms ensued; order became a heightened priority; and the individual students, teachers, and administrators were left to fend for themselves (Rosenbaum, 1979).

The ethnographies, of course, revealed this more complexly than the above statement reveals. Interestingly, they raised for NIE and the researchers the problem of how to reduce the detailed site-specific findings into a set of results that could be communicated to policy makers. In the end, two rather different approaches were attempted under the guidance of Murray Wax, an Anthropologist. One approach was to summarize the similar lessons from all sites (Wax, 1979a) by condensing the five final reports submitted (one contractor did not submit a final report in time to be included). This approach was criticized by LeCompte (1979) for not providing credible and convincing support for the conclusions, owing to lack of detail. Additionally, she argued, it ignored the idiosyncratic differences that seemingly were also policy-relevant.

The second approach was to ask the research team to agree on a set of salient issues and conduct cross-site analyses based on the data from all the sites. This attempt did not include a set of commissioned critiques, as did the other attempt, but only a summary by Rosenbaum, an independent analyst (Wax, 1979b). (The preceding summary of the results is drawn from that attempt.)

Nevertheless, in large part, LeCompte's critique applies to the cross-site essays as well as to the final summary of the reports. She, we think, reasonably argued:

> The Wax summary of five ethnographic studies of desegregated schools promised a great deal but does not deliver as much as it promises. Both Practitioners and Academics reading such a document will be looking for answers— though of a different kind. Teachers, administrators, and politicians will be looking for guidelines and techniques that they can utilize toward the immediate solution of a pressing problem; academics will be hopeful of an explanation of the complex phenomena under examination, or at least a conceptual framework, consistently applied, which might explain variation in the phenomena. Neither are provided, although some useful insights can be teased out of the material presented. While it is difficult to quarrel with the well-stated initial premise—that ethnography is a particularly useful tool for studying processes such as those involved in desegregation of schools, and is a technique that provides insights garnered by no other means—the brevity of the report has obviated the richness of data and explanatory detail that is the hallmark of good ethnography and permits its conclusions to be well-grounded. What remains are some rather trite and atheoretical explanations for the failure of schools really to desegregate—such as the absence of effective leadership from the principals—and an idiosyncratic view of the whole process of desegregation which ignores some of the more important structural aspects of the conflict inherent in such a situation. In short, the article under review earns plaudits for what it attempts to do and some serious criticism for what it fails to do (1979, p. 118).

As condemning as this critique is, we believe it is instructive; it proposed that the summary attempt ended up being neither truly ethnographic nor informative. The desegregation ethnographies and the various attempts to communicate their findings (Clement et al., 1978; Collins & Noblit, 1978; Ianni et al., 1978; Scherer & Slawski, 1978; Sagar & Schofield, 1979; Rist, 1979; Henderson, 1981) all were able to offer adequate analyses of each site. How do we, then, account for the failure of the attempts to achieve ethnographic synthesis?

The Problem of Ethnographic Synthesis

The summary attempts (Wax, 1979a, 1979b) were essentially similar in their focus on attaining "general" conclusions. Wax wrote of the cross-site essay attempts:

> At a meeting in November 1977, agreement was reached that the investigating teams should participate in a small venture toward achieving more general conclusions from the ethnographic specifics of the separate cases. Each team proposed or was assigned a particular topic or theme, with the notion that its members could secure relevant data concerning each of the other sites. Thus, instead of five final reports, each of which might have mentioned something about a topic such as the relationship of lower-class black students to the school, there would be a single essay integrating the findings about the alienation of such students from schools that were supposedly desegregated (1979b, p. 1).

Wax also described the condensation summary, saying the following:

> The present work constitutes an attempt to summarize and integrate the major findings of those five final reports into a compass of about 30,000 words. The work was commissioned with the hope that the process of textual integration would serve to bring forward the common findings among the five investigators, while the shortened size would mean a wider audience than might be gained by any single report. Moreover, it was also hoped that the textual integration would lead to a deemphasis of the faults and virtues of the particular sites while focusing attention on the common problems entailed in desegregating the schools (1979a, p. v).

The summary attempts were experimental in that two different approaches, the cross-site essays (Wax, 1979b) and the integration of the final reports (Wax, 1979a), were pursued. The experiment did not vary *how* to summarize, only *what* to summarize: Both aimed to isolate the common findings and deemphasize the uniqueness of each site. Thus the experiment in reality compared the essay summary format with the full report summary format, with both focused on seeking common findings. While neither is an unusual way to summarize findings, they both entail an unstated theory of social explanation that focuses on aggregate patterns of results. As such, these summaries are akin to positivism, although we did not understand that at that time.

One might ask what is wrong with this approach. There is little wrong, except that the aggregation we engaged in (1) avoided a full exploration of context and (2) did not enable an explanatory synthesis. Since the publication of summary attempts, Stephen Turner (1980) has provided us with a "theory of social explanation" that enables us to better understand what went wrong and what might be done about it. Turner's formulation is based on Winch's thesis (1958) about the nature of a social science and is especially appropriate to ethnographic analysis. He builds upon Winch's thesis to propose a theory of social explanation based in comparative understanding rather than in aggregation of data.

The desegregation summary attempts seemingly belied the rudiments of an ethnographic approach by ignoring "meaning in context" (Mishler, 1979). As Rosenbaum (1979) concluded from the cross-site essays, desegregation did have many different meanings in the schools studied. In these, context became the *confounding* variable in the search for common findings. The logic of the summary attempts is essentially to place aggregation above understanding and left us in the difficult situation of attempting to discount the effects of context. Only Sullivan (1979) escaped this trap. By concentrating on community context and conducting a comparative analysis of the five sites, Sullivan was able to assess how context affected desegregation and vice versa. Unfortunately, Sullivan's attempt was so powerful in identifying the contextually distinct meanings of race and desegregation that it resulted in the decision to delete contextual descriptions from the other essays. This decision contributed to the overall failure of synthesis.

Sullivan's summary attempt is instructive in another way. His comparative analysis, much like Turner's proposal (1980), is the keystone to ethnographic synthesis. Not only does it maintain context as a salient component of analysis; it also avoids the aggregate issue. That is, he did not make general conclusions. The aggregation of uniqueness was simply nonsensical.

The aggregation approach to ethnographic synthesis that we employed in the desegregation ethnographies was not merely context-stripping. It actually impeded explanation and thus negated a true interpretive synthesis. The aggregation across-context procedure only defined and set puzzles. Further, the focus on commonalities probably resulted in inadequate definitions of the puzzles themselves. Better puzzle definition would have allowed context as part of the explanation. It would have required an explanation that "translates" the practices and conditions of one school into practices and conditions of the other schools. In short, LeCompte's critique (1979) of the final reports' summary (also applicable to the cross-site summaries, except possibly Sullivan's) is apt. We failed to provide the explanation that academics and practitioners might have wished. As is common in research, the failure is attributable to the methodology employed. We simply did not consider an alternative theory of social explanation.

Success from Failure
The failure to achieve an adequate synthesis for the desegregation ethnographies was, of course, disheartening to all involved. As scholars, we initially took it as a personal failure. However, if we make the effort to learn from failure, knowledge advances as much through failure as through success. In this case, there is much to be learned. On the one hand, this should teach us that even experienced ethnographers can be lulled into violating their paradigm when faced with an unusual task. As ethnographers, we carefully guarded our research from paradigm violations when we faced the familiar tasks of intensive, grounded research. As experienced and confident researchers, we approached the synthesis attempts with little trepidation and great enthusiasm. As is now apparent, research synthesis, especially ethnographic synthesis, must be more sophisticated than we imagined. By not having an explicit theory of social explanation to undergird the synthesis, we inappropriately relied on an aggregate theory.

This example is a revealing critique of the current state of ethnographic research. In general, we judge the quality of educational ethnography to be high. Nonetheless, the ethnographers' efforts to be grounded and empirical mean that we may eschew the more theoretical and philosophical issues that enable the paradigm to flourish and grow. If the paradigm seeks to create a knowledge base and inform practice, then we must find ways to synthesize our research. To regard these concerns as inappropriate and wrong thinking is a gross error. We can reduce our findings without being either overly reductionistic or falling prey to aggregate theories of synthesis. However, we must invest in the philosophy of our paradigm and elaborate alternative theories of social explanation to do so.

An alternative theory of social explanation that is appropriate to ethnography must be essentially interpretive. It must be both grounded and comparative. In the next chapter, we will use Turner's formulation (1980) of sociological explanation as translation. While our approach is comparative, we wish to dissociate our views from those of such anthropologists as Paul Shankman (1984). Shankman sees a comparative approach as enabling "generalizations" (p. 263). This is the essential flaw with the synthesis of the desegregation ethnographies. A comparative approach, to us, leads to *translations*, not generalizations. A meta-ethnography entails translating studies into one another.

The successes emerging from the failure of the desegregation synthesis attempts, then, are four. First, we have awareness of the nature of the issue. Second, this awareness also revealed a direction in which to proceed. Third, this direction led to meta-ethnography as developed here. Finally, as we will show in Chapter 5, we are not able to provide a synthesis for the desegregation ethnographies.

Understanding and Knowledge

In the positivist paradigm, knowledge is thought to accumulate and thereby improve. The review of existing research is a prelude to deriving research questions and is used to justify the proposed research project as adding to the knowledge base. In qualitative research, we have a different view. First, we are not as concerned with knowledge (as a set of axiomatic "laws") as we are with understanding. Our research reveals that social life varies dramatically by context: Research is to help us understand how that occurs. As Geertz (1973) argues, the goal of qualitative research is to enrich human discourse, not to produce a formal body of knowledge. Second, while prior studies should, of course, inform proposed studies, a review of the literature in qualitative research is usually intended to establish the discourse to be addressed. However, in the process of studying something, interpretivists often discover a new area of discourse—that is, a new topic—to be enriched by their research. In doing so, an unanticipated understanding may develop that teaches us the limitations of the discourse we originally intended to inform. Third, qualitative researchers do not see accumulation as the vehicle with which to inform their sciences. The accumulation of studies merely indicates an arena of enduring human discourse. It may or may not reflect a substantive improvement in how well we understand something. Taking Kuhn's notion (1970) of "normal science" as being work done with a para-

digm, qualitative researchers may argue that an accumulation of studies is a technical endeavor of simply playing out the paradigm or theory
rather than any real advancement. Finally, positivists see accumulation of knowledge as a means of developing predictions. That is to
say, once we have enough knowledge, the world will be predictable, if
not controllable. Qualitative researchers, informed by the sociology of
knowledge (Mannheim, 1936; Berger & Luckmann, 1967), see social
life and culture as emergent. Knowledge, as accumulated culture, is
always limited in its ability to predict since humans are reflective and
use knowledge bases to create new social and cultural forms. Through
understanding the sense of things, anticipation, rather than prediction, is the more reasonable result of qualitative research.

One Basis for a Meta-Ethnography

One alternative to the aggregative theory is what we call meta-ethnography. We use this term, in part, because of the analogy to meta-
analysis. We share the goal of those proposing meta-analytic and integrative research reviews of "putting together" all the research available
to us. We hold the "attitude" that Glass et al. (1981) suggest. Yet the
analogy ends there. We use the phrase *meta-ethnography* to highlight our proposal as an interpretive alternative to research synthesis.
For us, the *meta* in *meta-ethnography* means something different
than it does in *meta-analysis*. It refers not to developing overarching
generalizations but, rather, to translations of qualitative studies into
one another. This is a *meta*-ethnography in that it involves using the
nature of interpretive explanation to guide the synthesis of ethnographies or other qualitative, interpretive studies.

We are the first to concede that our approach is but one of many
possible approaches. The discourse about language and symbols in
ethnographic research makes it inevitable that other approaches, also
interpretive, will be discovered. As interpretivists ourselves, we look
forward to the debate and the alternative perspectives. We acknowledge that our translation-based meta-ethnography is but *a* meta-
ethnography.

A meta-ethnography involves some theory about how best to synthesize interpretive accounts. For this purpose, we have adapted
Turner's notion (1980) that all explanation is essentially comparative
and takes the form of translation. A meta-ethnography based in Turner's
conceptualization simply extends his argument by constructing syntheses by translating multiple qualitative studies into one another's

terms. In doing so, we must be careful to remember Turner's essential point. The analyst is always translating studies into his own world view. A meta-ethnography based in notions of translating studies into one another will inevitably be partially a product of the synthesizer. While positivists will be concerned, interpretivists will be less concerned. As Geertz (1973) argues, all ethnography is but interpretations of interpretations. The ethnographer is "inscribing" (p. 19) the cultural interpretations that others create and, in doing so, creates a reading of a culture. A meta-ethnography is but one more interpretation and largely takes the same form. Indeed, we propose that it is best to treat all interpretive accounts, as well as the synthesis, as metaphoric: It was "as if" we failed to achieve a synthesis of desegregation ethnographies, even though we accumulated data, wrote reports, and made cross-site generalizations.

A meta-ethnography based in translating studies into one another obviously does not yield the same type of product as do meta-analysis and integrative research review. Translation can be an elaborate endeavor. Meta-analysis has been critiqued for overly long syntheses (Cohen, 1980). This problem may be endemic to synthesis attempts in general. However, we demonstrate that meta-ethnographic syntheses of small numbers of studies need not be overly long. The product, the translation of studies into one another, enables readers to simultaneously understand how the studies are related. Some studies may be appropriately characterized in the terms of other studies; others may not be. In this latter case, the translation reveals how different the interpretations are. These differences become a substantive part of the synthesis. Reciprocal translations of studies into one another enable holistic accounts that, according to Spicer's criteria for an ethnographic approach, are comparative, emic, and historical.

A Meta-Ethnographic Approach

A meta-ethnography starts, like all inquiries, with an interest in some setting, topic, argument, issue, controversy, or opportunity. This interest, for interpretivists, need not be overly specific. Often it starts simply from seeing what different qualitative researchers have to say about something and being concerned with how to compare their accounts. As one pursues this interest by reading qualitative studies, what is of interest undoubtedly changes. It may be modified, specified, or elaborated as one discovers new accounts. Our comparisons of studies are usually the most problematic aspect of this research process.

Once we have a general topic and a set of accounts that seemingly pertain to the topic, we begin systematic comparisons. A meta-ethnographic approach is one form of systematic comparison; it involves the translation of studies into one another. The collection of the translations constitutes a meta-ethnographic synthesis. We believe a meta-ethnography is best thought of as a series of phases that overlap and repeat as the synthesis proceeds.

Phase 1: Getting started. This phase involves identifying an intellectual interest that qualitative research might inform. As Yin (1984) suggests, qualitative approaches "are the preferred strategy when 'how' or 'why' questions are being posed, when the investigator has little control over events, and when the focus is on a contemporary phenomenon within some real-life context" (p. 13). An intellectual interest is immediately tempered and given form by reading interpretive accounts. In this phase, the investigator is asking, How can I inform my intellectual interest by examining some set of studies? In part, this phase is finding something that is worthy of the synthesis effort. This concern does not go away as the synthesis proceeds, as intellectual interest becomes elaborated and studies are read. However, usually what is worthy about the synthesis effort will change. Following Patton (1980), a synthesis not worth doing is not worth doing well. There is no value in a synthesis that is not of interest to the author.

Phase 2: Deciding What Is Relevant to the Initial Interest. In meta-analysis and integrative research reviews, considerable effort is expended in developing an exhaustive list of studies that might be included. For interpretivists, such a decision needs some justification. If the intent is to synthesize *all* the ethnographies concerning island peoples, there must be some justifiable reason that such a synthesis makes sense. What can we learn from translating all island cultures into one another? The answer to this question seems to dictate gross generalizations that an interpretive meta-ethnography would find unacceptable. In a meta-ethnography, the translations interpretations can be generalized, but the simple accumulation of similarities and differences between cultural setting proves fruitless.

Deciding what studies or accounts are relevant involves knowing who the audience for the synthesis is, what is credible and interesting to the audience, what accounts are available to address the audiences' interest, and what your interests are in the effort. Certainly, it makes sense to be exhaustive in the search for relevant accounts when one's interest is not in the synthesis of specified, particular studies. Of course, as Cooper (1984), Hunter et al. (1982), and Light (1980) indicate, it is sometimes difficult to know when one is being exhaustive, given that not all studies are published and/or publicly available.

Hunter et al. (1982) provide a review of the abstracting services for studies, monographs, and articles. Ethnographic research in particular is likely to be in monograph or book form. Thus searches require use of standard library card catalogs, review of references at the end of related works, and probably discussions with scholars working in the general area. In the end, a meta-ethnography is driven by some substantive interest derived from comparison of any given set of studies. Studies of particular settings should always be regarded as particular. Unless there is some substantive reason for an exhaustive search, generalizing from all studies of a particular setting yields trite conclusions.

Phase 3: Reading the Studies. Most proposed methods for research synthesis move quickly to analyzing the characteristics of the study relevant to the topic of interest. In qualitative research, the synthesis is more dynamic and develops throughout the synthesis effort. Therefore, in a meta-ethnography, this phase is not so clear. Rather, we think it is best to identify this phase as the repeated reading of the accounts and the noting of interpretative metaphors. Meta-ethnography is the synthesis of texts; this requires extensive attention to the details in the accounts, and what they tell you about your substantive concerns.

Phase 4: Determining How the Studies Are Related. In doing a synthesis, the various studies must be "put together." This requires determining the relationships between the studies to be synthesized. We think it makes sense to create a list of the key metaphors, phrases, ideas, and/or concepts (and their relations) used in each account and to juxtapose them. Near the end of phase 4, an initial assumption about the relationship between studies can be made. Three different assumptions and illustrations of subsequent syntheses are developed in Chapters, 3, 4, and 5.

Phase 5: Translating the Studies into One Another. In its simplest form, translation involves treating the accounts as analogies: One program is like another except. . . . On the other hand, translation is more involved than an analogy. Translations are unique syntheses, because they protect the particular, respect holism, and enable comparison. An adequate translation maintains the central metaphors and/or concepts of each account *in their relation to other key metaphors or concepts* in this account. It also compares both the metaphors or concepts and their interactions in one account with the metaphors or concepts and their interactions in the other accounts. We discuss this process in the next section of this chapter.

Phase 6: Synthesizing Translations. Synthesis refers to making a whole into something more than the parts alone imply. The translations as a set are one level of meta-ethnographic synthesis. However, when the number of studies is large and the resultant translations numerous, the various translations can be compared with one another to determine if there are types of translations or if some metaphors and/or concepts are able to encompass those of other accounts. In these cases, a second level of synthesis is possible, analyzing types of competing interpretations and translating them into each other.

Phase 7: Expressing the Synthesis. The existing literature on research synthesis is biased toward the written word. While it is no doubt true that most syntheses are written for an academic audience, the written synthesis is only one possible form. When the synthesis is driven by some concern to inform practitioners, other forms may be preferable. The audience itself may be employed to make the translations and to create symbolic forms appropriate to it. Videos, plays, art, and music all seem to be reasonable forms, depending on the audience and the form they respect (Patton, 1980).

While meta-ethnographic syntheses may be conducted by individuals solely for themselves, any effort to communicate the synthesis involves some assessment of the audience. To be effectively communicated, the synthesis must not only be in appropriate form but must also use intelligible concepts. Every audience has a language. For the translations of studies to achieve a synthesis, the translations must be rendered in the audience's particular language.

The intention here is not to pander to the audience. To have our syntheses readily intelligible does not mean reducing the lessons of ethnographic research to an everyday or naive understanding of a culture. The focus on translations is for the purpose of enabling an audience to stretch and see the phenomena in terms of others' interpretations and perspectives. To do this means we must understand the audience's culture in much the same way as we understand the studies to be synthesized; we must represent one to the other in both their commonality and their uniqueness. This is Turner's basic argument about sociological explanations as translations. The problems of getting the synthesis to the audience are discussed in further detail in Chapter 6.

These, then, are the phases of conducting a meta-ethnographic synthesis. In practice, the phases overlap and may be parallel. Our substantive interests and our translations develop simultaneously. The synthesis is affected by its intended expression. Often, audience needs drive the form and substance of the synthesis. What is unique about a meta-ethnography, however, is not these phases, but the translation theory of social explanation that it involves. In the next section, we explore this theory of social explanation in more detail.

An Alternative Theory of Social Explanation

The methodological discussions of ethnography in educational research often define it as an "alternative" approach (Patton, 1975; Noblit, 1981). A meta-ethnography certainly seems to imply an alternative theory of social explanation. It is often difficult to imagine what a reasonable alternative to synthesis as aggregation could be. As noted, Turner (1980) explored the issue of social explanation and suggests some directions. His work is of interest here because, as we will show, Turner's analysis establishes a theory of social explanation that can be extended to undergird a meta-ethnography, avoiding the problems we witnessed with the desegregation ethnographies.

Of course, Turner sought a theory of social explanation for all of social science—positivistic, interpretive, and critical—and, as such, he did not primarily direct his work toward the advancement of ethnography. Nevertheless, the three basic elements of his argument are consistent with an interpretive paradigm and an ethnographic approach. First, Turner argues that all social explanation is essentially comparative, implicitly or explicitly. Experimental designs, of course, are explicitly comparative; it is also true that single case studies are, at their base, comparative in the sense that the researcher uses his or her experience, knowledge, and/or expectations to discern what is of interest in the case (See Gouldner, 1970. As Turner (1980) writes:

> We proceed as though we hypothesized that where we should follow such and such rule, the members of another social group or persons in another social context would do the same (p. 97).

That is, researchers implicitly or explicitly use a "same practices hypothesis" (p. 97) in research. We can, of course, expand this notion and allow for more sophistication on the part of researchers. We argue that researchers proceed by hypothesizing that what is of interest is that which varies from their own experience, knowledge, and expectations (i.e., a "different practices hypothesis").

Second, Turner claims that the breakdown of a "same practices hypothesis" (or a different practices hypothesis) yields an explanatory "puzzle." The puzzle seeks to explain why the practice differs from that explicitly or implicitly expected. The answer for Turner must be interpretive, citing different social and historical contexts, and differing values, norms, and/or social relations, as reasons. He is careful to show that statistical analyses are of limited utility in this process:

> Analysis of aggregate patterns can help set puzzles, and differences in aggregate patterns may require explanations that cite differences in practices. But the question "why the different practice?" is not touched by the analysis (Turner, 1980, p. 97).

While aggregate analyses can set puzzles, explanations that solve puzzles are based in "translation" of one case into another. In the case of an implicit comparison, we see that value explicitness on the part of the researcher is vital for this "translation" to be effected. Turner sees "translation" as having the general form of an analogy: "[T]he different practice in a social group or social context that raises puzzles is explained in a way that a different rule of a game is explained" (p. 97). In other words, he argues that we solve the interpretive puzzle (that raised by the observation of similar or differing social practices in interpretive accounts) by explaining how the observed social practice is alike and different from our own. We translate the observed practice into our practices by treating each as an analogy of the other. Thus it is impossible to synthesize ethnographic research by focusing on empirical observations themselves, as in a meta-analysis. We must focus on the translations.

It is important to consider the form of translation that Turner is proposing here. An analogy is not literal; rather, it conveys the sense of things. In semantics, translations (Barnwell, 1980) can be either literal (word-for-word) or idiomatic (translating the meaning of the text). An interpretive meta-ethnography would require the latter. The idiomatic translation of accounts into one another is the interpretive synthesis of these accounts. As with other types of translation, translations of studies will vary with the translators and we should argue about what makes better or worse translations.

Third, and finally, Turner argues that social explanation must be inductive and framed in terms of the comparison of cases that give rise to the puzzles. He writes:

> What is logically peculiar about . . . the question [concerning the necessity for a general framework in advance of the research] is that it seems to rest on the idea that "what is important" can be decided in advance of explanation or apart from it. It is illicit to prejudge the question of which facts about society are truly "fundamental." . . . Assessments of what is fundamental, if they are ever intelligible as factual claims, must be based on factual, valid explanation, and not vice versa (Turner, 1980, p. 77).

Each researcher will have different substantive interests, see difference comparative puzzles, and achieve different syntheses.

Turner's theory of social explanation, even though proposed for all of social science, is especially helpful in our quest for a theory of social explanation that will guide a meta-ethnography. It is evident that his argument is paradigmatically appropriate for ethnography. Spicer's criteria (1976) for an ethnographic approach, quoted earlier, are subsumed in Turner's argument. Turner gives new impetus to Spicer's concern that ethnography be comparative. Spicer's criteria of holism and history are preserved under Turner's notion of translation of one case into the other. For Turner, it is the explanation that brings the holism and history into social research. Finally, Spicer's "emic" criterion is mirrored in Turner's last point, that explanation must be based on what is studied, rather than on a framework decided in advance.

Not only is Turner's argument paradigmatically appropriate for a meta-ethnography, it also constitutes a methodology for the synthesis of ethnographies. First, it reveals that the "data" of synthesis are interpretations and explanations rather than the data collected through interviews and observations. Second, it shows us that in the same way that interpretation is a comparative translation, synthesis is the translation of interpretations. A meta-ethnography appropriately proceeds by translating the interpretations of one study into the interpretations of another. Finally, Turner's analysis gives us the basic form of the translation itself: an analogy.

We should be cautious, of course, in extending Turner's theory of social explanation into an area that he was not addressing directly, and in specifying it as method. Such extension and specification can lead to inappropriate conclusions. Although we hope that others will critically consider what we have proposed thus far and offer alternatives, we are aware of one issue that is especially problematic. That is, as we move from the translation of the data of cases to the translation of interpretations of cases, we change levels of abstraction. Nonetheless, it is not the case that a meta-ethnography is necessarily more "abstract" than a meta-analysis. Rather, it is that the abstractions of a meta-analysis, which are issues of theory and measurement, come early in the process. Since they yield numeric values, the technical meta-analysis is deceivingly "concrete." Conversely, consistent with the interpretive paradigm, a meta-ethnography is based in "grounded" explanations. It struggles to keep the issues involved in explanation conscious to the researcher and the reader. At the same time, the explanations are themselves being translated into one another. Thus the technical meta-ethnography is deceivingly less "concrete" than a meta-analysis.

The key issue here is the nature of the interpretations. Since interpretations come in the form of narratives, we must be concerned about issues of language and knowledge. Language may be seen as an expression that attempts to communicate to others; knowledge may be seen as what we know or think we know. When knowledge is communicated to others, it must be expressed in ways that the others can understand: The process of communicating knowledge is one of translating symbol systems between two or more parties. In short, interpretation, as a form of communicated knowledge, is symbolic and thus metaphoric. As Brown (1977, p. 77) argues: "In the broadest sense, metaphor is seeing something from the viewpoint of something else, which means . . . that all knowledge is metaphoric." Brown's extreme stance, that is, that knowledge is essentially metaphoric, may be objectionable to all but those highly committed to an interpretive paradigm. It is reasonable to argue that grounded explanations of any ethnography may or may not be essentially metaphoric. However, abstractions from grounded explanations must be; that is, by treating these abstractions as metaphoric, we prevent closure on their meaning (Goetz & LeCompte, 1984). Certainly, all generalizations pay the price of empirical accuracy to any particular case, but a metaphoric explanation maintains the complexity of the case, while at the same time facilitating reduction of the data. Further, it is common practice for ethnographers to use metaphors as organizers for their explanations (Miles & Huberman, 1984). Thus a meta-ethnography is likely to involve translating metaphors of one interpretation into another. The abstraction in a meta-ethnography seemingly requires that the synthesis will involve and employ metaphors, since metaphors are involved in "the fundamental questions of similarity, identity, and difference" (Brown, 1977, p. 79).

Metaphors and Meta-Ethnography

Critics of the interpretive paradigm often argue against its relativism. Positivists generally believe that some things are better than others and that there is a singular truth that can be ascertained. They seemingly lose all reason when faced with a paradigm that reveals the "multiperspectival realities" of social endeavors (Douglas, 1976). However, the relativism that positivists portray is a "straw" relativism. In practice, ethnographers rarely, if ever, find that "anything goes." Rather, different groups perceive differently and act differently. The interactions of all this make for some interesting, if often ironic, developments. Nonetheless, the range of perceptions observed is always limited by context and socialization. Thus the ethnographer reveals a limited relativism. Ethnographers can argue for and against conduct in terms of cultural appropriateness, vested interests, and desired end-states, even if they do not see prediction of such end-states as a reasonable endeavor (Geertz, 1984). No doubt, the discussion thus far of translations, analogies, and metaphors does little to reassure those who fear an extreme relativism that it is indeed possible to achieve a meta-ethnography with some criteria for what constitutes a good synthesis.

Fortunately, Brown (1977), Martin (1975), and House (1979) all consider this issue. Brown argues that there are three basic criteria for the adequacy of metaphors in social science; economy, cogency, and range. Economy is similar to the classic criterion of parsimony in theory. Essentially, a metaphor is adequate when it is the simplest concept that accounts for the phenomena and has a superior "ease of representation and manipulation" (p. 104). Cogency refers to an "elegantly efficient integration." A metaphor is adequate on this criteria when it achieves the explanation without "redundancy, ambiguity, and contradiction" (p. 104). Range refers to the "power of incorporating other symbolic domains" (p. 105), and metaphors can be assessed as to superiority of this "power." Martin suggests an additional criterion: apparency. He writes, "[T]his ability of language to (seemingly) 'show' us experience rather than merely 'refer' to it—I shall term 'apparency'" (p. 168). For Martin, an adequate metaphor is one that is successful in "the making apparent of connotations" (p. 208). Finally, House, in his consideration of the "aesthetics" of evaluations, suggest "credibility" as a fifth criterion. That is to say, while adequate metaphors for research are consciously "as if" and involve a transference between a literal sense and an absurd sense of a word or phrase (Brown, 1977), adequate metaphors also must be credible to, and understood by, the audience of the study.

In a meta-ethnography, the metaphors employed in the studies to be synthesized are assessed by these criteria and a determination is made as to whether the emic metaphors are adequate to synthesize diverse studies. Further, if new metaphors are necessary to accomplish the synthesis, then alternative metaphors and sets of metaphors similarly are considered and judged. A meta-ethnography treats interpretations as metaphors to effect the comparative translation of one study into others. The adequacy of the metaphors, and thus the meta-ethnography, is assessed by these five criteria.

The Judgment Calls

Richard Light (1980) discusses what he believes are the key judgment calls to be made in quantitative research syntheses. He argues that the "art" of synthesis involves the analyst's judgments at key decision points. The judgment calls in quantitative research synthesis are inclusion (which studies should be included), summary measures to be used, reliability of variables across studies, and the attitude brought to the judgments about the basic character of that being studied. Interpretivists are likely to see this list of judgment calls as clearly insufficient; they point to key decisions regarding what is of interest; how to compare, interpret, and synthesize; and so on. Thus a meta-ethnography is perhaps better understood not as key decision points, but as an ongoing process. Substantive interest and the studies relevant to the interests develop and change throughout a meta-ethnographic synthesis. Our translations are emergent and interactive as we search for adequate metaphors to express the studies and their relationships. Our syntheses are always merely a "reading" (Geertz, 1973). By experimenting with different readings, we further develop our metaphors, translations, and syntheses.

This is not meant to imply, however, that judgment calls are any less crucial to the art of qualitative research synthesis than they are to the art of quantitative synthesis. Rather, in qualitative research, the values of the researcher are ubiquitous. Typically, the issue of judgment calls in qualitative research is dealt with not as a problem, but as a necessary part of the interpretation. As Geertz (1973) argues, the ethnographer is akin to an inscriber; we inscribe our interpretation upon a culture. Thus each interpretation is both of the culture studied and of the ethnographer. In a meta-ethnography, this issue has one more level. Each account to be synthesized is already an interpretation of interpretations (Geertz, 1973). The translations of accounts raises this to another level: interpretation of interpretations of interpretations. The person conducting the synthesis is intimately involved in the synthesis that results.

In qualitative research, the issue of judgments and biases is accepted and included in the account created. The values and experiences of the interpreter are made explicit and often are intricately woven into the account. On the level of a meta-ethnography, the synthesizer must also be value-explicit and weave these into the syntheses. Similarly, the synthesis itself should be viewed as an interpretation and, as such, subject to critique and debate. Since an enriched human discourse is the goal of interpretivism, the nature of the debate, and not the synthesis itself, should be regarded as evidence of the success of a meta-ethnography. A judgment call of primary interest to the qualitative researcher is the assessment made by the audience of the worth of the account.

References

Asad, T. (1986). The concept of cultural translation in British social anthropology. In J. Clifford & G. Marcus (Eds.), *Writing culture.* Berkeley: University of California Press.

Barnwell, K. (1980). *Introduction to semantics and translation.* Horsleys Green, UK: Summer Institute of Linguistics.

Berger, P., & Luckmann, T. (1967). *The social construction of reality.* Garden City, NY: Doubleday.

Bossert, S. (1979). *Task and social relationships in classrooms.* New York: Cambridge University Press.

Bredo, E., & Feinberg, W. (Eds.). (1982). *Knowledge and values in social and educational research.* Philadelphia: Temple University Press.

Brown, R. (1977). *A poetic for sociology.* New York: Cambridge University Press.

Cahen, L. (1980). Meta-analysis: A technique with promise and problems." *Evaluation in Education, 4,* 37–39.

Clement, D., et al. (1978). *The emerging order: An ethnography of a southern desegregated school.* Chapel Hill: University of North Carolina Press.

Collins, T., and Noblit, G. W. (1978). *Stratification and resegregation: The case of Crossover High School.* Final report of NIE Contract 400-76-009.

Cooper, H. (1984). *The integrative research review.* Newbury Park, CA: Sage.

Douglas, J. (1976). *Investigative social research.* Newbury Park, CA: Sage.

Everhart, R. (1983). *Reading, writing, and resistance.* London: Routledge & Kegan Paul.

Geertz, C. (1973). *The interpretation of cultures.* New York: Basic Books.

———, (1984) Anti anti-relativism. *American Anthropolist, 84,* 263–278.

Glass, G. (1977). Integrating findings: The meta-analysis of research. *Review of Research in Education, 5,* 351–379.

Glass, G., et al. (1981). *Meta-analysis in social research.* Newbury Park, CA: Sage.

Goetz, J. & LeCompte, M. (1984). *Ethnography and Qualitative Design in Educational Research.* Orlando, FL: Academic Press.

Gouldner, A. (1970). *The coming crisis of western sociology.* New York: Basic Books.

Habermas, J. (1971). *Knowledge and human interests.* Boston: Beacon Press.

Henderson, R. (Ed.). (1981). Effects of desegregation on white children. *Urban Review, 13* (4; Special issue).

House, E. (1979). Coherence and credibility: The aesthetics of evaluation. *Educational Evaluation and Policy Analysis, 1* (5), 5–17.

Hunter, J., et al. (1982). *Meta-analysis.* Newbury Park, CA: Sage.

Ianni, F., et al. (1978). *A field study of culture contact and desegregation in an urban high school.* New York: Columbia University, Teachers College, Horace-Mann—Lincoln Institute.

Kuhn, T. (1970). *The structure of scientific revolutions.* Chicago: University of Chicago Press.

LeCompte, M. (1979). Less than meets the eye. In M. Wax (Ed.), *Desegregated schools: An intimate portrait based on five ethnographic studies.* Washington, DC: National Institute of Education.

Light, R. (1980). Synthesis methods: Some judgment calls that must be made. *Evaluation in Education, 4,* 5–10.

Lincoln, Y. S., & Guba, E. G. (1980). The distinction between merit and worth in evaluation. *Educational Evaluation and Policy Analysis, 2,* 61–72.

Mannheim, K. (1936). *Ideology and utopia.* New York: Harcourt, Brace & World.

Marshall, C. (1985). Appropriate criteria of trustworthiness and goodness for qualitative research on education organizations. *Quality and Quantity, 19,* 353–373.

Martin, G. (1975). *Language, truth, and poetry.* Edinburgh: Edinburgh University Press.

Miles, M. & Huberman, A. (1984). *Qualitative data analysis.* Newbury Park, CA: Sage.

Mills, C. W. (1959). *The sociological imagination.* New York: Oxford University Press.

Mishler, E. (1979). Meaning in context. *Harvard Educational Review, 119* (1), 1–19.

Noblit, G. (1981). The holistic alternative in policy research. *High School Journal, 65* (2), 43–49.

Patton, M. (1975). Alternative evaluation research paradigm. North Dakota Study Group on Evaluation Monograph Series. Grand Forks: University of North Dakota.

———. (1980). *Qualitative evaluation methods.* Newbury Park, CA: Sage.

Rist, R. (1979). *Desegregated schools: Appraisals of an American experiment.* New York: Academic Press.

Rosenbaum, P. (1979). Five perspectives on desegregation in schools: A summary. In M. Wax (Ed.). *When schools are desegregated.* Washington, DC: National Institute of Education.

Sagar, A., & Schofield, J. (1979). Integrating the desegregated school: Perspectives, practices, and possibilities. In M. Wax (Ed.), *When schools are desegregated.* Washington, DC: National Institute of Education.

Scherer, J. & Slawski, E. (1978). *Hard walls-soft walls: The social ecology of an urban desegregated high school.* Rochester, MI: Oakland University Press.

Schlechty, P. & Noblit, G. W. (1982). Some uses of sociological theory in educational evaluation. In R. Corwin (Ed.), *Policy research.* Greenwich, CT: JAI Press.

Shankman, P. (1984). The thick and the then: On the interpretive theoretical program of Clifford Geertz. *Current anthroplogy, 25*(3), 261–280.

Spicer, E. (1976). Beyond analysis and explanation. *Human Organization, 35*(4), 335–343.

Strike, K. & Posner, G. (1983a). Epistemological problems in organizing social science knowledge for application. In S. Ward and L. Reed (Eds.), *Knowledge structure and use.* Philadelphia: Temple University Press.

————. (1983b). Types of syntheses and their criteria. In S. Ward and L. Reed (Eds.). *Knowledge structure and use.* Philadelphia: Temple University Press.

Sullivan, M. (1979). The community context of five desegregated schools. In M. Wax (Ed.), *When schools are desegregated.* Washington, DC: National Institute of Education.

Taylor, C. (1982). Interpretation and the sciences of man. In E. Bredo and W. Feinberg (Eds.), *Knowledge and values in social and educational research.* Philadelphia: Temple University Press.

Turner, S. (1980). *Sociological explanation as translation.* New York: Cambridge University Press.

Ward, S. (1983). Knowledge structure and knowledge synthesis. In S. Ward and L. Reed (Eds.), *Knowledge structures and use.* Philadelphia: Temple University Press.

Wax, M. (1979a). *Desegregated schools: An intimate portrait based on five ethnographic studies.* Washington DC: National Institute of Education.

————. (1979b). *When schools are desegregated.* Washington, DC: National Institute of Education.

Winch, P. (1958). *The idea of a social science and its relation to philosophy.* Atlantic Highlands, NJ: Humanities Press.

Wolcott, H. (1980). How to look like an anthropologist without really being one. *Practicing Anthropology, 3*(2), 56–59.

Yin, R. (1984). *Case study research: Design and methods.* Newbury Park, CA: Sage.

Part 2

ETHNOGRAPHIES OF EDUCATION AND RACE

Chapter 6

Cultural Degradation and Minority Student Adaptations: The School Experience and Minority Adjustment Contingencies

George W. Noblit and Thomas W. Collins

The controversies over school desegregation have largely focused upon the problems of whites in desegregated schools and the problems of school systems in successfully implementing desegregation. These controversies have largely overshadowed the original concern of desegregation with providing equal educational opportunity for minorities. Somehow we have assumed that school desegregation has solved the educational problems of minorities. Unfortunately that is not the case. The many concerns that emerged in the urban education debates of the 1960s are still quite salient. Schools still are somewhat alien and alienating for minorities. Their cultures are degraded and they respond. This chapter examines this situation in a Southern desegregated high school.

Research Procedures

The data for this investigation were drawn from an ethnographic study of a desegregated high school with approximately five hundred students in the South. The study, funded by the National Institute of Education, took place over two years, and was primarily geared to investigate the process of interracial schooling. The data were gathered by intensive, unstructured interviews, observations, and document review conducted primarily by the authors of this paper.

It is important to review the nature of ethnographic research, since this technique is often misunderstood by nonanthropologists. Spicer (1976) argues that ethnographic research is emic, holistic, historical, and comparative in nature. That is, it gathers data directly from the people involved in the categories that are relevant to them (emic); it places events in context of the total experience under study (holistic); it incorporates history as a natural event in the studied experience (historical); and it considers and compares the various classes of events that make up that experience (comparative).

Further, the collection and analysis of ethnographic data are conducted under rigorous rules of analytic induction. The most significant of these rules for data analysis concerns data exhaustion. Simply put, a hypothesis that is inductively derived must explain all the data relative to the relationships and classes of events contained in the hypothesis. If the "heuristic" hypothesis does not meet this standard, then either it must be modified so that all data are exhausted by it or a substitute hypothesis must be formulated that satisfies the standard. In short, an ethnographic analysis and/or synthesis is "true" for all relevant data collected, even though it may not be generalizable across other settings. Further discussion of the ethnographic technique and a response to its critics can be found in Noblit (1977).

Finally, it should be noted that ethnographic data is best used to gain an interpretive understanding of an experience or event, and as such is vital to deriving a scientific proof concerning the nature of the experience or event. Both interpretive understanding and causal explanation (as derived from enumerative research strategies) are necessary to satisfy the notion of a scientific proof (Turner & Carr, 1976).

The School

Crossover High School (a pseudonym) was built in 1948, and graduated its first class in 1951. The structure was built on a 35-acre tract of land for the expanding residential areas of a southern city. From the beginning, its program, kindergarten through twelfth grade, was established as a sort of college-prep school for the children of this economically affluent area of the city. In reflection of the political character of the community, the district boundaries were simple gerrymandered to exclude most children of working-class parents. And, or course, the dual system that existed under local racial segregation excluded the black children from the neighborhood of Crossover located two blocks to the north, just across the tracks.

With this highly homogeneous school population, the academic program of Crossover High School (CHS) developed a reputation for excellence. Regularly, 95 percent of the senior graduating class enrolled in college. In one year during the 1950s, there were eleven Merit Scholar students in one graduating class. Many of the local influential middle-management executives, professional people, and political leaders are graduates of CHS. During the 1950s and 1960s competition at the school was intense across the gamut of academics through the available social activities, and parents supported the school financially and spiritually.

The all-white faculty found the teaching situation highly attractive at Crossover. They received the best equipment and generous volunteer support. Only select teachers were permitted to transfer to Crossover, and only the very best maintained a position. Hence, the teacher turnover up until 1969 was minimal.

In a 1972 desegregation plan, the black neighborhood of Crossover, located just across some railroad tracks from CHS, was included in the school district. Not unlike other black enclaves in residential areas of Southern cities, the community was established early in the century to house a labor force for service in white homes and businesses. While the sense of community is strong in the neighborhood, it is plagued by property, violent, and victimless crimes. In many ways, it can be characterized as a "street corner society."

The former black high school (now a feeder junior high school for CHS) was a source of pride for the neighborhood. Business and parent groups, as with the segregated CHS, were active supporters of the school.

Needless to say, both black and white communities were apprehensive about the pairing and desegregation of Feeder School and CHS, and responded with mixed emotions. When desegregation was ordered in 1972, most white parents with children in the senior high permitted them to remain and graduate. But many parents with students in the junior high, particularly girls, removed them to private schools rather than send them to what was considered an inferior black junior high school. The black community had no choice but to comply. The white principal at Crossover High School resigned rather than face the inevitable problems of desegregation. Thus, the black principal at Feeder, with half his staff, moved to take charge of a desegregated Crossover High in September 1972.

Results
The incompatibility of the education and desegregation goals for education led to interesting patterns in Crossover High School. As it turned out, the efficacy of the desegregation efforts became highly depen-

dent upon keeping whites, students and instructors, in the school, for without them no desegregation would have occurred. This requisite had two effects. First, it prompted the principal to allow the white students and teachers some disproportionate influence in the school setting. Even as the school became majority black, the student council, clubs, and honors remained controlled by an elite white student network while the athletic program became largely black. The white, "old guard" teachers became the protectors of the academic standards ("education") and the accelerated courses, which provided the skill backgrounds that were of use to those who planned to continue on to college. The black teachers and a network of inexperienced teachers, black and white (whom we came to call the "motleys"), were relegated to the standard curricular offerings and, as the principal saw it, to "integration." The net result of the incompatible goal was simple resegregation essentially along lines of ability. The "old guard" taught the elite, white students and a smattering of black students, and advised the school organizations that these students controlled. The black teachers and the motleys taught classes populated by lower-class whites and blacks, with the latter being in the majority. Desegregation had its most meaningful test in the standard curriculum since there were few selection criteria for such courses. The accelerated course had more stringent criteria and included few blacks.

The resegregation was the result of two factors: the requisites for selection and success in the accelerated curriculum and the contingencies that face the minority students who wished to satisfy those requisites.

Negotiating Success. Obviously, it can be argued that there are formal and informal requisites for selection to, and success in, the accelerated curriculum. However, the students, particularly those students who had some difficulty in negotiating the attainment of the requisites, were most likely to "ground" these formal requisites in their interactional context and thus saw the distinction between formal and informal as blurred if not nonexistent. The "old guard" and elite white students saw a high grade point average, teacher's recommendations, and a determination of the students' interest and abilities (often by the guidance counselor) as the formal requisites, and promoted strict adherence to these standards even when it resulted in the enrollment in these classes being so low that they could no longer be offered. When accelerated courses began to be eliminated because of low enrollments, the "old guard" held their standards and watched their curriculum dwindle. In this context, the minority students suffered not only from degradation, but also from the emergent contingencies that were imposed on them by the school.

Suttles (1968, p. 58) argued that the ethnic ownership of schools defines the adaptation expected of the less powerful group:

> Schools . . . are consigned to ethnic groups on multiple criteria: location, precedent, the ethnicity of staff and the ethnicity of the student body. Where all these criteria coincide, the minority group students may take on the ingratiating manner of a humble guest. With this behavior they can survive and sometimes even advance. . . . If they do not accept this status they must fend for themselves.

His analysis is especially poignant in the case of CHS, as suggested by two comments by black students: "If we had stayed at Feeder [the former black high school] none of this would have ever happened. Everybody wouldn't be turning black and white." "Once we went to Crossover, everybody cared about what the white folks were doing." The black students were rarely admitted to the accelerated courses; the grade point averages, the teacher recommendations, and the counselor's estimation of interests and abilities were sufficient to relegate most black students to the basic or standard course offerings. However, many blacks wished access to the college preparatory curriculum, and those who desired such access "understood" that their success required "acting white." These students made a conscious effort to "take on" or emphasize those attitudes and traits that characterized elite white students. This emulation included behavior, dress, and linguistic patterns. Membership in certain school clubs and participation in selected school activities were seen as mechanisms with which to solidify their claim to academic and, ultimately, economic success. Nevertheless, the whites controlled the advanced curriculum and the prestige clubs and activities. All in all, the proficient black student was required to publicly renounce his or her ethnic heritage for the chance of success. Those students who had few prospects for the accelerated curriculum, high social status, and college saw this transition. As one of these students argued:

> Carl—his kind is trying to act white. Do you know Susan? She forgot she is black. She dresses white, she acts white, she even talks white. Darryl is an Oreo; he's busy getting his titles. Blacks working in the office ain't really black—just look at Greg. Paulette turned white for a while, but now she has turned back black. David is just like a white boy.

However, this is not just the biased account of one of the losers, for the school continued to be a threat even for the more successful. For example, even if admitted to the accelerated curriculum, the successful black student still had to face standardized college entrance examinations, often noted for their cultural bias. As one of the more successful students explained:

> I know I'm just a token for the whites as chaplain for the Student Council. I want desperately to go to college, but there's no way I can pass the ACT. I belong to several clubs so it will look good on my college application and in the yearbook. I made a 7 on the ACT, but I will retake it, and if I can make a 12, I want to go to the State University. If not, I will try for the local community college and transfer to the State University.

Another successful black student concurred:

> I belong to several clubs because I need this for my application for college, I have a 3.0 grade average.

The proficient black students found it necessary to manipulate the building of their credentials in many ways. Almost universally, however, it was required that these students "act white." A commonly expressed opinion by black students was:

> White students have more freedom and are disciplined less. If you want to get ahead you have to act white. The teachers like you if you act white. If you act white, you get better grades.

The relatively proficient black students found success and their ethnic heritage to be in direct contradiction. They had to reject their culture for the purposes of schooling; the contingencies of success at CHS required it and they adapted. Nevertheless, the adaptation taught many lessons, not the least of which was to distrust whites:

> This is all in just learning how to deal with these devils. Even in petty things . . . they will use trickery if need be.

The examples of distrust of whites were many in the accounts of the interviews with these students:

> He said black students loved to participate in club meetings, but the majority of meetings where you really had fun or really got into something were held at white students' houses that were far from the school. These meetings were usually held at night, and black students did not have transportation to get to

them. He thought this was just another extension of the white people being tricky. He felt that they knew that black students couldn't come out to their houses, so therefore they couldn't have that much input into the clubs the whites wanted to control.

Even tokenism was thought to indicate trickery:

Cordette Crane was a black student. She was on the student council; she was a majorette and homecoming queen. She had lots of activities. She was the only black asked to participate on the prom committee. She was appointed, it was believed, as a joke. It was argued that these white people knew Cordette would not actively participate on the prom committee because she was out for popularity. She just had too many activities to want to really get into the prom committee.

One of the black members of our research team commented in her account of an interview with one of the highly successful black students,

These are my personal comments on Clark Dane. Clark is not a bitter student; he may seem so from the conversation given you, but this is taken out of context. Clark is not bitter, does not hate white people. He likes white people, but it stresses him that you have to treat these people with a long-handled spoon. Anytime you get a white friend, you just cannot trust him. He talked about Mary Wells. This was one of the so-called white liberals. He said that even he had caught her at certain things that she wouldn't want her black friends to know. He said he would never want to go back to the segregated environment because integration had taught him how to deal with white people, what they expected. He felt they had taught him how to smile and at the same time be able to stick them in the back. He said he was now able to do this—now able to play their games, of smiling on the front and having no good intentions on the back. I [the black researcher] think this is a realistic observation. This is an observation that I carry to this day, and I do not include all white people in this category, but there are a lot of white people that you have to treat with a long-handled spoon as Clark is saying.

Peer Pressure. The successful black student has to pay more costs than personally denying his or her cultural heritage by acting white and developing a distrustful eye for those whom he or she has had to emulate. The successful black students were subject to derogation by their own who had not achieved academic success. Those who were relegated to the basic, or standard, curriculum, as noted earlier, chided their more successful peers for "acting white," and occasionally attempted to call for ethnic allegiance. These students had generally developed street repertoires and were regarded as a threat to the proficient black students, who had cultivated an image contrary to the stereotypes of blacks held by whites. The proficient blacks argued:

> That bunch in the low-income housing projects don't like whites and just hate them to death. They are always smoking dope in the projects. Almost every girl in the project has a baby.

The peer pressure was great and often forced the students to choose between acting black and acting white not only in school, but more holistically. The unsuccessful black students would not allow their more successful compatriots the luxury of degrading black culture for school purposes. They saw it as an either-or proposition; either you act black or you act white. Ethnicity was behavioral and cultural in their minds; one's genetic heritage was not sufficient to define ethnic identity. One female black student explained her experience of these pressures:

> *Student:* I'm kind of paranoid. You know, people give me such a hard time. I just kind of stay away from people that I'm not sure about or I know don't like me.
> *Interviewer:* Why do you think the black students are like you say?
> *Student:* They don't give you a chance. This started in the tenth grade. This white girl in my classroom was very talkative, very pretty, and you just couldn't be mean to her. And her name was Mary, and she lived in the nicest block in this white community, and we became very close. If you saw one of us, you saw the other. And after that . . . Well, no one liked me anyway because my momma dressed me real nice. They used to say I thought I was white before I ever talked to a white person. When I started being with her, they were just getting all motivated . . . and they beat me up every evening anyway and this gave them even more reason. But after that they wouldn't speak to me. I could count my black friends on one hand. That made me feel bad, because I know I'm black, but, you know, after you start being with people so much, you start acting like them and talking like them. I became changed, using kind of white slang and dressing like Mary did. I just thought because my black friends weren't giving me a chance.

Another student commented, "You know, it's weird, nobody likes me at school, and it's more blacks than whites."

Discussion

In the late 1960s and early 1970s, the dialogue concerning education was rather focused on the problems of minority students in a middle-class school. It was in that era that the critiques of public education were common and that the academic problems of minority students often were framed more as structural problems with the organization and process of schooling than problems with student capabilities (cf. Pearl, 1972, and Carnoy, 1972). These critiques have continued to today, but little has resulted from them in the way of educational change. In part, this can be attributed to the reluctance and probable impotence of educational institutions to change their fundamental logic of sorting (Katz, 1971), and in part to a lack of specificity on the part of the critics to provide guidelines so that small-scale educational innovations could be designed that would challenge that fundamental logic.

Perhaps the most direct challenge to the sorting logic of public schooling that emerged from these critiques has been court-mandated desegregation. Seemingly, this desegregation has imposed incompatible goals upon public schools.

Education and Desegregation

Obviously, it is necessary to demonstrate that the goal is compatibility of education (as embodied in American public schools) and desegregation. There are many ways to do this, but probably the succinct argument is based in history. Katz (1971) and Karier, Violas, and Spring (1973) demonstrated historically that public education in the United States was designed and functioned to serve the industrial and economic order, and not to promote equality, since its goal was to maintain stratification while prompting industrial skills.

The Interaction of Stratification and Schooling in the United States

Katz (1971) has argued most convincingly that the "Great School Legend," as Greer (1972) calls it, does not seem to have much historical veracity. Indeed, Katz portrayed the origins of public education in the United States as part of a movement to maintain Protestantism over Catholicism as the dominant form of religion in this country. The force of this movement was bolstered by the demands of a Protestant-controlled economy that was rapidly becoming industrial.

The industrialists saw the urban immigrant masses as a potential source of workers. However, most immigrants had come from agrarian backgrounds and simply were lacking in skills that industry needed. Yet, even more problematic than this lack of skills, since experience could easily give skills, was the potential of these masses for urban unrest and more specifically an attitude that was not conducive to working in industry. The necessary attitude, according to the industrialists, was one of acceptance and docility. Mass production required workers who not only had skills, but who also accepted their lot and were not divisive elements in a work setting that required acceptance of routine and authority. The Protestant industrialists, according to Katz (1971), viewed public education as the appropriate vehicle through which to inculcate these skills and attitudes in the poor.

There was some dissension, however, over how to best provide these educational services. Katz documented the range of experimentation and discourse to highlight the significance of the final choice of "incipient bureaucracy" as the organizational form that was believed to be most able to achieve the desired goals.

Intriguingly, bureaucracy has been seen as the most "rational" form of organization (Weber, 1964). This "rationality" was precisely what the industrialists saw. Bureaucracy maximizes order and control. It more nearly regularizes the distribution of power and authority than do other forms of organization. Thus, when looking at the task of instilling a particular set of skills and values into an extensively heterogeneous mass of immigrant groups, the selection of bureaucracy by those in control was indeed "rational" for their interests. They were pushing integration into the industrial order, if not American society.

It could be argued then that the history of mass education in this country is a history of conflict over the meaning of integration. As Katz (1971) showed for the nineteenth-century origins of public schooling in this nation, Karier, Violas, and Spring (1973) and Spring (1976) demonstrated for education in the twentieth century; the persistent logic of the public school movement has emphasized assimilation over intellectual development, with the often explicit goal of teaching "the norms necessary to adjust the young to the changing patterns of the economic system, as well as to the society's more permanent values" (Karier, Violas, & Spring, 1973, p. 7).

The assumption of bureaucracy as the organizational form for public education was, thus, a design to forcibly, but subtly, assimilate the newly immigrated into an emerging industrial order that was dominated by Anglo-Saxon Protestants. Further, this "assimilative logic" has persisted and often seems to have been heightened by the increasing bureaucratization of public education.

It may be argued that, if anything, the "assimilative logic" may have been heightened over time through an institutional accrual of power. The assumption of bureaucracy as the organizational form for public education seems to have led to an insulation and isolation of the institution from those which it serves. Inasmuch as the preeminent feature of bureaucracy is internal control, problems that emerge within the organization are routinely resolved internal to the bureaucracy with only gross incidents referred to formal linkage to the community, the school board. Further, given that the pattern of democracy in this nation is simply majority rule, it is often the case that the school board is more representative of local industrial interests than of the general community. Even when this is not the case, school board decisions are often based upon information and recommendations of the "experts" who staff the bureaucracy. Even the formation of state accrediting regulations reflect this pattern.

The institutional accrual of power by education seems to have been supported by the professionalization movement among educators. As with other occupations, professionalization appears to be a mechanism which "cools out" outside influence and control through the development of colleges of education that determine, under legislative mandate, who can be a teacher and who can be an "expert" in the field of education.

Interestingly, some of the characteristics of bureaucratization, differentiation and specialization in particular, have seemed to neutralize the possibility that anyone can be "expert" on all facets of the educational process. (Not only are educators specialists but schools have differentiated various curriculum blocks, administrative specialists, and levels of authority.) This trend seems to have been effective not only in reducing community influence and involvement, but also in thwarting the emergence of any large body of intellectuals who are "knowledgeable" across the gamut of educational philosophy, theory, policy, curriculum, instruction, and so on.

In short, public education, seemingly through increasing bureaucratization, has accrued such power over the past century that it may consciously only minimally represent even the industrialists. Yet the mold seems to have been cast in the 1880s, and education may never be able to escape its allegiance to the early industrialists, and its assimilative logic, if it never escapes bureaucracy as the dominant organizational form.

Desegregation is a challenge to the assimilative logic of public education because it serves the interests of those who have been denied a quality education because of their lack of assimilation. It represents a direct attack on public schools because it puts the burden of proof, and therefore accountability, upon them for "integrating" those who have not been "assimilated." Further, given that bureaucracies by design maximize control, "integration" into the conventional world and the promise of economic sufficiency are the rewards for being assimilated and accepting the parameters of behavior and style promulgated by the institution. The threat of punishment used by public schools for promoting "assimilation" is the denial of access to conventional economic opportunity by denying access to educational certification. As a result then, desegregation, when imposed as a goal for public schooling, challenges, the major social control mechanism of public schools. The goal of education as embraced in the American public schools is in direct contradiction with desegregation and equality of educational opportunity. The implementation of these incompatible goals has effects upon the everyday life of a public school and upon the adaptations of minority students to the public school.

Contingencies and Adaptations. Minority students face many contingencies in attempting to negotiate schooling successfully. Many who do not meet the "standards" find an ethnic identity available to them, but those minority students who more-or-less meet the standards are in a more precarious position. First, the standards are a constant threat. Not only must one make the grades, but one must do well on standardized tests. Not only must one compete academically, but one must compete socially for club memberships, honors, and teacher recommendations. Second, one must also challenge ethnic boundaries. The white-controlled activities often are the most prestigious, and striving black students must emulate whites to be socially acceptable. Nevertheless, they will not escape their ethnicity as far as the whites are concerned; white students have employed the blacks for their own ends. Therefore, the striving black students dare not trust those whom they emulate, while on the other hand, they lose the trust and respect of those less successful students who are of the same ethnic heritage. While they are not allowed to be white, they are also not allowed to be black.

The proficient black students are isolated when most adolescents are consumed by the peer group. They are threatened because there can be little trust. They are alienated and anomic in the classic sense of the concepts: without norms, they guardedly tread upon schooling; without available identification, they must structure their personal selves; and without participation, they must attach themselves to the structures of a somewhat alien culture. Adaptation seemingly requires of them the degradation of their culture and the emulation of another in which they will never be granted full status.

Responding to the Costs of Success. Unfortunately, educational programs are based upon a naive assumption that those who publicly appear to be assimilated into the mainstream of our society have fewer problems that need attention than those who are not being assimilated. It seems appropriate to reconsider this assumption on at least two grounds. First, those who are not being assimilated seemingly have different problems from those who are. The high priority for the unassimilated should be in the procurement of "hard" services like income and health care that directly affect the quality of their lives. Those who are being "successfully" assimilated into a majority culture have different needs. They may well need the support of "soft" services like counseling and guidance, for they are in a situation where guidance and understanding is hard to come by. Second, it may be that we have conceived the problem incorrectly. Usually, most professionals would argue that, in some form or another, lack of access to success is the problem, although this may be the result of our own ethnocentrism concerning assimilation. Because we were able to negotiate success, we believe it must be a problem for those who were not able to do so. If the results reported here have any validity, the problem is more the assimilative logic employed in our society and in our schools, whether they be desegregated as in the case here or segregated by race. The black students respond to the contingencies they face due to assimilation. Some fail the test of assimilation, cultural degradation, and resolve the problem by adopting a larger "street" repertoire that is available to them. Some degrade their culture, and find none fully available to them.

If the assimilative logic is the problem that ultimately needs remedying, this, obviously, would be a monumental task. It involves restructuring American schooling, if not the economy, and seemingly requires some form of cultural pluralism that as yet has not found easy reception in our society. As we explored earlier in this paper, desegregation was a challenge to the assimilative, stratifying logic of education. The data presented unequivocally demonstrate that even that has not been successful in its challenge. All in all, both remedial services and a concomitant change effort would probably be the most effective strategy at this point. Nevertheless, more emphasis on black students' adaptations to those contingencies seems to be appropriate. People adapt readily, but society changes slowly. The latter needs more of our attention.

Summary

In this chapter we have tried to better understand the situation of minority youth in the desegregated schools that are constitutionally mandated. These students, as our data reveal, are under great pressure both from the requisites for academic success and from their culture as embodied in their peer group. Schools seemingly coerce the minority student to modify the significance of his or her culture, and the minority student adapts by developing new cultural routines.

Desegregated education has done little to reduce such pressure upon the minority student. In part, this is because desegregation as conceptualized and enforced by federal courts has not been able to successfully modify the assimilative logic of public schools. Desegregation has resulted more in blacks and whites engaging in a competition of cultures than in a more pluralistic respect for diverse cultural styles. The minority student is still disadvantaged in these settings.

This disadvantage is rather complex. Not only are there actual skill differences, but also differing definitions of appropriateness of behaviors and linguistic patterns. Further, the minority student is buffeted between desires for socioeconomic ability and the heritage and support of his or her family and culture. The black students' legacy, their disadvantage, and their emotional survival are all contingent upon how well they are equipped to resolve these competing demands.

References

Carnoy, M. (1972). *Schooling in a corporate society.* New York: David McKay.

Greer, C. (1972). *The great school legend.* New York: Basic Books.

Karier, C., Violas, R., & Spring, J. (1973). *Roots of crisis: American education in the twentieth century.* Chicago: Rand McNally.

Katz, M. (1971). *Class, bureaucracy, and schools.* New York: Praeger.

Noblit, G. W. (1977). Ethnographic approaches to evaluation. Paper presented at the National Conference on Criminal Justice Evaluation, Washington, DC.

Pearl, A. (1972). *The atrocity of education.* St. Louis: New Critics Press.

Spicer, E. (1976). Beyond analysis and explanation? *Human Organization, 35*(4), 335–343.

Spring, J. (1976). *The sorting machine.* New York: David McKay.

Suttles, G. (1968). *The social order of the slum.* Chicago: University of Chicago Press.

Turner, S., & Carr, D. (1976). The process of criticism in interpretive sociology and history. Paper presented at the American Sociological Association meeting, New York, NY.

Weber, M. (1964). *Theory of social and economic organization.* New York: Free Press.

Chapter 7

Cui Bono? White Students in a Desegregating High School

George W. Noblit and Thomas W. Collins

Men are not disturbed by things but by the view they take of them.
—Epistelus

One of the characteristic difficulties in conducting research on social problems is establishing what the "problem" actually is. Humans use issues of fact loosely and symbolically in everyday life. Further, as Simon (1976) suggests, the distinction between fact and value may be problematic in itself. A "fact" may possibly not be independent of its value connotation, and certainly everyday life provides many examples of this. One good example is the issue of the benefits of school desegregation for white students. The symbolic meaning of this issue makes it quite difficult to establish just what issues need to be addressed by research.

Let us reflect on the context in which the issue emerges. It is certainly one of those "second-generation" issues (even though it is misleading to argue that we are in the second generation of school desegregation). This issue shares the symbolism of calling desegregation "busing." It is presented as a legitimate concern with a significant basis. Unfortunately, it is all too easy to accept this issue framed in this way. As a result, many argue that we must do something to "sell" desegregation to whites: We must demonstrate some benefit to whites.

However, it may not be necessary to "sell" desegregation to whites. After all, school desegregation is a constitutional requirement that has no direct expectation of benefits for whites. Furthermore, there is little reason to have ever expected desegregation to benefit whites, since desegregation ideally was meant to distribute the resources that were disproportionately assigned to whites in a more equitable fashion. Nevertheless, if we are careful to avoid the potential trap of looking only to those differences due to desegregation that whites would consider "beneficial" in their normative framework, we may be able to learn some of the effects of desegregation due to its implementation process. That is, if we reframe the issue, it may be possible to use an assessment of benefits to whites as a potentially negative indicator of the effectiveness of the desegregation process in any particular setting. If whites have accrued benefits that would not be expected to result from desegregation, then this may be a basis on which to critique the implementation of desegregation as it occurred in that setting. Let us attempt such an analysis using ethnographic data from a two-year study of a desegregated Southern high school that was also the basis of chapter 6. To conserve space, we have not repeated the research procedures used in this study, but have repeated and expanded the description of the school as it will help the reader understand this analysis.

The School

Crossover High School (a pseudonym) was built in 1948 and graduated its first class in 1951. The school was built on a 35-acre tract of land to serve an expanding and affluent residential area in Memphis. From the beginning, its program—kindergarten through twelfth grade—was established as that of a sort of college prep school. The school district's boundaries reflected the political character of the community, for they were gerrymandered to exclude most children of working-class parents. And, of course, racial segregation excluded black children from Crossover, even though black families lived in the immediate vicinity of the school.

With the highly homogeneous school population, the academic program of Crossover High School (CHS) developed a reputation for excellence. Regularly, 95 percent of the senior graduating class enrolled in college. In one year, during the 1950s, there were 11 National Merit Scholarship winners in the graduating class. Many of the influential middle-management executives, professional people, and political leaders in Memphis are graduates of CHS. During the 1950s and 1960s, competition at the school was intense, and parents supported the school financially and spiritually.

The white faculty found the teaching situation at Crossover highly attractive. They received the best equipment and generous volunteer support. Only select teachers were permitted at Crossover, and only the very best maintained a position. Hence teacher turnover was minimal.

In a 1972 desegregation plan, the black neighborhood of Crossover, located just across some railroad tracks from CHS, was included in the school district. Like other black enclaves in residential areas of Southern cities, the community had been established early in the century to house a labor force for service in white homes and businesses. While the sense of community is strong in the neighborhood, it is plagued by property crimes and violent and victimless offenses. In many ways, it can be characterized as a "street corner society."

The black high school (now a feeder junior high school for CHS) was a source of pride for the neighborhood. As in the case of CHS, business and parent groups were active supporters of the school.

Needless to say, both black and white communities were apprehensive about desegregating the black school (Feeder School) and CHS, and they responded with mixed emotions. When desegregation was ordered in 1972, most white parents with children in the senior high permitted them to remain and graduate. But many white parents with students in the junior high, particularly girls, removed them to private schools rather than send them to what was considered an inferior black junior high school. The white principal at Crossover High School resigned rather than face the inevitable problems of desegregation. The black community, on the other hand, had no choice but to comply with the desegregation decision. Thus, the black principal at Feeder, with half of his staff, moved to take charge of a desegregated Crossover High in September 1972.

The black principal was faced with the unenviable task of merging not only two racially different populations but also two populations with widely different socioeconomic levels and concomitant lifestyles. Several of the white parents maintained informal contact with board members of the school system, making for a potentially hostile board and complicating the principal's task. To add to this situation, the local media selected CHS as a sort of barometer for measuring the response of the entire district. Thus, the school received continual attention from the news media. The principal stated it concisely when he spoke to the student body the first year: "We are living in kind of a fishbowl on how desegregation can work."

One of the primary sources of school stability—community support—was lost from the beginning. The black community looked on CHS as a white institution controlled by forces they could not match, and the Feeder community would not identify with the new school. White community support was already strained by long litigation over desegregation before 1972. The major political issue in the 1971 mayoral election was busing. Thus, when desegregation did arrive, many white parents sent their children to CHS with a sense of defeat. Their school support was less than dramatic. As might be expected, adult attendance at sports and at musical and dramatic events dropped. Within three years, parent organizations ceased to exist. Parents were critical of the administration but offered little aid.

To add to the principal's difficulties, it was necessary to reorganize the curriculum to meet the needs of the two different school populations. However, any adjustment in course offerings was met with suspicion by the old-guard teaching staff, who established themselves as "the protectors of academic standards." When the principal attempted innovations in relaxing codes of dress and demeanor and in providing "recreational" study hall for students who did not choose to be quiet or study, this was interpreted by the old-guard teachers as somehow being related to lower academic standards. Therefore, the first principal often found himself without the full support of his own faculty. Given all these obstacles, he admitted quite early in his tenure that it would be only a matter of time before he was transferred to another school. This prophecy proved correct in 1976, and a new principal took his place.

The second principal, also a black, began his tenure with four years of experience with desegregation and with the white/black student ratio at CHS at 30 percent/70 percent. Moreover, school district policy was changing, and CHS was increasingly taking on the image of a vocationally oriented school, whether the new administrator and his staff were willing to accept it or not. A vocational skill center, one of six in the district, had been built adjacent to CHS. Although the center was administratively separate, the vocational programs were attractive to a large percentage of CHS students, if for no other reason than that they provided a half-day break from the routine of academic work. This loss of students weakened the program at CHS by increasing the teacher/student ratio to the point where some of the staff were declared nonessential and transferred from the school.

White Students and the Desegregation Process

The preceding description of CHS during its implementation years highlights the problematic nature of school desegregation for a wide range of school participants. School desegregation was a highly political process within CHS, and for the most part, those who had power maintained their power. However, power is not the most salient issue to be examined here. Let us instead address a set of questions that will allow us to keep a tight focus on the benefits to white students. The first question seemingly has to be, How much desegregation actually occurred? For if extensive desegregation did not occur, then it is harder to ascribe "benefits" or "losses" for whites as being due to desegregation. The second question then is, What did whites lose (if anything) as a result of desegregation? For if whites experienced few losses as a result of desegregation, then the issue of benefits to whites would seem to be less salient. The third and last question obviously is, What benefits did whites experience as a result of desegregation? Of course, to answer these questions we must be careful to account for how the interpretations of desegregation employed by whites (and not desegregation itself) may have shaped the results of desegregation and to remember that, potentially, implementation of desegregation at CHS may actually be better understood as a critique of the implementation process.

How Much Desegregation Occurred?

The U.S. Civil Rights Commission (1979) survey of forty-seven school districts found that about 47 percent of all minority students still attended at least moderately segregated schools. Further, we are increasingly aware that within-school segregation often results from the traditional educational practice of ability grouping. At Crossover High School, essentially two schools coexisted under one roof. With desegregation came a heightened emphasis on "levels of instruction." The desegregation plan was implemented in 1973, and a central office memo to secondary school principals indicated that within-school segregation was to become mandatory:

> It is imperative that we have more uniformity in our academic program as we enter into our desegregation program in the fall of 1973. Many procedures which were optional must now become standard policy.

The memo outlined the four newly "standard" levels of instruction that included basic, standard, enriched, and advanced placement, in order of increasing "ability" requirements.

This policy played into the hands of a newly desegregating faculty. The "old guard" with their concerns for "standards" continued to teach, at the enriched and advanced placement levels, the "higher-ability" students, who ended up being largely white. The black teachers, more concerned with "reaching the student," taught the basic and standard courses and the black students for the most part. With the establishment of this policy, both the principal and the teachers were faced with decisions concerning who should be teaching whom. Neither faction thought the other capable of assuming its role, so the faculty also segregated itself and taught largely segregated classes.

From the viewpoint of the teachers, segregation was necessary to protect "their" students (either black or white) from the other faction of teachers. From the principal's viewpoint, segregation by levels of instruction was a way to match the teacher to students with which he or she had the most experience and interest in teaching. The viewpoint of students and parents varied by the levels to which the students were assigned. White parents were largely satisfied with their children's assignment, since whites were largely assigned to the enriched and advanced placement courses with teachers who had always taught these courses to these types of students, but they bemoaned the fact that there was so little flexibility in offering these courses. There simply were not enough "high-ability" students (by some immutable set of standards) to justify maintaining, for example, Latin as well as French and Spanish, and later even French. Black parents were less satisfied. They had teachers from their old school and thus were satisfied with them. They were not satisfied with the within-school stratification that resulted in fewer minority students being the "top" students than obviously would have been the case had the black high school continued to exist.

The usual practice of scheduling advanced placement courses first so that they would be fully available to the "better" students exacerbated the problem. The practices favored those who were of "higher ability" in a range of subjects but penalized those who were of "high ability" in only subject. The higher-level courses were scheduled in sequence, while the other-level courses were not in the same sequences. Thus to take one enriched or advanced placement course could entail the cost of not being able to schedule all the courses one needed from the other levels.

In any case, while the high school was desegregated, there was little desegregation in classrooms. As one tenth-grade white student put it:

When I was in junior high, I had lots of black friends, but when I got over here they were just not in any of my classes. I never saw them. We kind of lost touch with each other.

As a black student saw it:

It's possible to go all through the years of high school and not have a single white person in your class.

As one teacher explained:

Well, I only have two blacks in here. This is standard English, and they have a hard time getting out of basic.

How much desegregation occurred? Not much. Those who experienced some classroom desegregation were working-class whites who were not college-bound and the more middle-class blacks who were college-bound, both relegated to the lower level of instruction. Nevertheless, classrooms were substantially segregated.

What Did Whites Lose (If Anything) as the Result of Desegregation?

We have seen that white students essentially retained their teachers, their curriculum, and their advantage in the desegregation of CHS. Therefore, this question requires some additional thought. Riedesel (1979, p. 120), in considering the question of the economic benefits to whites of racial segregation, simply notes: "The hypothesis that whites derive important economic benefits from discrimination against blacks and other minorities has long held sway." Thus it could be expected that desegregation should have cost whites something. However, desegregation was implemented at CHS so that within-school segregation resulted, and therefore the costs to whites were minimal.

However, whites could argue that, even if there was little change in the academic experience of their children, there could be a dramatic change in the "social life" that accompanies high school. At CHS, white students often complained about this. They argued essentially that blacks were infringing upon the just territory of whites when competing for school honors. The white students argued that splitting honors (e.g., "best dressed white, best dressed black"; "best white student, best black student") cheapened the honor, even though these honors were voted on by the student body who, being majority black, could have controlled the elections if not for the honors being race-specific. White students again had the advantage in election to the student council, which was contingent upon grades, good conduct, and teacher recommendation.

White males withdrew from the football and basketball teams and found havens in golf and cross-country running. But note that this was the result of their choice. They chose not to compete with blacks for positions on the squads and maintained that they could not win the competition for starting slots as long as the coaches were black. The principal had encouraged the coaches to desegregate the starting squads. While the coaches made some effort to do this, apparently the whites were not up to the competition.

Apparently whites did lose some social advantages at the school, but seemingly they lost less than their numbers would have demanded.

The social life of a school also is within classrooms, and seemingly this needs a close examination. One obviously would expect that, since little desegregation actually occurred within classrooms, this social life would have been affected only minimally. In fact, this seems to have been true. The classrooms which were largely white were almost cari-catures of white school culture. Let us look at one of these carica-tures, chosen not because it is representative of classroom life and the educational experiences of the students, but because it reveals the social life of white students when a teacher allowed the class to be largely informal.

The teacher noted that she was going to give some in-class time to study for the test for tomorrow, since "there is a game tonight, and they are all squawking." As it turned out, there were only six students in the class; the rest were in the auditorium buying their rings, and the six students worked diligently on their "memory assignment." In speak-ing with the teacher, even when only six students were in class, a white female, Lisa, raised her hand for permission. A white male, Bill was less respectful. The teacher asked, "Bill are you finished with your memory work?" He said, "Uh?" She repeated her question, and he replied, "I'm just sitting here proofreading it." He seemed openly defiant and that defiance seemed to bring no response from the teacher. The teacher encouraged them to complete the memory assignments as soon as possible so they could work on their vocabulary for the test the next day. As they finished, each one went to a small typing table, placed a single sheet of work in an in-box, and returned to his or her seat. The teacher went over Bill's work with him and then spoke with another student, Paul. She noted the study questions that were the work assignments for the test. The information discussed was about the history of early American literature. The teacher discussed the study questions a lot with Bill and Paul. And while she was doing this, Lisa and another white female cheerleader (Lisa was dressed as a cheerleader also) were talking in low voices, and she shushed them.

After discussing the study questions with the teacher, Bill went up to compare answers with the two white females as the teacher walked to her desk. Her back turned for a moment, and Lisa squirted Bill in the face with a green squirt gun which she had held behind her back, and actually up under the skirt of her cheerleader outfit. The students then engaged in a lively discussion with the teacher to cover up. There was no public indication of guilt. Lisa was even able to pick up her purse and hold it in front of her and slip the gun in her purse while she was talking with the teacher. It was another good example of the white students' manipulation and the teacher's complicity with it.

I noted the classroom had a small bookcase full of the *American College Dictionary* in the rear east corner of the room. And the students were free to use it in their work. I had not noted this in other English classes. A few students entered from the auditorium, all female, and it was quickly apparent that the only black students in the class were also both female. The white English teacher talked about discussing the literary techniques of imagery and antithesis. She had discussed imagery before and it was the subject of one of the study questions, but antithesis was what she had wanted the students to discuss after they had heard the speech by Patrick Henry. As it turned out, it became apparent that all students had assigned seats. Bill went to the office and brought back a package of newspapers. The teacher thanked him. He stopped by Lisa's desk, and the teacher lightly turned him in the direction toward his seat. (She walked over, put her arms on him, and just redirected him down the aisle.) The teacher began to unpack the papers. Paul walked up and volunteered to do that for her. The teacher relocated one white female student to her assigned seat, which meant moving her up approximately three seats in the row she was already in. She sighed as the student moved up the row. The relocated student looked back at the other girl with some kind of longing in her eyes. Seemingly they wanted to communicate.

The three cheerleaders constantly looked at each other, especially in showing disrespect for the teacher through snickers, raised eyebrows, and other such techniques. Two white males entered the room. One was wearing a red baseball cap. The teacher said, "Cap, Greg." Greg said "Oh" and removed it. Quickly he said to the teacher, "I got my hair cut, do you like it?" This was a transition to manipulate the teacher out of a disciplinary mood, and the teacher was complicit enough to say, "Well, it looks better," and discipline procedures ended there.

The students who were too late to do their memory work before the end of the class were told to come in before school the next day and do it. No one complained. I found that interesting, and in fact they seemed to treat it as being fine with them, that coming in before school didn't present any problems for them. Apparently, the white students were enjoying this informal class session and were enjoying school enough to not complain about coming in early. The scene is a lot like an Archie comic strip: a depiction of the social life of white schooling.

It was noted earlier that desegregated classrooms were experienced by college-bound blacks and non-college-bound whites. These classes represented the logic opposite that proposed by those who are concerned that whites are losing something as the result of desegregation. If we are to assume that gains accrue from association with those more motivated and talented (as some have argued to be the basis of current desegregation policy), then obviously whites should have benefited from these classes. The talented blacks chose lower levels of instruction to maximize their grades. One black student explained his choices in this way:

> Why should I work hard to get a C in accelerated English when I can get an A or B in standard English? I keep up my grade point average.

In short, the "standards" of the "old guard" guaranteed that even the white students who did not qualify for enriched or advanced placement courses took courses with black students who did qualify but opted for higher grades over a higher level of instruction. If blacks should have gained from an association with more motivated and talented whites, so should these white students have gained from an association with more motivated and talented blacks.

A related issue may concern what was taught in these desegregated classrooms. At CHS, a majority black standard English class (thirteen black and four white students) with a black teacher had a supplementary reading list of classics (to whites). Selections were from Jane Austen,

Charles Dickens, Oliver Goldsmith, John Steinbeck, John Donne, William Somerset Maugham, George Orwell, and Ossie Davis. Martin Luther King ("I Have a Dream"), Harriet Beecher Stowe (*Uncle Tom's Cabin*), and Margaret Mitchell (*Gone with the Wind*) were also on the list. In short, whites were not short-changed on the curriculum even in desegregated classrooms.

What did whites lose as the result of desegregation? At CHS, they lost little.

What Benefits Did Whites Experience as the Result of Desegregation?

The preceding analysis makes this question almost trivial. Desegregation had little effect upon the schooling of whites. They benefited from that which they always would have benefited. They had the same teachers, and a classic curriculum, and they received more honors than their numbers would have justified. Even whites who experienced desegregated classrooms had the benefits of associating and learning with more talented and motivated blacks.

However, desegregation must have given whites some new experiences, as it was implemented at CHS. But again these were the benefits that accrue to those of privilege: the benefits of segregation. White students argued that they experienced benefits. Since they had more contact with blacks because the school was desegregated, they were more knowledgeable about minorities. However, they argued that this did not necessarily lead to a reduction in prejudice. The elite white students maintained they were still prejudiced, while the other white students who experienced desegregated classrooms were more likely to indicate a reduction in prejudice. This effect may, then, be explainable by social-psychological theory. Distance and lack of knowledge may be related to prejudice. However, such an explanation is too simplistic. The elite whites also saw blacks as the competition for the social rewards of schooling. Their prejudice was the prejudice of enemies. They gained little respect for their enemies because there was little direct competition. They relied on stereotypes of blacks for their own in-group solidarity.

These elite white students, in short, gained in political sophistication. They saw their status threatened, organized to maintain their advantage, and did so for about four years, when they abandoned the school because they had lost their disproportionate advantage. They learned to manipulate the criteria for admission to activities and the rules for governing activities, to establish coalitions with other factors (the "old guard" teachers), and to manipulate the environment (the opinions of their parents). They often bemoaned that they had to "run" the school, but they never considered letting someone else do so. In short, they learned the politics of class and caste.

Conclusions

Blau (1980, p. 786) writes:

> Having associates whose backgrounds and experiences differ from one's own reduces prejudice, improves objectivity and increases tolerance, as Simmel pointed out in his analysis of the stranger and Laumonn found in research on friendships. Members of small minorities are more likely than majority members to be involved in outgroup associations that broaden horizons and furnish intellectual stimulation.

The whites at CHS, for the most part, did not reap the benefits Blau proposes, in part because Blau's statement is conditional. It assumes that the minority has less advantage. At CHS, this was not the case. There was little classroom desegregation, and thus little association with black students. The elite whites gained neither broader horizons nor intellectual stimulation, for the implementation of desegregation at CHS did little to increase meaningful associations. Whites who experienced desegregated classrooms were more tolerant, more objective, and less prejudiced in their view toward blacks and of desegregation, and they also potentially gained from association with the talented and motivated college-bound black students. The white elites profited from the "best" teachers, the smaller classes, and political control. Desegregation did not lead to an equitable distribution of these resources. As we argued in the beginning, benefits to whites may be a negative indicator of the progress of desegregation. If so, then the implementation of desegregation at CHS may indicate little progress in remedying segregation and providing equal educational opportunity. The real question remains, How can people of color benefit from school desegregation? Obviously, not from a desegregation process like that of Crossover High School.

Note

The research on which this paper is based was funded by the National Institute of Education, Contract 400-76-009. The views expressed do not necessarily reflect the views of that agency.

References

Blau, P. M. (1980). A fable about social structure. *Social Forces, 58*(3), 777–788.

Riedesel, P. L. (1979). Racial discrimination and white economic benefits. *Social Sciences Quarterly, 60*(1), 120–129.

Simon, H. A. (1976). *Administrative behavior.* New York: Free Press.

Spicer, E. H. (1976). Beyond analysis and explanation. *Human Organization, 35*(4), 335–343.

Turner, S. P., & Carr, D. R. (1976, August). The process of criticism in interpretive sociology and history. Paper presented at American Sociological Association meetings, New York, NY.

U.S. Commission on Civil Rights. (1979, February). Desegregation of the nation's public schools: A status report. Washington, DC: Government Printing Office.

Chapter 8

Patience and Prudence in a Southern High School: Managing the Political Economy of Desegregated Education

George W. Noblit and Thomas W. Collins

It is probably unfortunate that educators are held accountable for school desegregation, for it is hardly an educational issue.[1] Rather, school desegregation is better understood as an issue of the political economy of this country. For example, the constitutional justification for school desegregation assumes that the real issues are not educational ones but issues of access and opportunity in the world of work. Were it otherwise, equal educational opportunity would not be a major public policy debate but an aesthetic discussion of academicians. Nevertheless, public schools are more vulnerable than the economy and, given the interface of schooling and employment in this country, are destined to be the vehicles of public policy, albeit indirect, to amend the political economy.

Further, the political economy analysis has great credence on the local level. A close analysis of local desegregation controversies suggests that, at least in the South, the debate centers more on the political and economic implications than upon educational issues. Blacks and whites alike understand Southern school desegregation to be closely tied to the development of political power. Though some have maintained that desegregation threatens the political self-sufficiency of blacks (cf. Hamilton, 1968, and Chisholm, 1975), others see desegregation as a major vehicle to reapportion the availability of socioeconomic mobility relative to the races. One administrator for the school district in which this study took place argues that the public schools have traditionally been a vehicle for white mobility both to the city from rural areas and to the middle class. Desegregation of school staffs opened this mechanism to blacks, and with limited school budgets the mobility of whites was consequently being limited.

Further, this same administrator and other school district personnel argued that school desegregation threatens to make each Southern city "another Atlanta." This fate is ominous to whites inasmuch as it signifies the loss of political dominance by whites as well as the loss of control over public funds and employment.

Conflict Theory

Although school desegregation may not be properly conceived as an educational issue, it is the schools and the school systems that will be held accountable for its implementation and success. This creates a significant problem for school administrators, since "success" has various meanings. To satisfy the courts, a numerical balance must be maintained. To satisfy federal policy makers, a boost in the academic achievement of minorities, or at least a possibility of such, seems to be required. To satisfy the local community, however, quality education and discipline must remain sacrosanct, and this accountability falls largely on the individual schools and principals.

As a result, the individual principal is largely left to manage a complex set of pressures and forces. Principals, however, are hard pressed to find guidance for their response to the challenge and threat of school desegregation. Normative texts like Lipham & Hoeh (1974), for example, ground the principal's role in existing social theories but only hint at the notion that the individual principal in a desegregated school setting will have to manage the vested interests of the local political economy. Of course, some would argue that this is not an impossible task, since schools have always served the existing political economy well. Katz (1971), Karier et al. (1973), and Rist (1972) all point out that the practices and procedures of American education have historically perpetuated the stratification of our society. Nevertheless, desegregation has the potential to redistribute educational rewards and skills and in the long run could affect the local political and economic order, and local communities understand it in this way.

Seemingly, then, a school principal has a massive task with desegregation. He or she must manage the challenge of desegregation to the local political economy, integrate desegregation as a major educational goal (even though it is not an educational issue), and ultimately integrate immediate desegregation into an existing logic of education that is based upon notions of stratification and long-term assimilation.

Patience and Prudence

Wolcott (1973) has portrayed the school principal as a "man in the middle," buffeted about by superiors, the demands of the educational setting, and the various participants in the school. Coupling this with a noteworthy lack of role clarity on the part of principals, Wolcott sees the school principal vacillating between "patience" and "prudence" in responding to the challenges that must be faced. (Patience represents a concern with the normative, ethical, and moral, and prudence represents a concern with the practical and functional.)

In the eternal searching for an "improved" role, patience, in Wolcott's terms, is "the one possible hope in which most of them are willing to invest energy as well as concern" (p. 296), even though there is little expectation that it will ever be achieved. This preoccupation with the changing role of principals has two components. One emphasizes the historical changes in duties and responsibilities. The other reflects a more normative upgrading of the principalship in quality and as a profession. As Wolcott notes for this latter component:

> This quest was echoed constantly in the recurring rhetorical question that principals ask: What *should* we be doing as principals (p. 297, emphasis in the original).

Prudence, on the other hand, is described as "how to survive the principalship," and "survival does not seem to entail doing the job outstandingly well—no one can persistently satisfy so many individuals representing so many divergent interests—but rather doing it well enough to remain in the position at all" (p. 306). Further, Wolcott notes:

> The school principal is successful in his work to the extent that he is able to contain and constrain the forces of change with which he must contend as a matter of daily routine; whatever force he exerts on the dynamics of the school contributes to its stability, even when he wants to act, or believes he is acting, in a way that will encourage an aura of change (p. 304).

Ethnographic Study

Data from an ethnographic study of a desegregated high school in the South[2] provide an opportunity to better understand administrative styles and their consequences in a qualitative manner. On occasion, natural sequences of events that are the substance of ethnographic studies also allow unique research experiences. In the high school studied, Crossover High School, the dynamics of desegregated schooling prompted a change in principals during the two years of data collection. Each principal had his own administrative style. The first man, dedicated to the "improved" and humanistic role of the principal, embodied Wolcott's definition of patience. The second was more practical, more prudent. His goal was pragmatic—survival. A comparison of these two styles and their effects will reveal the dynamics of desegregation and provide some direction for school desegregation policy.

The Demise of Patience

As is obvious even to those unused to school routines, principals play a major role in the dynamics of schooling. To the students, parents, and teachers, he or she is both a threat and a protection. He is empowered to make decisions that can almost destroy a student's or a teacher's school career, while concomitantly serving as a moral and behavioral guardian responsible for the inculcation of appropriate values and skills in children. He is responsible for an orderly instructional and educational setting, which has become the hallmark of quality education, while knowing that such order is not necessarily educational or responsible behavior. Nevertheless, the principal's charge is to manage the career development of the parents' children and the teachers, and he is empowered to act as both an advocate and a police officer.

School desegregation makes the resolution of the principal's charge even more problematic. It was with this realization that the white principal of CHS retired prior to the beginning of the 1972–1973 school year. The central administration turned to the black assistant principal of the former black high school that was to become the feeder junior high school to CHS, and offered the principalship to him with the provision that his decision be made within two days. He accepted the position.

From the outset, it was evident to him that he was potentially a marked man. The central administration regarded CHS as a showcase for desegregation.[3] Further, the news media chose to use CHS as a barometer of desegregation and regularly invaded the school. As the principal told the newly desegregated student body: "We are living in kind of a fishbowl on how desegregation can work."

The primary problem as far as the central administration was concerned was to keep the lid on—no matter what. The principal recognized this and further realized that one faction of the student body and one faction of the faculty were particularly influential within the community. The "honor students," as we call them, came from elite families within the city who, while being liberal enough to "try" desegregation,[4] were not above using their influence. The "old guard" were the remains of the faculty who had served this elite class and, given their recognized reputation as the best teachers in the system, were capable of mobilizing influence in the community as well as within the school system.[5]

Recognizing the power of these factions and their allegiance to each other, the principal allowed them considerable influence within the school. The old guard received the better classes (populated by the honor students) and were the last to receive the additional teaching assignments that later became necessary. The honor students were allowed control of student government and student honors. Whenever possible, whites and blacks received separate awards for "best dressed," "best student," etc. The selection of representatives for the student council was controlled by minimum grade and behavior requirements, teacher approval, and finally, student elections—all of which gave the elite white students an advantage over the other students.

For about three years, the lid stayed on. The school and the principal maintained their showcase designation. Further, although white enrollment dropped dramatically in the system and fewer and fewer students were promoted to CHS, the white students were not leaving CHS in any large numbers. Desegregation, a cause in which the principal believed fervently, was seemingly being accomplished. However, it should be noted that desegregation meant the retaining of white students—not black. Black students were regularly suspended for offenses for which whites were merely reprimanded. The lack of discipline exercised toward the white students was commented upon by both the teachers and the white parents. As one teacher put it: "When I send a student—white—down to the office, the student is right back in my class again." The disgruntlement of the school participants was evident; nonetheless, the lid stayed on.

By the time we began our observations, optimism was fading fast. Small enrollments had prompted the elimination of some advanced placement and foreign language classes. The old guard teachers had begun to transfer to suburban schools. Black students and parents had been and continued to be alienated from the school. White parents complained about a lack of discipline within the school.

In this setting, the demise of the "marked" principal was effected. The white female social science teacher, a member of the old guard, transferred to a suburban school and was replaced by a black female who had been in a professional development program at the central administration office. Though no one knew it at the time (except possibly the principal), this teacher had been administratively transferred a number of times and was regarded as incompetent by at least one of her superiors in the central administration.

Almost immediately, the honor students became dissatisfied with her teaching. She assigned homework, required them to pay attention in class, and chided them for their laziness. Though her competence may have been questionable, it appears that what caused the students disgruntlement may have been her "standards." Their performance on her examinations was poor; they rarely completed their homework; and she was unyielding to their demands. Nevertheless, she was lax in returning homework and examinations and was reluctant to take class time to go over basics and errors the students had made. She maintained they should already know such things in order to be in the advanced classes or, at the very least, should be able to sharpen these skills on their own.

Many of the honor students were angry and complained directly to the principal, who decided to support the teacher. After continued complaints to the principal were met with support for the teacher, the majority of the honor students declared war. They went to the old guard, whose allegiance would seem to require a sympathetic response. The old guard began to complain but were reluctant to confront the principal, even though they made it known whose side they supported.

The honor students had not previously mobilized their parents for support. In fact, parents had all but ceased to exist as far as the school was concerned. The PTA had not yet met that year. The Principal's Advisory Committee, consisting of parents, had been essentially recruited by the principal and rarely met. To this point, parents had been successfully "cooled out." The honor students had been so secure in their power that even though they might complain at home, they requested their parents to stay out. One mother related her daughter's response to an offer of intervention: "Mother, I can handle it."

With their influence stunted, however, the honor students initiated the mobilization of their elite parents. The parents were concerned. They called the principal, came to the school, and talked with both the principal and the teacher. The teacher wavered but little in the face of the onslaught, and the principal stood firmly in support of her—after all "standards" were at stake and the old guard had repeatedly demanded that standards be maintained. Unfortunately, in retrospect, it appears that only their standards were to be immutable.

The elite parents were in a dilemma. As they had originally viewed it, their liberal ideology supported desegregation even though it might result in some possible educational costs to their children, but were the costs now too high? With the support of their children, they decided that the teacher incident was an indication of the ineptness of the principal. They recounted the discipline problems and the principal's low-key response to their complaints. They noted the erosion of the academic program as fewer and fewer accelerated classes were offered.[6]

It seems that the development of these two issues was a major determinant of what further action, if any, was to be taken. Being influential people in the community, the parents were not going to take on the school just to resolve the incidents their children brought to them. The result of their search for the "basic issue" was that there were significant quality-of-education problems at Crossover. Of course, this conclusion was based largely upon the reports of the honor students to their parents.

The parents went to the area superintendent with their complaints instead of to the principal. They interpreted his response as protecting the principal. The area superintendent explained the course offering problems, recited his faith in the principal, and promised to look into the situation further. As a result of this action, the only PTA meeting of the year was called. It was hoped the meeting would result in once again placating the parents. Both the principal and the area superintendent spoke about the problems, actions that had been taken, and the recalcitrance of some problems. The parents, black and white, were not convinced and left still disgruntled.

The elite white parents decided to use their influence. They utilized their social networks and developed a direct "white line," as the principal was later to term it, to the central administration and the school board. In most instances, they began to bypass the principal and the school and went directly to the sympathetic ear of a school board member. Finally, however, the school board member convinced the parents that for the concerns to have a proper hearing, they would have to go through channels and appeal through the lines of authority within the bureaucracy.

At the school level, the principal and parents understood the problems in the same way, although the principal argued he was powerless to make the necessary changes. When the white elite parents worked their way up the bureaucracy to the school system's central administration, they were pressed to define precisely what they meant by "quality of education." The parents were certainly ready to agree that the principal was a problem, if not the major problem, and the central office administrator argued that what was needed was a principal who could enforce the bureaucracy and thereby guarantee "quality" education, or, in other words, someone who represented prudence over patience.

The parents left the central office meeting with assurances that something would be done. Their impression was that the principal would be removed, probably, by transfer to an elementary school.

Toward the end of the year, the old guard became aware of the possible transfer of the principal. They began to realize their influence had persisted through the desegregation process only because he had allowed it. The old guard was aroused and circulated a petition to retain him. They maintained they had not anticipated the transfer outcome, they had only wished for the principal to be more susceptible to their influence.

The honor students showed only slight remorse. The lower-class black students who had been disproportionately subject to the principal's discipline were, in many cases, glad to see him go. The principal was transferred during the summer. He was not even officially notified. He learned of the transfer from his secretary, who obtained the information from the secretary who wished to transfer to CHS with the newly assigned principal. A call to the superintendent confirmed the transfer.

The reputation of the new black principal preceded him. He was known to be a "tough cookie" who ran a "tight ship." The coaches had heard through their network that he was a "student's principal." Other schools began to recruit the old guard teachers, hoping to "skim off the cream." A few transfers resulted, and the new year began with apprehension.

The pragmatic new principal believed the problems at CHS were twofold—discipline and quality of education. His strategy was to attack the former immediately and develop the latter. His discipline was strong, which, in his mind, was what the school participants had demanded.

He cleared the halls of students. He dismissed a guidance counselor after declaring her "surplus" and then replaced her, even though the impropriety of this action was noted by many of his staff. Although the first principal had lacked dramatic community support, he was at least well connected in the black networks within the school system and in the black neighborhood that CHS served. The second principal, while having achieved great administrative success in the past, lacked the support of networks in and out of the school. He was not as much a part of the black school system network and not part of the black neighborhood network, lacked immediate teacher support, and quickly lost the support of even the honor students by eliminating their preferred status within the school. However, the elite white parents were full of praise, even as some of their children transferred to other schools for a higher-quality education and for access to student honors. In any case, these problems were not attributed to the new principal but to desegregation, the past principal, and the school system. The new principal reassigned the coaches from study hall duty to large sections of social studies classes, and he increased teaching loads, even to the point of assigning each of the two guidance counselors two classes a day in addition to their guidance responsibilities. He was very visible within the school and very coercive. He said he would eliminate anyone, teacher or student, who was "not on the program," and he did.

The school became uneasy, quiet, and closed. Students initially feared him, as did the faculty. No allegiances could be counted on for protection against possible punishment. Student assemblies were patrolled by teachers as the principal chided the students for misbehavior and noise. His assembly dismissals were dotted with paternalistic praise for their cooperation. If control was lacking in the past and the previous principal had "failed" because of it, the new principal was going to succeed by establishing order.

As the year progressed, the new principal received tacit support from most networks, since their interests required at least some support from him, although, once again, the halls were not clear of students during classes. Teachers put in for transfers and students transferred, withdrew, or were pushed out, even though some students did develop friendly ties with the new principal as they became accustomed to his procedures. One teacher even commented that "things were fine," but he also noted that he had been unaware of the problems attributed to the former administration.

Rules and Enforcement: Elements of Administrative Style

In order to understand the two administrative styles and their consequences, it is necessary to define what actually changed over the two-year period. Each principal had a distinct personality; each also perceived, and had, a somewhat different setting and context in which to act. Nonetheless, the similarities outweigh the differences. What varied was the philosophy required.

An analysis of the two styles must be grounded in the observations and accounts that constitute our data. The analysis and an assessment of what changed in the setting are best captured by developing characterizations of "order" as engendered in the administrative styles of the two principals. A consideration of the rules and their enforcement in Crossover High School will help ground these characterizations and provide the basis for an assessment of most direct effects of change on the school participants.

In any school there are rules that attempt to prompt "appropriate behavior." As with most rules in our society, school rules are based on the assumption that penalties will deter illicit behavior. Unlike much of the research on deterrence, which reveals it to be a complicated issue (Tittle & Logan, 1973), the rationale for deterrence in schools is rather simplistic. Each principal of CHS argued that order is necessary for learning to take place in the classroom and that schools should be safe places for students to attend. Yet they varied in how they saw rules and in their understanding of "deterrence."

These differences between the patient and the prudent principals can be elucidated somewhat in an analysis of rules and rule enforcement. In any setting for which rules have been developed, there appear to be at least two distinct sets of rules. One set of rules is more or less universalistic and impartial, considered legitimate by most of the constituents, and when it is enforced the offender will display more vexation at being discovered than at the existence of the rules. The second set of rules is negotiable. The legitimacy of these rules is challenged by some body of constituents, usually on the basis of unfair discrimination against a constituent group or against youth in general. Moreover, the administration sees it as in its best interests to withhold enforcement selectively so that the offender is indebted to the administration. In this way, nonenforcement of these negotiable rules is intended to elicit students' commitment to and compliance with school authority.

Thus, for both principals, deterring illicit behavior through rules and rule enforcement involved two levels of understanding of deterrence. On one level, and for the impartial rules, it was argued that deterrence was promoted by strict and universalistic enforcement of rules. The involving of penalties for the infraction of these rules was believed to reduce the likelihood that students would engage in illicit behavior. On the second level, the negotiability of some rules was allowed so that commitment to the school could be fostered by the students' personal indebtedness to the administration for the nonenforcement.

It is now possible to better understand the implications of the two styles for the everyday operation of the school. The second principal is characterized by more reliance on impartial rules (which we will call bureaucratic order), and the first is characterized by more reliance on negotiable rules (negotiated order). The styles of each type of order are distinct, but they have many similarities and are bound by the parameters common to all public schools. As seen in this school, bureaucratic order assumed both the legitimacy of the principal's authority and the recognition of that legitimacy by all constituents, and thus, overall, rules were enforced with impunity. Negotiated order, as we observed it, did not take that legitimacy as given, but rather as something that had to be developed and cultivated, even as rules had to be enforced.

The types of order were characterized by different enforcement strategies. Bureaucratic order was enforced by the principal himself. He administered discipline and patrolled the halls. Further, the bureaucratic principal developed an informal record-keeping mechanism. He allowed students three "unofficial visits" to his office, which he recorded on cards in a file in his office. By and large, these visits dealt with infractions for which the formal administration of discipline would have been difficult, since evidence of the infraction was lacking or not collected. Thus, an "informal" disciplinary talk occurred. After three of these visits, the student became subject to suspension for an infraction for which evidence was present. Generally, without three unofficial visits, a student with a similar offense would not be suspended.

The negotiable principal enforced order through a network. He, the vice-principal, and the administrative assistant were all responsible for administering discipline. The vice-principal and/or the administrative assistant would do so, and they would call in the principal only when there were extenuating circumstances. Conferences among the three were frequent, however, as discipline decisions were made. Both principals patrolled the halls, but the negotiable one put more emphasis on the teachers' enforcing order in their classrooms and in the halls. Further, he gave the athletic coaches responsibility for maintaining order in the halls, a practice that was discontinued under the bureaucratic principal. The coaches under the negotiable one were informal disciplinarians. They would prompt movement on to classes, the removal of hats, and the elimination of jostling in the halls. Their approach, by and large, was to cajole students into compliance; only rarely would they actually refer a student for formal discipline. In practice, they engaged in supervision but not in disciplinary behavior. Thus, the negotiable principal attempted to enforce rules informally through the wider network of teachers and coaches, as well as through the formal discipline meted out by the administrators.

The styles, then, differed in some crucial dimensions: the degree to which authority was vested in the principal and the way in which informal discipline was managed. The bureaucratic-order principal was the disciplinarian of the school and managed both formal and informal discipline. The negotiated-order principal delegated his disciplinary authority and separated formal from informal discipline by asking the coaches to manage the day-to-day supervision and enforcement of minor rules and by allowing them discretion on enforcement. In essence, he delegated negotiable as well as bureaucratic authority.

The Dynamics of Power and
Order in a Desegregated High School

School desegregation in the United States found many educators unprepared for a multicultural educational setting, regardless of the educational rhetoric of the late 1960s and early 1970s. During the two years we observed CHS, both principals had to face the issue of student power, and each responded differently.

Desegregation meant a dramatic transformation for CHS. Not only had the school previously been all white, but it also had a history as a public "prep" school for the middle- and upper-class youth of the city. To the new negotiable black principal, the school represented both a threat and a promise. The promise was that if desegregation went smoothly at CHS, he would gain the publicity and reputation that would bring further advancement in the school system and prestige in the general community. The threat was that if it did not go smoothly, both he and desegregation, a cause in which he believed fervently, would be criticized.

The influx of black students and some school flight by the middle- and upper-class whites led to the development of four large student groups that were, for practical purposes, networks of students. We have termed these networks *honor students*, *blue-collar whites*, *active blacks*, and *lower-class blacks*. Each network was relatively distinct as to racial and class characteristics. The honor students were middle- and upper-class whites who, by and large, populated the accelerated classes offered at CHS. The blue-collar whites demonstrated less commitment to success in the school and more to the street, some were middle-class but most were from working-class homes. The active blacks were a small group of students relatively committed to success in school, and some were in the accelerated classes. These students were from higher-status families than were the lower-class blacks. Yet their social class was more akin to that of the blue-collar whites than to that of the honor students in that they came from essentially working-class homes and had parents who were stably employed. The lower-class blacks were from the housing projects in the neighborhood and were poor. They had a relatively strong commitment to behaviors and attitudes and styles that are common to the street.

In short, three variables differentiated the students: class, race, and commitment (school versus street). Blacks have been, and are, a numerical majority in the school (approximately 60 and 70 percent respectively, for each year of observation). However, as noted earlier, the first black principal was in the spotlight to make desegregation work, a task that entailed satisfying the educational and order requirements of all concerned. As a result, he, in his patience, established a system of negotiated order whereby each of the groups could have influence. But the honor students were from highly politically influential families whose loss from the school would demonstrate the failure of desegregation; thus, the principal felt obligated to grant some additional influence to the honor students. This influence ended up guaranteeing them essential control of student activities and honors. In those arenas where control was not complete, most notably sports and elected honors "best dressed," etc., the honor students either withdrew (as they did for most sports) or were guaranteed equal representation with blacks (elected honors had black *and* white victors). The honor students were able to maintain their support by mobilizing the teachers (who "respected" these students), the blue-collar whites, and the active blacks (who were attempting to gain admission into the honor student network). The lower-class blacks were the contenders in the student power confrontations and on occasion were able to pull some support from the active blacks, usually through ridicule ("You've been eating cheese" or "You're a Tom"). However, many of the active blacks felt it was necessary to maintain their street skills so they would be able to use that option if the school denied them access to success in academics and the world of work.

Thus, negotiated order and patience permitted issues of race to be salient to the process of schooling. Racial and cultural differences could be discussed, and tolerated to some extent, although the street culture was not tolerated to any significant degree. This carried over into the discussions of school crime and disruption; that is, it was allowed and common for each group to see the other as perpetrators and themselves as victims. Disagreements could be phrased as racial in origin, and the groups were allowed to segregate themselves in informal activities if they chose. The annex to the school was the "recreational study hall," which quickly became a black area; the library was the scene of the "nonrecreational study hall," which was largely white. An overly simplistic view perhaps, but two schools did seem to exist under one roof, a school for blacks and a school for whites. Each style was respected in the school.

Under the negotiated order, students seemed to perceive the rules as legitimate inasmuch as they were the product of the peace bond that had evolved to keep the lid on the desegregation of the school. The bond was continually evolving as the constituents of the school vied for influence. Thus, though there was no formal mechanism enabling students to participate in governance, their role in rule formation was evident. Further, since enforcement of rules was largely informal, the offenders rarely needed to consider whether to question the legitimacy of the rules, and thus they never developed a stance of defiance. Put simply, the penalties were rarely severe enough to cause a reconsideration of commitment to the rules of the school.

Of course, some students were forced to face that decision and were essentially uncommitted to the school. For students exhibiting a street style of behavior or an obvious lack of respect for "appropriate" school behavior, formal authority was quick to be imposed. Further, a student exhibiting such behavior and/or attitudes was not permitted the range of negotiability of enforcement that committed students had. One black student commented on what she thought was overly harsh treatment of the streetwise black youth: "They do all the dudes [in the housing project] like that." Although these accusations of discrimination are alarming, most persons familiar with schools will realize that they are not really unusual. But there is something significant about the accusation in this case: School participants under the negotiated order felt free to lodge complaints in the company of other participants, regardless of whether they shared the same network. Negotiated order allowed participants to express their opinions quite freely.

In many ways, it was this freedom that damaged the first principal's credibility and led to his transfer. The second was led to believe that the failure of his predecessor was due to lack of order. Since desegregation had thus far failed at CHS, and since that was believed to have resulted from a weak administration, the new and prudent principal centralized authority in his own hands and began to formulate and enforce rules. His concern was to "turn the school around" and increase the quality of education at CHS. Success in these endeavors seemed to require the opposite of what was assumed to have caused the failure. Therefore, rule enforcement was to be less negotiable and more impartial. The principal ran the ship. His administrative assistant (a black female) and the vice-principal (a white male carry-over from the former principal) were assigned to curriculum development and attendance, respectively. Teachers and students alike were held accountable and were disciplined for infractions.

The same networks of students were evident, although some of the faces had changed. Overall, the white population had decreased, even though the new principal brought in four classes of multiply handicapped students in what seemed an effort to boost the white enrollment. This white loss was most evident in the number of honor students, who suffered the greatest loss in terms of the size of their network. Seemingly more important than the shrinking size of this network was the power loss the honor students suffered under bureaucratic order. Because rules were impartial, the quotas for white representation in elected honors were no longer in force. The honor students at first were not dismayed because they felt that the blacks, who were even more in the majority this year than last, would continue to respect them and in the end vote so that both whites and blacks would receive honors. However, the blacks did not vote for many of the white candidates, and in the eyes of the honor students, the elected honors of the school no longer went to the "best" students.

Though race was no longer a salient issue as far as the bureaucratic principal was concerned, the school's identity became more firmly black in the eyes of the students. Whereas under the first principal it had been easy to discern the variables that differentiated the students— that is, class, race, and commitment—it now became more difficult.

These variables continued to be important to the teachers, who used them to refer students to the principal; and with the centralization of authority, the referrals of students by teachers increased. Note, for example, the following episode:

> A black male entered the room wearing a stocking cap. The teacher (a white female) ordered him to remove it, which he did. However, as he removed the hat, he assumed a stance with his shoulders held back, arms falling straight down a little behind his sides, his chin thrust forward, and sauntered back toward his seat. The teacher, at the sight of this, ordered him to the office. Within one minute a white male entered wearing a baseball cap. She said in a stern tone, "Robert, your hat!" He responded by whipping his hat off, and turning his head to show the sides and rear of it, said, "See my new haircut." The teacher responded, "Yes, it's very nice." He strutted to his seat triumphantly.

Thus, life in the classroom still granted more negotiability to the higher-status, white, and committed students, and as had been done during the negotiable principal's reign, these students continued to use, or "hustle," the discretionary interpretations of their behavior in the classroom. Further, students were quick to discern, but did not openly or freely discuss, that grades, achievement scores, and conduct history (another indicator of school commitment) were the crucial factors in the disciplinary decision the new principal made for any particular infraction; that is, the punishment decision depended not so much on the actual infraction, but on the student's history. Though corporal punishment continued not to be the policy of the school, the bureaucratic principal did introduce a form of punishment that previously had not been used. The academic and conduct history of a student beyond the age of compulsory attendance determined, in large part, whether a rule violation would result in suspension or being dropped from the rolls. For example, a student guilty of fighting who had low grades and a history of at least three unofficial visits to the principal's office would simply be withdrawn without official expulsion from public schooling, whereas a student guilty of fighting who was a good student and did not have three unofficial visits would receive a short suspension.

As a result of the more formalized enforcement of rules, prompting of acceptable behavior by school staff was replaced with action and punishment by the principal. Students were more and more often faced with the decision of whether or not to comply willingly with school rules. They had to face and evaluate the cost incurred by remaining committed to the school. They had openly complained about racial discrimination under negotiated order but now did not openly complain about the injustice they felt from the new principal's unilateral discretionary power. They saw the bureaucratic principal as having discretion, but they were not allowed to attempt to negotiate it. As he himself put it:

> No one can argue with me . . . when I have all the cards [records of unofficial visits] in my hand. I don't kick them out of school; they do.

Under bureaucratic order, students seemingly did more questioning of the legitimacy of rules and the principal's right to enforce them. The student role was passive and weak. The increased severity of penalties (withdrawal from school) and the relative lack of negotiability under bureaucratic order seemed to lead to the emergence of an unofficial front challenging the school. In general, street-type clothing styles were worn more often within the school, and hats, particularly hats that connote "pimp," became more common. Further, open defiance of rules was more prevalent and organized. Male students, black and white, from the vocational school behind CHS refused to wait in the auditorium for the bell indicating time to change classes. Whereas students under negotiated order would skip and hide, they now stood at the doorway in the center of the hall that the classrooms open upon, wore their hats, and glared down the hall. They did not scatter or move back as the principal approached; they stood quietly and defiantly. In one of these encounters, witnessed by the author, the principal demanded, "Why aren't you in the auditorium? Don't you know the rules?" One student responded, "You weren't there." The principal retorted, "You mean I have to be there for you to obey the rules?" There was no response from the five males, except quiet and emphatic defiance. The bell rang and the principal shook his head sadly. The students went on to class.

In short, under bureaucratic order the rules of the school became "his rules"—the rules of the principal. Their legitimacy was not established, and the students responded with defiance.

Although principals are hardly omnipotent in defining the school milieu, it does seem that, within the limitations of school system policy and expectations and "good educational practice" as defined by staff and others, the principal does negotiate order and decide how to conduct the school. It could be expected that a change in style or order would most affect students, since they usually are not permitted to place strict limits on the principal's behavior. We have seen how the first principal allowed students to set limits because he believed that to be the only way to retain whites and keep the situation under control, and seemingly this plan worked. The controversy that had erupted led the second principal to believe that the problem was one of too much student freedom. He saw discipline as the answer. Each attempted to manage the political economy of the school as each saw it.

We would expect the change in style of order to have less influence on the teacher and parent networks. Teachers are insulated somewhat by the principal's need for the support of the staff, unionization, and other sources of power available to lower participants in an organization. The parent network is obviously independent of the principal and therefore represents a source of threat to him, particularly in the case of Crossover High School. Nevertheless, the change in the style of order did have some effect on both networks.

The teachers, like the students, were subject to a new bureaucracy within the school. Impersonal rules were applied to them as they were to the students. Teachers were required to be on time for work, to have more class preparations, and to submit lesson plans, which they had never been forced to do at Crossover. They argued that until the second principal took charge, they had been respected as professionals who did their jobs with minimal supervision. They were disgruntled at this encroachment upon their professionalism and saw it as an almost personal affront. The coaches were moved from study halls and hall patrol to large social studies classes in which their teaching effectiveness was observed and reported to be minimal. Faculty meetings became nothing more than forums in which the principal addressed his teachers without any expectation of feedback. The staff became reluctant to be seen talking informally in the halls for fear that he would charge them with abdicating their responsibilities.

However, the bureaucratic rules that were newly imposed upon the faculty did not bind the principal himself. At the beginning of the school year he confronted a black female guidance counselor who seemingly did not keep the records demanded of her position. He declared her "surplus," since enrollments had declined (the first principal's request to dismiss a counselor on that basis had been denied by the central administration), and after her reassignment replaced her with a new guidance counselor. The teachers were miffed but were obviously threatened by the action and therefore were silent. This event seemed to prove to them that rules were something by which they had to live but by which their principal did not.

The teachers began to see that there was a totalitarian element to the new bureaucratic order, and at first they sought only to maintain a low profile in order to avoid ridicule and punishment. As the year progressed, however, the situation was not as well tolerated, particularly by the old guard. Transfers were sought and retirements taken, all seemingly with the tacit approval of the principal. The teachers who initially did not seek transfers were somewhat repressed, but they also believed that the tightening of school rules was beneficial. However, some of these faculty were later reported to have wished they had put in for transfers early enough so that they would have been able to seek an acceptable position in a different school.

The parents, white and black, who had complained about the school were quite happy with the change. The school was the tight ship that in their eyes marked a quality educational program. The other parents, as they had done before, stayed out of the school except for the occasions when the principal invited them to come and meet with faculty.

On one such occasion, report cards were withheld until Parents' Night, when parents were to pick them up from the homeroom teacher and discuss their children's progress. Although many parents, particularly white parents of at least moderately good students, were glad to participate, the black parents felt somewhat affronted because the black community had a Parents' Night tradition of turning out the entire family with an element of celebration. Turning the evening into a long series of teacher-parent conferences was thought inappropriate.

In his opening remarks the principal chided the parents for not enforcing their children's attendance and for their lack of respect for time and thus punctuality. The principal took on the black neighborhood, and the uncomfortable and disgruntled black parents had no recourse.

Numerous black families with children who received low marks responded by picking up the report cards and embarrassing their offspring by using this forum—with the homeroom teacher and other parents and children as witnesses—to demand that they promise to shape up. These confronted students acquiesced, but resentment was high.

Though the white parents who had demanded the change were happy with the new principal, they did not wait for the new situation to develop fully before pulling their children from the school. The number of honor students dwindled with transfers to private schools and other city schools with better programs. Intriguingly, many of these transfers were the result of the new principal's style. Although the lack of curriculum flexibility and accelerated courses was the chief reason that white parents continued to withdraw their children, a new reason emerged a few months into the second school year. White parents reported that their children were quite unhappy at the lack of social life at the school because the honors that CHS had to offer were now going to the undeserving. By removing the stipulation that awards were to have black and white recipients, the new principal allowed democracy to prevail in a majority black school. Whites were rarely elevated to office or to rewards. The rewards of being a white honor student at CHS had disappeared, and the honor students and their parents begin to seek alternatives at other schools.

Conclusions

It is not the intent of this study to report two tales of failure, for neither principal actually did fail. Given their goals and conceptual frameworks for understanding the situations they faced, they were indeed successful. The first upheld his humanistic orientation as he searched for his proper role, and the second developed a functional system that reduced the complaints of parents.

Different administrative styles seem to create distinct school climates. Further, school desegregation seems to heighten emotionally the pressures a principal must face and may well heighten the consequences of any particular approach to the principalship. Since school desegregation is understood by both blacks and whites to be a political and economic issue, school principals will be challenged on more than the educational justifications for their decisions and therefore must understand educational stratification not as an objective reflection of a student's aptitudes and motivations, but as a preselection mechanism for the labor market and ultimately as an agent of power maintenance by society's elites. Desegregation has the potential to challenge the maintenance of this power by the existing elites, and ultimately may be the primary vehicle to alter the economic disadvantage of minorities.

There is an alternative implication of this study that needs some discussion. The first principal fostered something like cultural pluralism as the goal of desegregation, and even though he attempted to make it politically acceptable to the whites by allowing them disproportionate influence, it was ultimately unacceptable to the powerful whites: It did jeopardize their control. On the other hand, the second principal embraced assimilation as the goal of desegregation, a policy that ended up allowing the black student majority more control. This, as it turned out, was also ultimately unacceptable to whites—even as they praised his middle-class emphasis on orderly schooling. Further, the alienation of the somewhat disaffected students seemed to increase. In short, our previous suggestion that principals need to better understand the political economy of schooling as they face desegregation may be a moot point. Inasmuch as desegregation challenges white supremacy, it may not be possible to make it acceptable to whites who understand their status to be based on the control of a limited economy.

Some Policy Considerations

This chapter has attempted to be policy-relevant even in its emphasis upon one school and two principals. Let us examine some of the policy implications that can be extracted. First, it is evident that desegregation when seen as a district-level phenomenon will not necessarily promote equal educational opportunity. The federal courts have usually assumed that equal opportunity between whites and minorities can be achieved by placing white and blacks in the same school, and therefore by implication blacks will receive equal opportunities. There is great variety in how school systems, schools, and principals can respond to desegregation. As we have noted, though system desegregation has occurred in the city in which this study took place, the first principal established two schools under one roof, and the second allowed a black majority-controlled school that led to more school flight by whites. In either case, resegregation resulted. Desegregation needs to be monitored in individual schools as well as at the district level.

Second, existing school system practices (e.g., levels of instruction and minimum enrollments) and beliefs concerning the limited potential of minority students play a large part in the resegregation of students, and furthermore are highly political. That is, parents and students will define quality education as segregative, at least by ability, unless other models are available and convincing. Without such models, it may be impossible for schools to meet the challenge of desegregation, since it seems that desegregation is at odds with quality education as it is currently defined. Such mainstreaming models and justifications need to be developed, and school systems, principals, and teachers need to be able to defend them when the local political economy challenges them as ineffective.

Third, negotiated order and bureaucratic order are but two possible organizational formats in desegregated schools, and cultural pluralism and assimilation are but two possible models for integration. Other models and combinations of models need exploration and evaluation, particularly in the face of desegregation.

Fourth, regardless of the years of research and rhetoric, parents and schools are still at odds. Indeed, parents are probably the main threat to the principal and the school. It would seem that desegregation might even exacerbate this problem. Since, even after desegregation, schools have a specific clientele, further consideration of community involvement and control as a vehicle for effective desegregation is needed. If parents and community are committed to making desegregation work, it is more likely to succeed.

Fifth, academic standards as currently defined seem to be a major roadblock to desegregation within a school. Logically, it would seem that standards, like laws, are meant to be discriminatory in that they are invoked only when one does not behave in ways that more powerful people would prefer. As a higher authority to define quality education, standards promise to be a thorn in the side of principals who must manage a multicultural setting. Nevertheless, teachers seem to need guidelines, and alternative standards need to be developed.

Last, there are implications for policy formation in general. We have revealed that a desegregated school is a complex social setting; however, it is more than complexity that is at issue. In human settings, multiperspectival realities are common (Douglas, 1976) and difficult to analyze, so that clear and specific policy implications are problematic. Maybe in the end what the two principals in this study have demonstrated is that social research can best inform policy by delimiting the many perspectives and viewpoints of a setting or issue.

Notes

1. The research upon which this article is based was performed pursuant to Contract 400-76-009 with the Field Studies in Urban Desegregated Schools Program of the National Institute of Education. It does not, however, necessarily reflect the views of the agency.

2. For more detail on the setting, please see Chapters 6 and 7.

3. This, indeed, was one of the major reasons why this site was suggested to us. We asked for a "good" school, and they gave us the one they thought was the best at that time. The central administration has since amended this assessment.

4. *Try* seemed to have two simultaneous meanings of "attempting" and "putting to the test" to these parents. Thus desegregation was at risk for these parents.

5. As will later be shown, the principal actually underestimated the power of these groups.

6. School system policy specified minimum enrollments for classes to be offered. The small number of white honor students, when distributed across the desired number of accelerated classes, and the active blacks, desire for higher grades, which led them to enroll in standard classes, conjoined to eliminate accelerated classes from the curriculum. Nevertheless, the principal was held responsible.

References

Chisholm, S. (1975). Desegregation and national policy. *Integrated Education, 13*(1), 122–126.

Douglas, J. (1976). *Investigative social research.* New York: Sage Publications.

Hamilton, C. V. (1968). Race and education: A search for legitimacy. *Harvard Educational Review, 38*(4), 669–684.

Karier, C., Violas, P., & Spring, J. (1973). *Roots of crises: American education in the twentieth century.* Chicago: Rand McNally.

Katz, M. (1971). *Class, bureaucracy, and schools.* New York: Praeger.

Lipham, J., & Hoeh, J. (1974). *The principalship: Foundations and functions.* New York: Harper and Row.

Rist, R. C. (1972). *Restructuring American education.* New Brunswick, NJ: Transaction Books.

Tittle, C. R., & Logan, C. H. (1973). Sanctions and deviance: Evidence and remaining questions. *Law and Society Review, 8* (Spring), 371–382.

Wolcott, Harry F. (1973). *The man in the principal's office.* New York: Holt, Rinehart and Winston.

Chapter 9

Cultural Ignorance and School Desegregation: Reconstructing a Silenced Narrative

Van Dempsey and George W. Noblit

School desegregation was a classic case of educational policy accompanied by ignorance. Burlingame (1979) has argued that this is often the case with policy decisions. To act at all, policy makers must act "as if" they do not know things that could divert them from their intended agenda. The issue here is not being unknowing, but rather acting as if they were ignorant in order to pursue some policy. Certainly this was true in school desegregation. Policy makers acted as if they were ignorant of the fact that desegregation was disproportionately burdening African Americans with the bulk of busing, with the closure of African-American schools, and with the demotions and firing of African-American educators (Irvine & Irvine, 1983; Smith & Smith, 1973).

There were many levels of ignorance at play. Proponents of desegregation were ignorant of the taken-for-granted assumptions made by whites and the courts. For example, whites and the courts assumed that African Americans would benefit from merely associating with the dominant culture and would assume more desirable status and beliefs (Coleman, et al., 1967). Desegregationalists were equally ignorant of the culture of African Americans. Indeed, school desegregation, in many ways, ignored the possibility that there could be desirable elements in African-American culture worthy of maintenance and celebration. In practice, desegregationalists seemed to ignore that there was an African-American culture at all. The result was that they could not even consider that school desegregation could have destructive consequences for African-Americans, that school desegregation could actually destroy important elements of African-American culture. Irvine and Irvine (1983) refer to such destructive consequences as "iatrogenesis," a medical label for the creation of an unhealthier situation brought on by the remedy that was meant to cure the disease in the first place. Irvine and Irvine suggest that iatrogenesis may apply to our efforts at school desegregation.

In each of these cases, ignorance was based on assumption more than on a lack of knowledge. There were people who disagreed with the Coleman report (Moynihan & Mosteller, 1972), people who understood that we were desegregating schools on white terms (Bell, 1975), and people who were concerned that school desegregation could be cultural genocide of African Americans (Hardy, 1979). Yet we proceeded to ignore these issues in earnest pursuit of school desegregation, acting as if they were not reasonable concerns. To us, this is a special kind of ignorance, a cultural ignorance, driven both by the assumptions of the majority group and the logic of educational policy. Cultural ignorance is presumptive in that it devalues aspects of what is known so that we act as if these were not known. It is an ignorance based in intention—the intention to make something happen, regardless of reasonable concerns raised about the intention. The tragedy is that, in this case, the intention was about race equity, and it required us to act as if the culture of African Americans was of no concern at all.

Had we been more sensitive to African-American culture, or even culture itself (Eisenhart, 1989; Bellah, et al., 1985), we might have reconsidered desegregation and fashioned a remedy that was less destructive of African-American beliefs. Possibly, we could have prescribed a remedy that enhanced the communicative competence of African Americans to change and maintain their culture (Bowers, 1984), rather than make their culture reflect the dominant one. But we did not. We did not, even though some minority communities resisted school desegregation because they saw the remedy fashioned in the courts and in policy as destructive (Cecelski, 1991). Educational policy makers, and whites in general, were not only ignorant of African-American culture, they chose to ignore efforts by African Americans to enlighten them. As Burlingame (1979) argued, educational policy seems to require us to act as if we were ignorant and moreover to reject opportunities that would educate us. Now, more than forty years after *Brown v. Board of Education* (1954), it is time for us to better understand what we chose to be ignorant of and follow the lead of African Americans who seek a fresh understanding of desegregation and a new approach to educational policy about equity (e.g., Bell, 1980).

Our ignorance about desegregation and its impact on African-American culture has persisted partly because we have failed to recollect and celebrate the stories that were lost in the desegregation era. We thus lost important lessons about how we might become more sensitive to diverse cultures in schools today. Across America, thousands of schools, and in some cases communities, were lost in the movement to provide equity in education. Also lost in those communities and schools were the stories of their cultures, of their lives, and of how education worked for them. It is one of those stories on which we will focus here. It will reveal a cultural narrative almost lost by our cultural ignorance.

In the fall of 1987, the authors were part of a research team of four invited into a small Southern elementary school we called Liberty Hill. The principal had asked us to help him build a sense of unity among his faculty. New to the school, he was concerned with the amount of tension that existed within the faculty, both among themselves and between the school and its community. We suggested that the faculty and the research team produce a history of the school as a cohesion-building project. In the process of creating that history, we found that the school, which opened in 1915, was the oldest school in the city still in operation. Liberty Hill School had a long and proud tradition as one of the best schools in the city, referred to consistently in our interviews as being "like a private school."

This, by the way, is not the school we will be describing at length. In the process of researching the history of this school, we found that a nearby school, Rougemont, has played an inextricable role in the history of Liberty Hill. To reconstruct the histories of the two schools, and understand what life was like in and around them, we examined various documents, including board of education minutes dating back to 1919, PTA minutes, journals, scrapbooks, personal records and artifacts, church histories, and public archives. Our richest data by far, though, came from over seventy-five interviews we conducted in the Rougemont and Liberty Hill Schools and communities. These included current teachers at Liberty Hill; former students, teachers, and principals of both schools; and members of the school communities. (All names and references used here are pseudonyms.)

Our role was to help reconstruct the narrative silenced by school desegregation. We should always remember not to confuse narrative for factual history. Narratives are ways for people to be linked to the future and to have the meanings they value become part of a wider human discourse. That is to say, the narrative that follows is part of the Rougemont community's effort to construct and reconstruct its culture. This construction is sentimental because the community's project is constructing sentiment itself. It is likely that everyday life in Rougemont was much more contested than the narrative reveals, but sentiment recalls that which people wish to be perpetuated in their narrative and is thus selective. For us, the significance of the story that follows is that people wish this to be their story and, as such, are no longer silenced.

Because our initial focus was on Liberty Hill School, our entry into the field for research about Rougemont School did not begin in earnest until almost one and one-half years later, in January of 1989. We were introduced to the Rougemont community in a rather dramatic way: through an interdenominational church service in Rougemont. We were there to introduce ourselves and to have our history project sanctioned by the community. We had already done some interviews with people from Rougemont but in general received a lukewarm response. We learned a telling lesson: The remaining vestiges of a formerly close-knit community with strong and visible leadership and a powerful sense of identity were its churches. There was no other way for us to be introduced to the community than to go to the one gathering still reflective of community: the interdenominational service that incorporated all the churches that served Rougemont whenever there was a fifth Sunday in the month.

The fifth-Sunday service rotated through the five Rougemont churches and this night met in a church that was geographically centered in the community. The church seated about two hundred people, with half that in attendance, including those of us representing the school history project. As we waited for the service to begin, an elderly woman inquired as to why we were there, and having learned of our intent, launched into a description of how the community had changed during her lifetime. "We didn't have to shut our doors," she began her portrait of the community that people nostalgically recall. A community without crime in its boundaries. Homes that could be left open without a fear of robbery or assault. Neighbors that were lifelong friends, free to go into each other's houses at will and encouraged to supervise and discipline each other's children. She said her feeling of safety ended about fifteen years before, when her husband died just as the community began to change. It was about fifteen years before when Rougemont school was closed as the city desegregated its schools.

The diminished sense of safety is part and parcel of the changes in the Rougemont community since its school was closed in 1975. There are other related changes. Home ownership has decreased, and the population is more transient. The children of the community no longer see the neighborhood as the idyllic community their parents were raised in and move to other neighborhoods to raise their families. There are no longer visible leaders of the community or cooperative efforts to help those in need, the aged, or the infirm, as was the case in the past. Yet the church service was evidence that there still was some sense of community; it was a testament to Rougemont's struggle to survive.

The service was the most moving introduction to a community any of us had ever witnessed. It came at a time during which we were afraid that we would fail to be able to write a history of Rougemont School. We were having difficulty identifying people who worked at and attended the school, and even when we could identify them, few were willing to talk with us. That evening one of the church elders took it upon himself to arrange a Saturday meeting at the church where people could come and talk with us. Another woman offered to share a history she had assembled about the community that focused on the churches. Others recounted how central the school had been to the community and how much they wished it was still in operation. People repeated that its closing marked the beginning of decline in the community. We were well on our way to learning what Rougemont School could have taught us about education, had its voice not been silenced. Rougemont was trying to hold fast to its traditions even as outside forces rent the boundaries and soul of the community.

A Place for Us

As Relph (1976) argues:

> People are their place and a place its people, and however readily these may be separated in conceptual terms, in experience they are not easily differentiated. In this context places are public—they are created and known through common experiences and involvement in common symbols and meanings. (p. 34)

Rougemont had been created as a pocket of opportunity for African Americans. There was employment, largely at a nearby university, and home ownership was its material base. But what made Rougemont a community was its park, its school, its churches, and its political organization. All of these provided for common experiences, symbols, and meanings. And, importantly, they were all created by the community as essential to their social and cultural lives. With only the churches left, it was becoming harder and harder to find people who identified themselves as "from Rougemont." Even place was dissolving.

Rougemont was settled in the late ninteenth century when Randolph College moved from Trinity County to the outskirts of Treyburn, a Southern town growing, at the time, around the tobacco industry. Charles Walters, an African-American employee of the college, decided to move with the college and built a home in a nearby woods. He cleared a path between home and work that was destined to become the main thoroughfare of Rougemont. Other African Americans similarly found employment at the college and built small homes. The path became a dirt street, and eventually the farmland became a neighborhood with definite boundaries. In the era of enforced segregation, Rougemont was in part bounded by other neighborhoods, including College Park, built by white employees of the college and by white professionals and business people of Treyburn. It was also bounded by the college itself on the south and a notorious district of gambling and bootleg houses on the north. The boundaries were so rigid that people recalled the special meaning of Mr. Fred Brewer's hayrides for the children. They were billed as a "trip around the world," because Mr. Brewer dared to take his horse-drawn hay wagon full of children beyond the reaches of Rougemont, circling the entire city.

Rougemont was not then a community of poor African Americans, but neither was it a neighborhood of higher status African Americans. The latter community was across the city, surrounding Treyburn State College. Rougemont, rather, was a community of stably employed people, originally at Randolph College and later in the local mills or as maids and servants in the adjacent white neighborhoods. Though the vestiges of this are still evident, residents lament the influx of unemployed people and transients.

Rougemont was a "close-knit" community, and "everyone was one big family," according to residents. Friends visited, and neighbors helped each other out. If someone was sick, neighbors pitched in and took food to the home. As a long-time Rougemont resident described it:

> I used to joke, especially when I started driving . . . "I wish I had a third hand." Because knowing everyone in Rougemont [meant] when you went down the street, I would have liked to have two hands just to wave as I went by and have my third hand on the wheel. But walking or riding or whatever, you knew everybody.

The elderly were looked in on, and the elderly looked out for the children. Child rearing was also seen as a community venture. If an adult saw a child misbehaving, generally the adult would punish the child and then report the infraction and the punishment to the parent:

> It would not bother your parents at the time if someone took you in their house and gave you a spanking if they saw you doing something wrong. And when you got home you got another one. There was that kind of closeness.

Another resident remembered the epitome of the close-knit discipline network—"Ma Franklin":

> All the families were close, close-knit families. There was a lady there all the kids called Ma Franklin. She's still living, she's about ninety years old now. We still call her Ma Franklin. She was everybody's mama. If she caught you doing something wrong or fighting she might spank you and then take you home. . . . She was everybody's mom.

Rougemont was a community of strong and shared values: hard work, religious faith, discipline, and individual and collective responsibility. They took care of their own and expected each to look to the others' welfare. It was their place, and they shared responsibility for it.

The neighborhood included all the amenities of a small town: grocery and clothing stores, barbershops and beauty salons, churches, scout troops, and recreation centers. The citizens even reclaimed a garbage dump to create a park for the residents. It became a place for children to play, for adults to stroll and visit, and for families to picnic. It was also the site of community celebrations. It symbolized just how much Rougemont was a place especially of and for them.

Rougemont was not an incorporated town and was not active in the wider political world of the city or of the African-American population of Treyburn. It enjoyed few community services and had no representative in the wider political structure of the city, neither unusual for African-American neighborhoods in cities, especially in the South. Isolated from the wider political apparatus, Rougemont created its own. The "Bronze Mayor" and his "Board of Directors" took care of everything from voter registration to helping people in trouble. These positions were honorary, going to the men with the "most money" and "know-how" in the community. The Board of Directors organized community projects and lobbied with the local political structure for needed public services.

Rougemont was a community unto itself, with boundaries, churches, stores, and a political system. It was solidly working class, even if such employment was limited to domestic and service employment. Traditional employment patterns continued as Randolph College employed Rougemont residents as custodians, cooks, and dormitory workers. Some were employed in the local mills and tobacco companies, but in general, Rougemont people had little exposure to the wider African American and white communities. Connections with the other African-American communities in the city were largely through the teachers at Rougemont School, who came from the middle-class neighborhoods around Treyburn State College where they also had studied. In this, Rougemont was one step down from the influential African-American community and from the white communities. All contributed even more to Rougemont's insularity. Their struggle was defined as being stalwart, hardworking, and investing in education, religion, and their community. They struggled to improve their lives, their churches, and their school, but engaged little in the wider struggles for civil rights in the community.

This insularity was nowhere more evident than in the 1960s, when civil rights was a major issue in all African-American communities. Rougemont kept a "very low profile" in civil rights protests, according to a resident. "Our first lady," one person commented, knew how to deal with people, and Rougemont adopted the posture "Just let Lillie do it." Lillie, the Bronze Mayor's wife, would go to meetings and talk with people. The community saw her as effective in getting the things the community desired, but there came a point when Rougemont recognized the need for collective action. In the early 1960s, African American leaders from other areas of the city came to Rougemont and held a meeting at St. John's Church to plan and elicit support for a boycott of downtown stores. The community voted at that meeting to boycott. However, it was also recognized that it would be necessary for African Americans to become more active in the electoral process if they wished to have a voice on the local political scene. The Bronze Mayor and the Board of Directors organized voter registration drives in Rougemont and campaigned to get out the vote. Rougemont, however, was a minor actor in the local civil rights movement inasmuch as the leadership came from other neighborhoods. Equally important was Rougemont's basic insularity. They continued to invest in their community, never realizing that the investment would contribute to the community's demise and ultimately to the demise of the most significant project in the history of the community, Rougemont School.

A School of Our Own

Though we were unable to find its exact date of origin, the Rougemont School dates back to roughly the turn of the century. The first classes were held in a church in the community, with a schoolhouse being constructed eventually with the help of the Rosenwald School movement. Rougemont School became a symbol of the community through its exclusive service to students from Rougemont, from its presence in the neighborhood, from its longstanding faculty, by its reinforcing of community values, and by its identity as "a school of our own." Rougemont School was the community's ultimate cultural symbol and reflected the basic patterns and beliefs of Rougemont. Rougemont community was characterized as a "family," and this was also true of the characterizations of the school. Rougemont expected its school to "educate the children and to be involved in the community" even though most of the teachers lived outside Rougemont. The teachers at Rougemont fulfilled an educational and ideological role in the community Beyond the usual responsibilities of teaching, they were expected to be present every time there was something at the school. They had to attend all picnics, celebrations, and community meetings held at the school. The teachers were clearly to be role models for the children. They were to dress well, to be respected and exemplary citizens, and to foster close relationships between the school and community. They were, for example, expected to attend church services in Rougemont periodically. The community reciprocated by treating them with deference and respect equal to that accorded to the ministers of the churches they would attend. At the services, their presence would be publicly announced and ministers would take time in the service to thank them for attending. According to one resident:

> You have to remember, too, that for many years . . . and this was certainly true when I was a child . . . for many black people, for most black people, the teacher was the person in the community. . . That was because primarily [teaching] was the profession that most blacks went in if they wanted to get ahead and so forth. So, when the teachers came to church, then everybody took a back seat and they were always allowed to speak . . . It was really a big thing when they would come [to church].

A former Rougemont School student recalled, "There was prestige. My parents thought preachers were good, but teachers were great!"

Rougemont teachers had expectations of their own, mostly directed to their students. Teachers attempted to instill in children a sense of importance of success in school. As a former principal explained:

> They expected kids to learn. They expected high performance, and the kids gave it. Kids responded like that. [Rougemont School] wasn't somewhere to run and hide and be lazy.

Another former principal elaborated:

> The teachers wanted their kids to be proud of themselves. They wanted their kids to have an understanding of their culture and history, and what they were doing . . . what they were needing to do.

Teachers expected students to approach school with purpose. Teachers wanted their students to "want" to learn and to do well. Rougemont teachers were of one mind. According to a former student:

> You knew when you went to school that morning that you will be doing whatever you were told to do and you were going to stay there until you finished it. That was another thing . . . you didn't finish your work, you didn't go home when the other kids went home.

She continued to explain what the teachers communicated to the students: "You're going to learn. You're going to do well. You're going to excel, and you're going to compete with anyone." They did not take excuses lightly.

Growing from a faculty of two in 1921 to a faculty of eighteen by 1974 had little effect on the stance of the teachers or how they were regarded by the community. As one mother whose children attended the school across the three decades of the 1950s and 1960s and 1970s recalled, "They had a good group of teachers, some of the best. They were extra good." One former principal who worked at the school during the early 1970s summed it up succinctly: "I found a lot of good teaching going on." Another explained how the teachers got the children to believe that they were able to live up to the high expectations. "There was a lot of praise; there was a lot of boosting. But not illegitimate praise, not a facade, not a false sense of pride trying to be instilled."

Community School Atmosphere

> "I have heard every teacher and principal who has been at Rougemont say that there was really something special about that community, but I think the relationship between the school and the community existed because the parents really took an interest in the children and really worked together."

Students, teachers, principals, and community members all expressed feelings similar to this one about the relationship between

Rougemont School and the community: "It was a community school, and everybody seemed like they loved it." This teacher continued:

It was a wonderful community [where] people [stuck] together, that cared about each other, that loved each other. It was just great. They were fully involved in the school. Whatever went on they were there.

The close bond between Rougemont School and the community was best expressed in a description of the spring carnival in Rougemont Park, across the street from the school. As a former teacher recalled:

We had, I remember, the parents there. They always planned the social gathering in the spring over at the park. That was beautiful. It reminded you of a family type of situation. This was in the spring. This is where the parents would, like in the olden days, I guess. . . . I'm from the country where people would pack picnic lunches, go to church, and spread. Well, they would do these things in the park for the kids. They would grill food and things of that sort. That was a very good relationship. It was other things. You could almost feel, how you know people care. You could just feel the warmth.

The school and community also came together at school fund-raisers such as the school carnival. Grade mothers would work with the teachers in planning events such as movies, hot dog stands, and sock hops. All of the materials were donated to the school by the community, and the profits were used to buy instructional materials. As a former student said, "I remember that well when I was a little girl. It was a closeness, a sense of family because of some of the projects like that."

One student remembered the carnival as the "biggest event at our school." The carnival was something everybody looked forward to. Students would play games such as "go fish" for prizes:

You might pull up a baby doll on a fishing pole, or some spectacular gift, not a little spider or things like we do now. But the parents in the neighborhood went way out, because that was the main event of the year at our school. Like people have baby dolls and stuff; they clean it up at home and make new clothes for it. And if you were lucky, you'd pull up a baby doll or a yo-yo, which was a big thing then, or a bat and ball, you know, little things. And you might pull up a booby prize, but, you know, you're lucky to pull a good prize.

The Rougemont parents were integrally involved with Rougemont School on a daily basis, not just at special events. As one teacher described the parents' effect on the school:

They were special. They would come to the school. You didn't particularly have to go to them. They would come to you to want to help to do. For parents that is good, you know. They'd want to know how they could help. What can they do? If you had a problem at school, or maybe if you needed something and you would say, "Oh, I need such and such a thing," they would try to get it for you. If there was a problem with a child, they would do that. If we would say, OK, we're having some particular thing at school, whether it included the total school, whatever was needed, they would get it. Would help to try anyway.

A former principal said:

The parents liked the school. The community enjoyed their school. The community would come in to visit and to eat with the kids. It wasn't like pulling eye teeth to get people in.

Another principal said:

The PTA was there one hundred percent. They always had a large crowd. Any principal or leader would call, and they would help out. The attitude toward the teacher was different. The parents wouldn't say anything negative. It was a family school, like being a member of a family.

As mentioned earlier, the family atmosphere of the community made disciplining children a shared responsibility. Teachers were allowed to make full use of that network. As a principal stated:

I knew it was a tight-knit community that had always been tight-knit. Folks helped each other. Relatives lived a couple of blocks away, so there was extended family in the area. There was a grandmother or uncle nearby. I was just as free to talk to them as to the parents. Whatever you said would get back to the parents verbatim, and in some instances the relatives would just handle it.

Students were fully aware of the parental support teachers received as disciplinarians:

Well, in those days, we got a spanking. Your teachers spanked you and called your mom, and then you went home and knew what you were going to get when you go home—the same thing!

Another student recalled:

If you were disobedient, oh yeah, the call was made that very day and you didn't want your parents to know that you had misbehaved because the rule was, If you got it at school, you got it again when you got home.

Many teachers and principals discussed school-community interaction in terms of problems brought into Rougemont School by students from home. Children would at times bring in problems first thing in the morning, to which the teacher lent a friendly ear. Though students generally got along well in the school, sometimes problems were brought in from the previous evening or weekend, and teachers would attempt to diffuse the problem early.

Teachers visited the homes and would eat with the families. The relationship was strong enough for teachers to go to homes whenever necessary. One teacher commented:

> And I guess the parents, as I said, [were] right there whenever there was a problem. I had a little thing where I would walk home. At 2:30, if I had a problem with a kid that day, then they knew, "I'll walk home with you today." And I guess this was one thing that kept the children from having so many problems.

As stated in this teacher's comment, having a parent so near to the school cut down on a great many discipline problems. When parents were so close by, in many cases walking children to school, they had ample opportunity to converse with teachers. Required home visits by the teacher, as well as voluntary ones, helped to build a great deal of rapport between the parents and the teachers, strengthening the connection between home and school.

> Primarily if [teachers] would visit in the afternoon after school, it was because of a problem that was going on, and they would try to get with the parents before it got out of hand, which again I think is really important. And I think that personal touch really showed the concern, the interest.

One teacher remembered a particularly poignant example of teachers going into the community to deal with a problem.

I remember one year, Sarah [another teacher] and I were involved with a family that was in—I think one of the kids was in her room and one was in mine. This particular child—this is where the teacher would enter to help with the family. We noticed that the child needed assistance, and they were not getting it from Social Services. We went in to help. . . .It was cold this particular day, and very rainy. We went by to see the parents, and this was a little old lady. The little fella, and his sister [were] living with their grandmama. She was too old to care for the children. So after going in there, we found that they didn't have any heat, and at that time we came across [the city] to Scott Coal Company, got coal, went home, got blankets, and things of this sort.

A Comparison of Two Cultures

Accreditation reports provided one of the sources of information through which we could triangulate data and enhance our description of Rougemont and Liberty Hill Schools. During the 1973–1974 school year, both schools underwent Southern Association Accreditation. The accreditation process involved self-study, whereby committees of teachers and administrators evaluated all aspects of their school, including not only academic programs such as social studies, math, and science, but other areas such as "the children served by the school," "philosophy," "organization for learning," and "facilities." All schools that underwent the accreditation process followed the same plan and carried out the evaluation in the same amount of time. The self-studies, although a selective data source in themselves, can help in our reconstruction of the silenced narrative of Rougemont School. In many ways, they provide text to the context we have discussed above.

Rougemont and Liberty Hill Schools were both required to undergo the accreditation process in the 1973–1974 school year. At the time of accreditation, both schools had nearly achieved a 50/50 African American/white racial balance through the altering of attendance lines. There were important differences in context between the studies. One was prepared at a historically African-American elementary school with a predominantly African-American faculty, whereas the other was prepared at a historically white elementary school with a predominantly white faculty. Another key difference was that the Rougemont community was more weighted toward middle- and lower-income neighborhoods, whereas Liberty Hill tended toward middle- and upper-middle-class neighborhoods. Because the schools were evaluated at the same time, the self-study reports by each school in April of 1974 provide an opportunity to examine the two faculties' responses to the same questions about the same educational issues at the same time. The studies provide an opportunity to compare the two schools from roughly the same vantage point. Given that the two reports were written at the same time, and were written about schools only six city blocks apart, it is easy to assume that similarities would appear, but it is the difference in the tone of the two documents that makes the comparison interesting. Following are comparable sections selected from each study that help enhance understanding the contexts of each school and community.

Rougemont

In the section on the children served, Rougemont referred to attendance and absenteeism by stating "The general health of the students at Rougemont School is good, and a high rate of absenteeism is not a problem." The Rougemont document made a general reference to the state of manners and language of the children: "The manners and language usage of the students are fair, but some improvement is needed in this area." To further describe the children in the school, more specifically their aspirations for their futures, the Rougemont School authors of the study asked the student "What would you like to be when you grow up?" Following are some student responses: teacher, 1; veterinarian, 4; doctor, 4; secretary, 5; dentist, 1; policeman, 6; nurse, 13; pilot, 4; athlete, 8; oceanographer, 2; artist, 8; and janitor, 1. The Rougemont study also contained children's answers to "What do you do after school?"

—Play	107
Work at home, then play	16
—Do homework	33
—Watch TV	47
—Read	2
—Work at a job	4

Rougemont seemingly found the children to be worthy of providing information, and teachers took the time to include them as part of information gathering.

The Rougemont philosophy, another self-study section, described how the school helped children cope with the world at the present.

We at Rougemont Elementary School believe that the challenges of speed, complexity, and impersonality of modern day living in today's changing world are frightening experiences for many of our elementary school children.

At issue was how the child's understanding of the world affected the fulfillment of her or his needs as a student. "Therefore, an atmosphere must be obtained in which a child's social, emotional, intellectual, physical, and moral needs can be met on an individual basis." The Rougemont philosophy viewed the school as part of the community. "We believe that the school is an integral and vital part of the community. Therefore, the school should strive to serve the needs of the community." School and community were partners in the education of children. "Only when both the school and the community acknowledge their responsibility to support and develop each other can the needs of children in school be met." The community was viewed as a participant in the educational process, not just a beneficiary of it.

Emergency School Assistance Aid (ESAA), another section of the self-study, described the use of funds provided to school districts in the early 1970s to help alleviate problems brought on by desegregation. (Both Rougemont and Liberty Hill used ESAA funds to attempt to improve math and reading performance among students.) The Rougemont study stated in the ESAA section that "racial tension still exists in our community and probably will for a number of years. . . . The fine work of professional groups, student groups, and several community groups, has given the community a relatively good base for human relations."

The Rougemont study also gave background to their problems in areas pertaining to ESAA. "Many participants come from homes which are economically, educationally, and socially disadvantaged and many have (1) poor attendance records, (2) low self-concepts, (3) low aspirations, and (4) lack of motivation in the home environment." The Rougemont study went on to describe the children on whom this project was focused:

> Children are born with intellectual curiosity as proven by the thousands of questions they ask from the time they start talking until they are turned off by some who ridicule, laugh at, or belittle them. We feel that the project teachers and aides, with the help of the central office staff, will rekindle this curiosity.

In the "Language Arts" section, Rougemont teachers recognized variance in ability levels of children and attempted to "accept the child as he is." Oral expression was to be developed according to student needs, with encouragement to "broaden his vocabulary and cultivate a more fluent, correct usage of the English language," thus making the student part of the standard.

In a discussion of the "teaching-learning process" at Rougemont School, factual knowledge was valuable because of its present utility, not its potential utility.

> A sound approach to the learning process will recognize that learning is the interaction of the learners with a situation which includes, among other things, a problem, material to help solve the problem, and in the case of the child, an adult to help and guide.

This was "the best preparation for living in the future." The teacher's purpose was to help the child find value in knowledge. "It is the teacher's

privilege to help the child establish goals and clarify hazy purposes."
By taking advantage of the personality of the student, "the teacher
can bring the goals of the children and the objectives of the school
into closer harmony."

Liberty Hill

Under the section "The Children Served," the Liberty Hill study, referring to dropouts, states, "The children like Liberty Hill as a school
and are loyal to it. There are no dropouts here in elementary school."
Liberty Hill implied that dropouts were nonachievers, uninterested in
college, and disloyal, with no association between absenteeism and
health. In their description of the children, the Liberty Hill study associated poor language with a particular group, drawing a distinction
between those who use proper language and those who don't:

> Most of the students are cooperative and polite. A very few, due to poor
> home environment, use language that is not up to our standards. Constant
> efforts are exerted to improve this.

Liberty Hill used language and manners to group students, one
being problematic for the school, whereas Rougemont portrayed its
students as one body, albeit in need of improvement.

It is also interesting how the future plans of the children at Liberty
Hill are discussed: "Most of the children who attend Liberty Hill School
are eager to achieve. Quite a number plan to go to college and some
plan to go to technical schools." There was also quite a difference in
the discussion of leisure time between the two schools. Liberty Hill
gave one statement that "Teachers encourage pupils to have things to
do in their leisure time." Liberty Hill made a general statement about
the children in the school, whereas Rougemont used a more emic
approach.

The Liberty Hill philosophy treated school as a prerequisite to
children's lives and their later integration into the community:

> The faculty at Liberty Hill School believes that the elementary school should
> aid in the development and adjustment of the child for the assumption of his
> personal role in American society. Our philosophy is that each child is an
> individual who should be helped toward a self-realization of his potential as a
> member of his community.

At Liberty Hill, education was preparing to be as opposed to being.
The goal of language arts at Liberty Hill was "clear diction, correct

grammar, and a good vocabulary." The authors set as the standard the socially accepted way children were supposed to express themselves "in both formal and informal situations," a standard both monolithic and external to the student.

Liberty Hill stated as its goal for the Emergency School Assistance Aid "preventing a gradual regression of a pupil's achievement level in the math and/or reading area." Its target is "the slow learning child." Also in this section, and in sharp contrast to a critical statement made in the introduction to the Rougemont self-study, the Liberty Hill study claimed, "Integration was no big problem here." Although it is possible that one school may have experienced tensions and the other not, it is interesting that being as close together as these schools were geographically, with significant overlap in populations, their perception of racial tension would be so different. It is also ironic that the tone of the Liberty Hill study implied a dichotomized student body, brought about through the identification of a disadvantaged group in the school. The Rougemont study implied at least the perception of a more unified school. Rougemont did not scapegoat the child and had a more ambitious goal for ESAA than "preventing a gradual regression of. . .achievement level."

At Liberty Hill, the teacher dominated the teaching-learning process. "The faculty of Liberty Hill School believes that the teacher is the key to the learning process." There was no mention of the student's place in the process other than "pupil-teacher planning" and "teacher-pupil-parent relationships."

A Comparison of the Two Schools

Both Liberty Hill School and Rougemont School created texts to tell about themselves. Both stories focused on communities that each school considered "home" to the school. Each dealt with a population that was extremely different from that historically dealt with at each school. Here the similarities end. The Rougemont text told "who we are." It was in some instances an interpretive text, but it also offered a description from which the reader could build his own story about the Rougemont community and school. Rougemont told a candid story of who children are.

The Liberty Hill study told a different story, one where the authors dichotomized "us" from "them," and "we" from "they." Those who achieved were singled out from those who did not. Successes originated in the school, whereas failures originated elsewhere. The Liberty Hill authors interpreted for the reader. There was little description; the story was built. The Liberty Hill text was managed, one where the image was created for the audience. When the Liberty Hill text became specific, it was to place blame. Liberty Hill told who parents are and what children will be.

The Rougemont text was about one community. The Liberty Hill story was about two. Liberty Hill School saw itself as serving two communities and thus told two stories when the difference between the two warranted recognition. There was, at Liberty Hill, one group that achieved and had achieved. There was another that did not and had not.

Ultimately, the self-studies are not about factual description of the two schools. They are, nonetheless, narratives of the two schools. In these representations, the language of the Liberty Hill self-study manifested the kinds of cultural ignorance and nonrepresentation to which we point. "Factual" or not, the dichotomizing and marginalizing language embodies the ignorance.

Rougement Closing

Differences in the cultures of schools and in the tone of documents reflecting those cultures, such as the self-studies described above, provide valuable insights into the stories that institutions such as schools have to tell about themselves. For schools and school cultures such as Liberty Hill that have survived institutionally, such documents are important. But, in the situations where schools and their cultures may have been lost to social and political events and needs—or ignored— the ability to reconstruct the stories becomes crucial for the maintenance of those schools' narratives and their cultural identities.

As noted above, the self-study reports were released by Rougemont School and Liberty Hill School in April 1974. In less than one year, Rougemont School became the subject of a much more significant process and report. On October 30, 1974, the U.S. District Court advised the city that new desegregation plans would be developed. Four schools in the city were under consideration to be closed, Rougemont being one of them. At the end of the 1974–1975 school year, Rougemont community's children were redistributed into other schools, one of them being Liberty Hill. The teacher who remembered the story cited earlier, of delivering coal to a student's home, finished her story by reflecting on that decision:

You know, these are things I miss from Rougemont because it was really—that was a very good atmosphere to work. I loved it. When that school closed, I cried for almost a week.

For Rougemont, the end of its school was at least in part the end of the community. Education in Rougemont had been in and of the community, and as one resident of the community said:

The closing of Rougemont was the end of social organizations, the end of home visits. Nobody knew what anyone else was doing. You didn't see people the way you did.

As one former Rougemont principal stated, "The kids in the heart of Rougemont went to Liberty Hill School."

One Rougemont citizen commented that the closing of the school had a definite impact on Rougemont. "It hurt the community, everybody. We had one of the best schools in [the city]. We had good teachers. Why did they want to change it?" It is ironic that the answer to this man's question might lie in the very community strength that had made the school successful for so many years. The Rougemont School and its community had done a very effective job of defining itself as a community—and in the harsh political realities of desegregation—as an African-American community (even though, ironically, by 1974 the school was 50 percent white). In the end, the insularity that had for so long served Rougemont led to its downfall. The insularity meant that Rougemont was both excluded by and had excluded itself from the wider community's politics surrounding desegregation. Rougemont community members were not participants in the politics of desegregation; rather they were the victims. The citizen who helped lead the community fight to save the school said:

The school was good. It was new with new facilities. It was set up as one of the best schools. Being in a black community closed it. We had good teachers. They took interest in children.

It is also ironic, and in a sense tragic, that the best evidence of the power of the relationship between Rougemont School and the community came in both institutions' destruction. A former principal described the closing of the school as the "destruction of [the] community focal point."

The unraveling of Rougemont School and the community reflects the importance of the relationship between place and people described by Relph (1976) earlier, and the damage that can occur by severing that relationship. For the children of Rougemont, who had for years known limited boundaries to their world, the abrupt expansion of boundaries that came with desegregation must have been traumatic. For the Rougemont community, relationships that had for years defined the community unraveled. Relph asserts that community and place reinforce the identity of each other in a "very powerful" relationship (p. 34). In an extension of this discussion of community, "the identities of places are founded . . . on the interaction of . . . three opposing poles of the I, the Other, and the We." (p. 57). The I and the Other are able to communicate with each other through the signs and symbols of the We. "To wish to separate the I, the Other and the We is to desire to dissolve or to destroy consciousness itself" (p. 57). In a sense, it was consciousness that was lost in the closing of Rougemont School, for the school was the one place where the signs and symbols of a community came together and were shared. It was at Rougemont School that all the threads of the "close-knit" were woven; where the Rougemont family could unite and reunite. Rougemont School was synonymous with Rougemont community. Much like Erickson's description (1976, p. 215) of loss of community through a natural disaster, the people of Rougemont were "enmeshed in the fabric" of their school and their community. Each one—community and school—was dependent on the other for completing its character and completing and holding together the "knit" in the Rougemont fabric. When the school was taken away, the fabric was shredded. The resident who talked about social disintegration above described well the danger of being forced out of community:

> Being poor was not a stigma [at Rougemont], they understood. [After the closing of Rougemont] people became afraid to come to school because of limited background or lack of education. Many students from the area stopped education after integration came. There wasn't a strong push. Things seemed to have broken down.

The teacher who shared the story of the gathering in the park and the story of the home visit that ended in delivering coal and blankets to children and their grandmother said of the school's closing, "It was just like you were losing a friend, which I did."

Conclusion

Featherstone (1976), in a discussion of the desegregation of the Boston schools, commented on the African-American experience with the process:

> Blacks inherit more than their share of American faith in schools; but in the
> past this was grounded less in naive idealism than in a shrewd assessment
> that schools were the only game in town that would let them in, albeit on
> condescending racist terms. Schools kept blacks out and oppressed them; but
> separate black schools and colleges served as havens, turfs, and sources of
> jobs (p. 191).

For the Rougemont community, their elementary school served in many senses as a haven and a turf, if not a source for jobs. In the period since the school's closing in 1975, that haven and turf were not only taken away, they were replaced with a school community that was "separate" in ways seldom envisioned in the desegregation movement. The Rougemont students were reassigned to schools like Liberty Hill, which resegregated them by scapegoating and stigmatizing the children. In the process of resolving the inequality between African-American and white schools, schooling for Rougemont children was separated from their community, from their history, from their traditions, and from their culture. The result of school desegregation for Rougemont was a cruel irony. The cost of being integrated in schools was the disintegration of community. The children were separated from their culture. Moreover, the community lost the only social institution that served all of them and celebrated their lives and beliefs. Today, it is only on fifth Sundays, when all the churches meet together, that there is a chance for community and a chance for shared cultural beliefs.

The lesson of Rougemont is a brutal one. It teaches African Americans to be wary of education policies that are intended to benefit them, for these policies may well be based in cultural ignorance. Cultural ignorance is more damaging than simply not knowing another's culture because it assumes the superiority of one's own beliefs. Sadly, cultural ignorance legitimates educational policy makers' treating other beliefs as detractors to the implementation of policy. The lesson, then, is that any educational policy that is not equitable in its development and implementation is unlikely to be equitable in its results.

It is, of course, impossible to turn back the clock, to act as if desegregation never occurred. Our intent, rather, is simply to try to reclaim a little of what was lost. Clearly, the story of Rougemont is but a reconstruction of a narrative of African-American life that was silenced by school desegregation. Yet the process of reconstructing such narratives is vital. In these stories is what remains of a culture that equated education with emancipation, that valued schools as cultural entities, and that built communities with schools. These are values worth upholding in all our communities. In better understanding the cultural consequences of school desegregation for African Americans, we may come to understand what we all need in our communities and from our schools.

References

Bell, D. (1975). The burden of *Brown* on Blacks. *North Carolina Central Law Journal, 7*(Fall), 27–39.

————. (1980). *Shades of Brown: New perspective on school desegregation.* New York: Teachers College Press.

Bellah, R., et al. (1985). *Habits of the heart.* Berkeley: University of California Press.

Bowers, C. A. (1984). *The promise of theory: Education in the politics of cultural change.* New York: Teachers College Press.

Brown v. Board of Education, 347 U.S. 483 (1954).

Burlingame, M. (1979). Some neglected dimensions in the study of educational administration. *Educational Administration Quarterly, 15*(1), 1–18.

Cecelski, D. (1991). The Hyde County school boycott. Ph.D. diss. Harvard University Graduate School of Education.

Coleman, J., et al. (1976). *Equity of educational opportunity.* Washington, DC: U.S. Government Printing Office.

Eisenhart, M. (1989). Reconsidering cultural difference in schools. *Education Foundations, 39,* 51–68.

Erickson, K. T. (1976). *Everything in its path.* New York: Simon & Schuster.

Featherstone, J. (1976). *What schools can do.* New York: Liverstone Publishing Company.

Hardy, C. (1979). Motivation: Making the extra effort!!! Again. *Southern Exposure, 7*(2), 94–98.

Irvine, R. W., & Irvine, J. J. (1983). The impact of the desegregation process on the education of black students: Key variables. *Journal of Negro Education, 52,* 410–422.

Moynihan, D., & Mosteller, F. (1972). *On equality of educational opportunity.* New York: Random House.

Relph, E. (1976). *Place and placelessness.* London: Pion.

Smith, J., & Smith, B. (1973). For black educators: Integration brings the ace. *The Urban Review, 6*(3), 1–11.

Chapter 10

Power and Caring

George W. Noblit

"You'll love me more after you leave me." Pam Knight (a pseudonym) was explaining to me what she always said to her second-grade students about their relationship with her while in her class. Pam had invited me to spend one day each week in her class as part of our study of caring in Cedar Grove School (a pseudonym) and was trying to educate me about her relationship with her children. I now regard this statement to be directed not only to her children but also to me. There is much in this statement. It first indicates that there is love between Pam and her students (myself included) but that the love will grow and change over time. There is a promise that this love will continue long after we have left her tutelage. There is also a message that the student has some learning to do about love, learning that will come with time and comparison with other teachers. Yet, as I will try to explain in this article, the learning also has to do with understanding what power and responsibility have to do with love. I now think of Pam as a person who understood the difference between power and moral authority. She understood what I could not see when I first joined her second-grade class: caring in classrooms is not about democracy—it is about the ethical use of power.

I also must admit that this article is my way—an academic's way—of trying to consider what she taught me. For this reason, my writing here is in many ways more about me than about Pam or her classroom. Clifford Geertz (1988, p. 73) would term my approach "I-witnessing." John Van Maanen (1988, p. 73) would call it a "confessional" tale. I have been trying to analyze and interpret my copious field notes from my year with Pam with the goal of understanding how caring relationships and student attachment are or are not linked.

What has been in my way has been me. Pam shook apart my smug little "learned" views about education, and I now need to put my new understandings in some order before I can proceed with other efforts at data analysis. This task is made only more difficult by my discovery in my field notes of something else Pam told me when I had asked her about caring relationships and student attachment. She said, "Aren't they the same thing?" I am now sure she is right, but like all intractable students I must come to that conclusion in my own way, and I must first understand what she taught me before I can begin to use what I have learned.

The Lesson Is in the Learner

Pam really hit all my buttons. She made me reconsider my lenses on power and on caring, the two concepts that probably encompass my whole intellectual history. Power, and my invariant linking of it with oppression, has been what I have thought, taught, researched, and written about for my entire career. I know about power conceived as the trait of individuals, power conceived as relations between people, and power as institutionalized in ideologies and structures (Burbules, 1986). I know about what some call the "informal" power of social networks. the power of patrons over clients and the power plays of factions and feuds (Schmidt et al., 1977). I have considered Michel Foucault's conception (1980) of power being indelibly articulated with knowledge ("It is not possible for power to be exercised without knowledge; it is impossible for knowledge not to engender power" (p. 52)) and his argument that "the genealogy of knowledge needs to be analyzed, not in terms of types of consciousness, modes of perceptions, and forms of ideology, but in terms of tactics and strategies of power" (p. 77) which Foucault called "the mechanisims of repression" (p.90). I have used power to analyze gender, race, and organizational issues. It has been my major lens.

Caring is part of my more recent intellectual history, beginning with my reading Carol Gilligan (1982) and Nel Noddings (1984) followed by my helping to form a study group of faculty and graduate students within our school of education to consider the idea of caring. We have pondered connection, nurturance, sustenance, dependency, and morality. Our considerations in turn led to our ethnographic research on caring at Cedar Grove School and my year with Pam. Pam made me look at how power and caring are connected and then at how I have been thinking, teaching, researching, and writing for my whole career. You may have already concluded that Pam is a powerful woman: that conclusion is the central theme of what follows.

What Powerful Teachers Can Teach Educational Theorists

Educational thought is not quite ready for powerful women. In this country we have a strong tradition of thought linking schools and democracy; the usual argument is that schools should be places where children learn democratic values. This train of thought has a long history. In contrast to Horace Mann's promotion of republican values, John Dewey proposed that schools should be structured to promote democratic values (1916). Indeed, Dewey's faith in a scientific method of problem solving was coupled with his belief that this process allowed for more democratic decision making and the development of an interdependence in social life and society (Bowers, 1987). Although they start from a very different assumption about the nature of scientific knowledge, critical theorists have joined in this refrain, proposing that teachers need to use their authority judiciously so as not to repress youth (Giroux, 1981). We see similar reasoning at the level of teaching practice by those who promote child-centered teaching in the name of democracy. Philip Cusick (1983) has possibly extended the analysis of education's testedness in notions of democracy and egalitarianism to an extreme. He argues from his studies of three public secondary schools that "the dominating element in the schools . . . was their obligation to the egalitarian ideal" (p. 106). I knew all this when I first went to Pam's class; indeed, it was the basis for my most prominent taken-for-granted assumption. For me, a good classroom was one that minimized the differences in power between teachers and students.

I also now understand another assumption I took into Pam's classroom; I understood caring as relational and reciprocal (Gilligan, 1982; Noddings, 1984). People volunteered into a caring relationship to be nurtured and sustained and to sustain and nurture. Each benefits and is committed to the other (Noddings, 1984). I had read Noddings on the "toughness of caring" and Gilligan on dependence as connection, and these readings helped me make my assumption (Noddings, 1988, p. 14). Although I was not so naive as to assume that a caring relationship was an equal relationship, I did not appreciate how much I was investing in the concept of caring. I, who saw power linked to oppression in everything, did not want caring to be about power, and thereby about oppression. Fisher and Tronto (1990) unwittingly helped me in this by arguing that power is often located in roles distant from actual care-giving, but it is important to remember that my interpretation of their work is perhaps nonstandard. I wanted the "ethic of caring" to be pristine, to be somehow beyond issues of power that I considered to be essentially hegemonic and masculine.

Taken together, my taken-for-granted assumptions about democracy in education and the nature of caring as apolitical were a powerful set of beliefs to bring to Pam's classroom. As an ethnographer of some experience, I was mentally and intellectually prepared to revise my beliefs when I went into the field, but I was not prepared for my experience in Pam's classroom to shake them apart. I was not prepared for a powerful woman. I was not prepared for her definition of caring as moral authority.

Pam came by her power naturally. As I have learned, some African American teachers have unique ideas of children and of teaching (Foster, 1991). As Shirley Brice Heath (1983) has explained, it may be that African-American adults consider children to be children and not small adults. Children are not equal conversational partners—they must be socialized to this end, and their teachers are expected to be significant socialization agents. This is not solely a belief of African Americans. It is shared by white teachers and parents in Cedar Grove School. Pam once explained that she saw herself and one white teacher, Christine (a pseudonym), as exemplars of the same general approach—teachers who are in charge of what their children do. At Cedar Grove School, this model of teaching pervades deeply. The most significant person in the history of Cedar Grove School is believed to have been Francis Gray Patton's severe and stern schoolteacher in *Good Morning Miss Dove* (1987). If you remember the novel, the play, or the film, you will understand that teacher-centered teaching at Cedar Grove School means assuming moral responsibility for the education of children.

I think you also need to know that Pam's power extended well beyond the classroom. She was one of the opinion makers in the building, was revered by white and African-American parents, and was the teacher who assumed charge of the school whenever the principal was out of the building. She was reputed to be the most effective teacher in the building, adept with "difficult" students and (I later concluded) with "difficult" parents. She never missed a chance to talk with parents and was frequently called by the school secretary to deal with parent complaints. Her power was such that she, in many ways, chose me to be in her classroom for the Caring Study, rather than the other way around. I was her guest, there at her behest, and even if my presence was occasionally more distracting or imposing than she originally imagined, she bore it well. This was further evidence of Pam's sense of self. It was her responsibility to make her classroom work, and she graciously extended that responsibility to making my research work also. I usually spent one full day a week observing in her classroom during the 1989–1990 school year (Merriam, 1988). In the course of the year, it finally dawned on me just how powerful Pam really was. I had gone from being a full professor of education at a major university to being her "oldest student." She took responsibility for my learning, and although I came to respect and love her as my teacher, as I write this article it becomes evident that I too "love her more after I left her." Apparently, Pam also had the power of prophesy.

Once the Opening Bell Rings

As students in Pam's class, our day started with going to our seats for quiet reading until all twenty-four (70 percent African-American, 30 percent white) students arrived and the opening bell rang. Pam and her assistant, Sharon, did not excuse themselves from this ritual. They usually spent this time reading over the plans and materials for the day as well as any school or district missives. I fell into the routine of taking my seat in the rear corner of the room, just in front of Pam's desk. Here I could quietly observe and take notes. I came to justify this as "writing to read."

After the opening bell rang, Pam would go to the board and review the plan for the day. In North Carolina, this is regarded as good teaching practice for the teaching evaluation instrument, but Pam took this as an opportunity to review what had been studied on previous days, discuss what they would do that day, and project what was planned for the days to come for each subject area. She also commented on the previous day's work, praising students and recalling unique performances. On my first day in Pam's class, I noted she owned her humanity, taking responsibility for a common student error from the day before: "Oh yes, yesterday I must have misspelled 'caterpillar' because you all did on your work." Humor was a constant in this classroom. Pam enjoyed her children and her teaching, and celebrated her enjoyment. As she later told me, it was only after she had taught for twenty years (she was in her twenty-fifth year of teaching) that she realized she "loved it." She framed this transition in terms of her overcoming doubts about whether she was doing the right things. I now understand she defeated her doubts when she became confident of her moral authority. She could laugh at a lot of the tribulations of classroom life because neither the events nor her enjoyment of her students threatened her authority. In many ways, they constituted her moral authority.

Pam's class had many collective rituals. On most days the first lesson started with the kids doing something with her. In the first week of class, when teaching consonants, Pam started by saying "Let's go over our cheer, our chant." The children then recited the consonants in a sequence that they learned from her, and this elicited praise: "This is the first time I've had a second-grade class come in and know all their sounds." She attributed their knowledge not to herself but to them, even though the chant was clearly her routine.

As is usual practice in many elementary school classrooms, reading in Pam's class was largely taught and practiced in reading groups. There were four homogenous groups, allowing Pam and Sharon each to take a group while the other two groups stayed at their desks doing "seatwork." This was also one of the periods of the day when both the gifted and remedial students were pulled from the classroom for work with special resource teachers. The reading groups were not permanent assignments, and a number of children changed groups during the year. Pam and Sharon had the children read, helped them with pronunciation, and ended each turn at reading with a series of questions about what the child had read, focusing on how things unfolded and asking the children to recount similar things that had happened in their own lives. The seatwork was usually related to language arts; asking the children to complete sentences, spell words, and so forth. When the seatwork was completed, the children were allowed to go to the bookshelves and select from a wide range of books for "free reading."

Pam or Sharon often taught other subjects at the blackboard, calling on children to give answers or to come to the board to demonstrate how to work the problem, spell the word, or write the sentence. This was followed by the class as a whole practicing the problems, or whatever, in a recitation format. Recitation was in turn followed by the students, individually or in groups, doing practice exercises from the book or on the worksheets Pam or Sharon had prepared. This routine was often supplemented with hands-on materials especially in the teaching of science and math, or supplanted by cooperative learning strategies. Indeed, I saw both of these used almost every day I was in the classroom.

Our day was partitioned by morning break, lunch, afternoon quiet time, and recess periods (usually taken outside). Music, physical education, art, and foreign language classes were taught by others and were usually offered two or three days a week. On days I was in the class, lunch was usually followed by storytime, during which I read stories to the children and repeatedly revealed my ineptness as a teacher. My inability was a source of delight to the children, who immediately took advantage of it in a good-natured way. They even taught me the way I should handle the session. I also believe storytime was a source of some amusement to Pam and Sharon, who, after helping me through a few sessions, left me on my own with the children. This was something I had asked for so I could talk with the kids about school and things related to caring Pam and Sharon would return, smiling and shaking their heads at the mayhem I was able to create in what was a few short minutes for them and a lifetime for me. I caused mayhem in the classroom on many other occasions and was repeatedly and good-naturedly rescued from the results of my labor.

I now realize that storytime was Pam's way of including me in another of the rituals of her classroom. Although students were clearly there to work, they were also there to serve the collective good. Pam had created a host of service routines that gave children a chance to perform helpful daily tasks. Children rotated responsibilities for reading the calendar; reporting on the weather; passing out and collecting pencils, papers, and books (different pairs of children for each of these); cleaning the board; sharpening the pencils; and so forth. Storytime was my responsibility, and I discovered that in Pam's class ineptness did not lead to your losing your responsibility. Instead, it led to a lot of coaching to get it right and a lot of room to figure it out for yourself.

Discipline in Pam's class was promoted in a number of ways. First, routines helped the children and me know what was expected of us and in many ways kept us out of trouble. Second, I soon learned that in Pam's class instruction had a dual meaning. On the one hand, instruction was about teaching the subject matter. On the other hand, it was about a meticulous process of making sure everyone knew what and how to do whatever was being assigned. The process often ended with what ethnographers call a "member check." Pam would ask one of the students to repeat the instructions to the class and, if the student was not able to do so, would ask: "Can someone help Clinton [or whomever] out?" Third, teacher talk was laced with reminders and admonitions to the students in an attempt to prevent more serious infractions. Finally, when all else failed, Pam had a form of "assertive discipline": A student who blatantly violated one of the written classroom rules (cooperation, consideration, communication, concentration) had to write his or her name on the board and subsequently lost the right to free time during the day. There was, however, what I came to consider the worst infraction in the classroom. If you did it, you did not write your name on the board. It was not a written rule, but all the children knew it. This violation made all the children, and myself, drop our heads in apparent shame. The worst infraction of all was to laugh if someone did not know the right answer to a question.

Discipline never really was an issue in Pam's class; rather, it was taken for granted. The children knew she expected them to behave, and largely they did. This was true even though Pam was likely to be given the children in the second grade with the major discipline problems. I counted four of her twenty-four students in this category (two boys and two girls, both races for each gender). She sometimes complained about the unfairness of such assignments, but also, I think, reveled in the testimony that these assignments represented to her abilities with children. I can attest to the difficulties these youths presented, and can I attest that these students did respond to Pam, generally behaved, and did their schoolwork. All of this was in marked contrast to what teachers and the principal reported had happened the year before with these students under other teachers. Pam's fundamental strategy with all the children (I noted in my field notes) was to lead the children to the right answers, to smile, and to praise their efforts. She showed she was proud of them, and they seemed to want that above all.

There was, of course, much more to Pam's class each and every day, but I think you can get a sense of what it was like in our class. In educational jargon, the class was more teacher-centered than child-centered, and Pam saw this as appropriate. She felt it was her responsibility to set the agenda for the children to learn, and to teach them. The children were responsible for doing their work and for not interfering with others' doing their work. I was responsible for my observation and note taking, and eventually learned that my attempts to "help" were often interference. We were all responsible for looking after the collective good of the class, and I had to learn how I could participate appropriately in this.

The Learner's Lens

I am convinced Pam knew I was not ready for her class. My beard and longish hair, my leftist tendencies, my lack of experience with children, and my job as a professor all attested to this. Yet she took me anyway. She showed me and told me what she knew—and watched my world shake and crumble. My crumbling was not easy on her, for she knew I was uncomfortable with her class, and I believe for a time she took this as an evaluation of her teaching. I now know that I originally did not accept her style, and what made it even more difficult for me was the fact that she generated evidence everyday that her style worked in her class. This compelled me to turn my evaluative eyes on myself and my taken-for-granted beliefs about teaching. This was hard—and is hard—as this article continues to attest. I first noted my shifting of views in a meeting of the Caring Study research team held during the late fall of my year in the school. The six researchers were discussing what we thought we were finding out about caring, and I began to defend Pam's style. Defending it opened my eyes. First, it showed me my lens on teaching was changing and Pam was changing it. Second, it showed me that the team had to deal with the issue of preferred teaching style as a substantive part of our research. Third, it showed me I did not know enough yet to deal with this change in my perspective. I was taking up Pam's defense where she would probably see none needed, and I could not put all of that into words.

I became a professor of education by a circuitous route. I had not been a classroom teacher. My Ph.D. was in sociology, and my first university job was primarily teaching about deviance, juvenile delinquency, and organizational theory with an occasional sociology of education course. I started studying schools when I received a grant to do an ethnography of a desegregating high school in Memphis. My interest at first was in race relations, but over time that gave way to an interest in education as an institution and schools as organizations. I went to the National Institute of Education with the Desegregation Studies Team. There I finally decided that I wanted to switch my discipline from sociology to education, and I did. My background meant that my knowledge of teaching was heavily influenced by the literature on how best to teach in what we then called interracial classrooms. As it turns out, I think this literature is better understood as how whites thought it would be best to teach interracial classrooms. Implicit in this literature, as Foster argues, is a denigration of the teaching of African-American teachers because their teaching capability was associated with the segregated school stigmatized by James S. Coleman et al. (Foster, 1991; Coleman et al., 1966).

The "knowledge" I had about teaching in multicultural classrooms assumed many things, but most of all it assumed that difference was *the* problem. Because the children were racially different, "good" teaching practice avoided competition, public demonstrations, and evaluations of knowledge. It favored cooperative learning and private assessments of knowledge. If the teacher called only on hands that were raised, some children would not get to participate and that would be, in part, because of the biases of the teacher (Collins & Noblit, 1976). There was much more to all this, but I now can see little reason to elaborate this "knowledge." Pam taught me that all this was not necessary practice if the classroom context was defined not in terms of individual achievement but rather in terms of "connectedness and solidarity" (Foster, 1991).

There were many instances in Pam's class that showed what is possible when classrooms are defined as collectives, individuals connected by responsibilities and obligations to the whole. What stood out in those instances were the children's definition of the situation as involving participation in a learning event and an opportunity for a personal connection with Pam. Let me share the event that demonstrated Pam's power to me. When I witnessed it, what I knew became obsolete.

Pam's Power

Like so many of the instructional strategies used in Pam's class, the strategy I now call to your attention had ritualized characteristics. That is to say, the strategy was about more than instruction and learning. It symbolized a shared world view, a shared belief system (Kapferer, 1981; Gehrke, 1979). Let me recreate the perspective I had as I observed this strategy for the first time. The event as I saw it then was a "public testing" event. I saw the event this way; it involved the teacher standing in front of the class, asking for answers to questions or problems that the children were to give for immediate and public evaluation.

The students were competing to get the right answer for any single question, and the one who got the most right answers would get a chance to draw from the "surprise box" of prizes Pam and Sharon kept full of trinkets. A question was asked, and Pam usually called on someone who had raised a hand. Wrong answers were usually greeted with the response, "Can anyone help [the student's name]?" Children often raised their hands as soon as they recognized the wrong answer, and Pam would then call on one of them. Although this rendition captures the action and reveals my lens at the time, it misses the meaning of the ritual entirely.

As I paid closer attention, I saw a completely different event. The event began with Pam's signaling the ritual: "We'll do this together." She would say this as she walked to the front of the room, and the children would immediately change their posture—they would sit up straighter, look to each other with wide eyes, and quickly focus on Pam. It really did not matter what the content of the questions concerned: math, social studies, spelling, science, or whatever. It also did not matter how the questions were asked. Sometimes she used flash cards, sometimes she would write on the board, and sometimes she simply made a verbal request. Pam would ask the first question, and hands would go up. Here was my first real shock. It seemed that all the hands would go up. On closer examination, I realized that was not totally true. There were some questions that had more hands than others, and some children raised their hands less often than others. Yet only one child, Tim (a pseudonym), did not participate. Tim was an African-American boy who earnestly tried to disappear no matter what the instructional event. I can picture him sliding behind other students to be unnoticeable, dropping his head to his desk with the hope that when he was not looking around no one could see him, and so on. He could even manage to "disappear" in cooperative learning groups. He performed no differently in this ritual than in other formats, but somehow he was more visible in this one for his nonparticipation. Pam would call on him even though his hand was not raised and try to lead him to a correct answer. Indeed she regularly called on students who did not raise their hands and regularly returned to students who had misanswered or had no answer to a previous question.

What is harder to convey with words is how the children raised their hands. They did so slightly raising out of their seats (although they were supposed to stay in their seats), waving their hands, and making eye contact with Pam. They raised their hands even if they had the wrong answer or no answer at all. Pam would respond to the latter cases with a gentle request: "Please do not raise your hands if you do not have an answer." The children would even raise their hands before the question was asked! To be sure, some children were trying to win a chance to pick from the surprise box, but most just wanted to participate, and hand raising was one way to participate. Repeatedly, children would simply look at their classmates with smiles on their faces after being called upon, whether or not they offered an answer. It was a moment in the sun.

Pam, of course, was the brightest sun even though the children would also look to each other for recognition. When Pam called on you, it was as if you were the chosen, and it seemed to matter little that many others would be chosen and that your moment was but brief. How did a public testing event become a moment in the sun? In a multitude of small things. In calling on the children, Pam would let the hands wave for a while—long enough to allow the maximum number of hands to raise. In this time, she would smile and make eye contact with all she could. She raised the event to a fever pitch and then chose. After the choice, her attention was focused on the chosen child. She smiled and often made a brief comment, sometimes praise but often just a comment about unrelated things. Sometimes she even shared a comment with Sharon and me about the child. Even if the child did not have an answer, she would connect for a brief moment with her eyes, words, humor, and attention. In some ways, this is the saddest part of classroom life. There is an insatiable demand for attention and connection, and in some ways every decision to connect with one child is a decision to not connect with another. Pam tried to minimize this through her fashioning of the collectivity with rituals like this. The students loved it. I repeatedly interpreted this as the students' favorite time in the classroom. Pam's power made the collectivity stronger and each child stronger as a consequence.

I also began to note when Pam used this ritual and soon discovered it was neither an accident nor simply an everyday routine. Pam often switched to this ritual when the collectivity was weakening, when the children were getting restless, when the content was proving difficult to manage, or when she was feeling a bit listless. All of these were threatening to the sense of one's responsibility and obligation to the collectivity, and her job was not to let that happen. It was her moral responsibility to keep us all together, and everyone loved her for it, myself included—once I got over having to revalue teacher-centered teaching.

What Control Has to Do with Continuity

Pam's power was used for many things: to keep order, to set up lessons, to evaluate performance, and so on. Not all these had the significance of the aforementioned ritual. Some were just the things teachers have to do. Yet the previously described ritual helps us see that patterns give not just consistency but continuity. I recognized late in my year with Pam that she used her power and her control often in the service of continuity. As Noddings (forthcoming) has argued, what is most missing in schools is attending to "continuity of place, people, purpose, and curriculum." I now see this is Pam's teacher-centeredness. What I have recounted previously demonstrates how routine and ritual established a continuity to the curriculum and instruction, and how the purpose of collective responsibility and work were continuous.

Pam also used her power to make sure we had a place that was secure. Outsiders came into her classroom only with her invitation. She met parents at the door and moved them out into the hall with her. I witnessed an incident in which the children were lining up near the door to the classroom to go to music class. The principal had come in to reinforce the students' doing their homework, something the teachers, including Pam, had asked him to do. He asked Pam, "Have they been doing their homework?" Pam, Sharon, the children, and I knew that not all of them had. Pam looked at the kids and then back to the principal, responding, "They've done well." Taken literally, she had not answered the question asked by the principal. The principal, in kind, said to the children something to the effect of "Keep up the good work." He left, and Pam reorganized the line of students to go to music, only to have it break down into a series of children coming to her and hugging her. She had protected them. In her place they were secure—they were her students.

Continuity of people was achieved largely by Pam's and Sharon's rarely missing a day of work, and by repeated recountings of what the class had accomplished. As I previously mentioned, even parents were kept out of the classroom for the most part. They were not part of the collectivity. Even when Pam had to miss a day, and a substitute was called in as required by law, Sharon ran the class, leaving the substitute with little to do. Even I was better than anyone else when both had to be out of the classroom for a few minutes. As Pam put it to me, "You know the children, and they know you." During such moments I also knew I belonged somewhere. My identity was connected to the class: the children, Pam, and Sharon.

Power and Morality

I now recognize how limited my understanding of power was before I began to explore an ethic of caring. I was well educated in the literature of power, yet I could not distinguish between power and oppression: They were one and the same. I believe I understood that an ethic of caring required me to distinguish between power used for its own sake and power used in the moral service of others. What I was not able to understand was the dramatic implications of that for my understanding of education and my intellectual journey. As has been written, caring is context dependent and reciprocal (Gilligan, 1982; Noddings, 1984). However, knowing about caring by reading about it is a poor substitute for experiencing it, either as a participant or as a participant-observer.

I now know that the conceptions of power I have used to understand education are but one part of the picture. Burbules (1986) says, and I once would have concurred, that power is based in a conflict of interests and is latent in our ideologies and structures. In this conception, without a conflict of interest, there is little reason to speak of power. On the surface, then, we may believe that caring meets this criterion. Because it is reciprocal and of benefit to both parties, caring would not seem to be about power. Yet in Pam's classroom there were conflicts of interest, especially in the short term. With respect to many things, students simply complied. For many activities, Pam set up rituals and structures that controlled our behavior. To me, it is now clear that we must speak of power *and* caring. As Noddings (1984, p. 64) argues about the educator, "her power is awesome. Somehow the child must be led to choose for himself . . . for his ethical self."

Noddings (1984, p. 64) argues that in a caring relation, power does not render the other into an object, but rather maintains and promotes the other as subject. "Power is used to confirm, not disconfirm, the other. It is not about competition, as is Burbules' notion (1986) of the zero-sum game in power, but about connection and construction." Yet caring is a "tough" relationship in that the care giver must be strong and courageous so that he or she can use the good to "control that which is not good" (Noddings, p. 100). Caring is reciprocal and unequal, but while patron-client relationships with these same characteristics disproportionately benefit the patron, power in the caring relationship benefits both parties. Each benefits differently, so that the linear concept of disproportion is nonsensical.

I now think that Noddings has given a new meaning to Foucault's admonition to all intellectuals:

> The essential political problem for the intellectual is not to criticize that his own scientific practice is accompanied by a correct ideology, but that of as-certaining the possibility of constituting a new politics of truth (Foucault, 1980, p. 133).

The project of feminist thought in Foucault's terms is "an insurrection of subjugated knowledge," but in this case the insurrection is against the accepted conceptions of power (Foucault, 1980, p. 80). Noddings, in *Women and Evil* (1989), with her notion of "pedagogies for the oppressors" (p. 173). She argues that Friere's notion of solidarity has no basis; it comes from nowhere. Even when Friere conceives of it as an "act of love," it is not about relations between people but about relieving objective conditions of repression. Noddings proposed her insurrection against our usual notions of power as "power that springs from weakness" (1989, p. 167). She argues that women's experience as the oppressed gives a better understanding of how to use power to transform oppressors than do existing theories of power, which she sees as requiring women to act more like men. She writes:

> The pedagogy of the oppressor must include at least lessons in mediation, moderation and sharing. We must provide far more opportunities for students of all ages to plead each other's cases, to stand between opposing parties in appreciative efforts to bring people together in common understanding. We also need opportunities to learn moderation and to embrace it as an ideal. We must relearn sharing—not as a special privilege of those who have and therefore may be further blessed for their generosity, but as a way of life that sustains everyone in mutual giving and receiving. Those who share even when they have little feel like whole and valued human beings (1989, p. 173).

Pam, of course, understood this as an African-American woman even if she did not articulate it in such ways. She practiced her pedagogy for the oppressor on me, on the principal, on some parents, and on other people who had more privileges than she. She mediated my connection with the children, Sharon, and herself. She made it impossible for me to impose my theory of education on her and her classroom, and persuaded me, not by words but by persistence and caring, to become connected. She moderated my extremes and the extremes of her other students, not in the name of mediocrity, but in the name of celebrating our differences and maintaining the collectivity that was her class. She shared, with me and all her students, her ideas, her faith in us, her commitment to us, and her caring. As this article attests, she was as effective in her pedagogy for the oppressor as she was in pedagogy for second-grade students. She never knew she was also engaged in an intellectual insurrection of our conceptions of power, but she certainly was effective at it. She effectively demonstrated what incorporating feminist ideas about caring will do to our learned theories of power.

Pam created a context for me to learn about caring, and it has forever altered how I think about education and about caring. It has also led me to conclude that it is maybe only through such opportunities that we are going to understand how power is implicated in caring. I see Pam as understanding and acting not with power, but with moral authority—an authority not only legitimated by the usual mechanisms of our society but also by reciprocal negotiation between people, in this case people of unequal power and knowledge. Pam's authority came from her willingness to take responsibility for creating a context for children to participate in, and from the children themselves who, after all, can and often do deny adults the right to control them. Some readers may wish to say that they would prefer that she be more child-centered, but I believe that this means that they do not understand caring as being constructed in the relationship between the parties to that relationship. In fact, we were dependent on Pam, yet all of us worked to construct Pam's class. It was our way to nurture and sustain her as well as ourselves. This means to me that it is time for us to reconsider the terms *child-centered* and *teacher-centered teaching*. They oversimplify and mislead.[1]

I have much to learn about moral authority, but I think I now know where to focus my efforts. First, I must try to learn more from African-American teachers. They may construct education and caring quite differently than teachers of my own race do (Foster, 1991). The emphasis on collectivity is promising as a corrective for the seemingly rampant individualism of Americans in general (Bellah et al., 1985). African-American teachers seem to still understand that schooling is about morality and continuity. They still understand their moral authority. Second, I must try to reconceptualize my image of power by trying to understand powerful women. Following Mary Field Belenky et al. (1980), I realize that women construct power rather than assume or usurp it. For powerful women, it may be that there is no important distinction between power and authority. Power that is socially constructed is socially legitimated. It may lack legal basis, charisma, or even the full force of tradition, but it is moral authority nonetheless (Weber, 1974). Finally, I have increasing interest in understanding morality not as ethical codes but as a construction of continuity between the many pasts available to us and the many futures possible. I now know that I, like Pam, can have the power to construct continuity, morality, authority, and caring.

She taught me well. The lesson was there every day for me. Every morning before school, children came to her room to see her. They came for a word, a smile, a hug. They were Pam's students from previous years. We all do love her after we have left her, and maybe, just maybe, love her more.

Note

1.   I wish to thank Inez Rovengo for her comments on an earlier draft and for this conclusion.

References

Belenky, M. F., et al. (1980). *Women's ways of knowing.* New York: Basic Books.

Bellah, R. N., et al. (1985). *Habits of the heart.* Berkeley: University of California Press.

Bowers, C. A. (1987). *Elements of a post-liberal theory of education.* New York Teachers College Press.

Burbules, N. (1986). A theory of power in education. *Educational Theory, 36*(2), 96–114.

Coleman, J. et al. (1966). *Equality of educational opportunity.* Washington, DC: U.S. Government Printing Office.

Collins, T., & Noblit, G. W. (1976). The process of interracial schooling. In *The desegregation literature: A critical appraisal.* Washington, DC: National Institute of Education.

Cusick, P. A. (1983). *The egalitarian ideal and the American high school.* New York: Longman.

Dewey, J. (1916). *Democracy and education.* New York: Macmillan.

Fisher, B., & Tronto, J. (1990). Toward a feminist theory of caring. In E. Abel & M. Nelson (Eds.), *Circles of care.* Albany, NY: SUNY Press.

Foster, M. (1991). Caring of African American teachers. Manuscript. University of California-Davis.

Foucault, M. (1980). *Power and knowledge.* (C. Gordon, Ed.). New York: Pantheon Books, pp. 52, 77, 90.

Geertz, C. (1988). *Works and lives.* Stanford, CA: Stanford University Press, p. 73.

Gehrke, N. J. (1979). Rituals of the hidden curriculum. In Kaoru Yamomoto (Ed.), *Children in time and space.* (pp. 103–27). New York: Teachers College Press.

Gilligan, C. (1982). *In a different voice.* Cambridge: Harvard University Press.

Giroux, H. (1981). *Ideology, culture, and the process of schooling.* Philadelphia: Temple University Press.

Heath, S. B. (1983). *Ways with words.* New York: Cambridge University Press.

Kapferer, J. L. (1981). Socialization and the symbolic order of the school. *Anthropology and Education Quarterly, 7*(4), 258–274;

Merriam, S. (1988). *Case study research in education.* San Francisco: Jossey-Bass.

Noddings, N. (1984). *Caring.* Berkeley: University of California Press.

Noddings, N. (1988). *Mapping the moral domain.* Cambridge: Harvard University Press.

Noddings, N. (1989). *Women and evil.* Berkeley: University of California Press.

————. (1992). *The challenge to care in schools.* New York. Teachers College Press.

Patton, F. G. (1947). *Good morning Miss Dove.* New York: Dodd, Mead.

Schmidt, S. W., et al. (Eds.). (1977). *Friends, followers, and factions.* Berkeley: University of California Press.

Van Maanen, J. (1988). *Tales of the field.* Chicago: University of Chicago Press.

Weber, M. (1974). *The theory of social and economic organization.* New York: Free Press.

<COVNTERPOINTS ▶>

Studies in the Postmodern Theory of Education

General Editors
Joe L. Kincheloe & Shirley R. Steinberg

Counterpoints publishes the most compelling and imaginative books being written in education today. Grounded on the theoretical advances in criticalism, feminism and postmodernism in the last two decades of the twentieth century, Counterpoints engages the meaning of these innovations in various forms of educational expression. Committed to the proposition that theoretical literature should be accessible to a variety of audiences, the series insists that its authors avoid esoteric and jargonistic languages that transform educational scholarship into an elite discourse for the initiated. Scholarly work matters only to the degree it affects consciousness and practice at multiple sites. Counterpoints' editorial policy is based on these principles and the ability of scholars to break new ground, to open new conversations, to go where educators have never gone before.

For additional information about this series or for the submission of manuscripts, please contact:

Joe L. Kincheloe & Shirley R. Steinberg
637 West Foster Avenue
State College, PA 16801